CREDIBILIT

CW00518233

"Creativity Spil
400 and 700% In Flow."

Harvard and Flow Genome Project
Result of various studies [1]

"Top Executives Increase Productivity
By Up To 500% In Flow."

McKinsey & Company
Result of a 10-year study [2]

"The Learning Process Becomes
490% Faster In Flow."

USA Department of Defence
Study with snipers and radar operators [3]

CREATIVITY & FLOW

Flow is the scientific term for optimal states of consciousness, where your sense of self vanishes, you merge with the activity you are performing, time flies, and you achieve ultimate performance. It is intrinsically connected to finding creative solutions to your challenges.

As you enter the flow state you become laser-like focused, without feeling high or wired. You will feel unusually clear, knowing what you need to do and how to do it.

You already know there is nothing quite like it, as we all experience getting in flow from time to time. What is fundamental in this competitive world is to be able to access flow more often at work, and as a bonus you will be more likely to access flow in your leisure time and have more fun in life.

Hungarian-American psychologist Mihaly Csikszentmihalyi ran one of the largest psychological surveys ever, asking people about the times in their life when they felt their best and performed at their best. No matter their age, occupation, or nationality, their description of peak performance converged to describe what getting in flow felt like and the term flow was created.

Scientific research to guide your access to flow is still surrounded by mystery, but now we can clearly define the characteristics of a flow experience, conditions for it to happen, and identify the triggers to achieve flow. We can also observe the radical change in body neurochemistry, brain activity and brain wave patterns while in flow.

Researchers believe that flow is behind the most significant progress in science, business breakthroughs and innovation in arts, not forgetting that gold medals and world championships are achieved as a result of athletes having an intimate relationship with flow.

Creativity is the most sought-after asset in the marketplace, but unlike skills it is almost impossible to train someone to become more creative. The great discovery contained in this book is that you can become more creative when you find your way to enter the elusive state of mind called flow.

REVIEWS AFTER
FLOW TRAINING
APPLIED TO LEARNING

Jim improved 93%.
"You gave me the why, not just the what."

Jim Albert
Managing Director UK – Adecco

Sridhar improved 71%
"I loved the training. Zander really helped me understand the process of reading and gave me tools to make it faster."

Sridhar Ramaswamy
Senior Vice-President – Google

Karim improved 94%
"Very interesting"

Karim L.
Vice-President – JP Morgan

Luca improved 88%
"Useful in terms of giving important hints of how to read faster."

Luca Tres
Vice-President – Deutsche Bank

Sherjeel improved 124%
"Taught me about the key areas I need to focus on to improve comprehension and speed."

Sherjeel Ahmed
Vice-President Finance – Barclays Bank

Nicole improved 108%
"Excellent course."

Nicole
Vice-President – Morgan Stanley Equity Sales

Nicola improved 100%

"I like science behind things too, so it was nice to have it explained."

Nicola Horton
Director Sanctions Operations – Barclays Bank

Wayne improved 67%

"Zander's enthusiasm and great presentation skills inspired me.

Wayne Miller
Director – Barclays Capital & Derivatives

Jennifer improved 100%

"Target improvement was 30% and actual improvement was 100%! Good techniques to practice. Thanks!"

Jennifer Bodie
Analyst – Goldman Sachs

Amr improved 116%

"I like the fact Zander made us think of what could inspire us to read!"

Amr Al-Yafeai
Director – Commerzbank

Nikki improved 318%

"I felt that these tools are good to really kick start a new passion for reading."

Nikki Jones
Executive Marketing & Sponsorship – O2

Chrissy improved 80%

"I can see the tangible results of the short training. Plus practice going forward, I am confident that my reading speed will be a lot faster!"

Chrissy Cao
Auditor – KPMG

Ramone improved 81%

"Yes, it helped speed my reading and other life coaching tips."

Ramone Param
Corporate Financier – PwC

Jide improved 112%
"Good examples, enthusiastic and love to hear more about memory skills."

Jide Odunsi
Trader – Goldman Sachs

Lindsey improved 86%
"Very insightful, scientific and easy to follow."

Lindsey Harper
Concessions Manager – Harrods

Thomas improved 165%
"Liked it because I feel as I can read faster and not feel as tired when reading."

Thomas Fonzo
Journalist – The Wall Street Journal

Petar improved 140%
"Great course, I definitely liked it! I learned some very useful techniques and concepts."

Petar Lipovyanov
Analyst – HSBC

Andre improved 176%
"I am happy I can read faster. Good tempo. Great presenter."

Andre White
Relationship Manager – Lloyds Banking Group

Tom improved 243%
"Excellent, interesting, quantifiable results in a very short period of time, value for money, clearly a well-oiled machine that seemed to work for all that attended!"

Tom Mc Grath
Project Manager – RBS GBM

Vanessa improved 88%
"Knowing how it all works is fascinating."

Vanessa Clarke
Hansard Editor – House of Commons UK Parliament

Sandrine improved 84%

"I saw I could read faster while actually improving my understanding. Ideas did stick."

Sandrine Andre
Assistant Vice-President – JP Morgan

Kellie improved 213%

"Don't know where to start. I learned much more than how to read faster. Amazing tools for life and I am inspired to be better."

Kellie Golboume
Sales Executive – The Walt Disney Company

Abhijeet improved 125%

"I did like the course. In true sense, the potential was not realised. Achieved quite a lot of understanding of different techniques and would try to improve it."

Abhijeet Kulkami
Engineer – General Electric

Emma improved 165%

"I think the techniques taught are very valuable and I'll be able to keep using them and improve."

Emma Gibson
Editor – Sage

Tim improved 117%

"Good coverage of techniques to improve reading speed."

Tim Bangemann
Director Fixed Income Trading – UBS

Ritesh improved 70%

"It forced us to think about our reading speed and encouraged improving this."

Ritesh Ramji
Infrastructure Finance Adviser – PwC

Martin improved 125%

"It was a fascinating insight into speed reading and I feel inspired to read more. I just wish I'd done this years ago. It was excellent!"

Martin Dannhouser
Policy Advisor – Home Office

HUMANS IN FLOW®

Unlock the flow state to boost your creativity in business by between 400 and 700%.
Achieve one of the most powerful human experiences by entering the altered state of consciousness behind most insights, breakthroughs and discoveries.

ZANDER GARCEZ

MIND'S EYE PRESS
Mind's Eye Press is incorporated as
Mind's Eye Training Ltd Reg. No. 08159615
Address and contact details can be found at
www.humansinflow.global

First Edition published in Great Britain in 28th March 2020
By Mind's Eye Press
Copyright © 2020 Zander Alex Garcez

Disclaimer.

This book is intended to question the way you read, write,
draw, think and focus in order to increase your mental
performance and get you into flow state.
I have tested many products and services that can be helpful
to you, and I recommend the best ones throughout the book. I
might receive a commission from some of them, so I advise
you to make your research and due diligence before deciding
about any purchase. I am not a doctor, and I do not
recommend any drugs mentioned in the book. I do not take
any responsibility for third party products and services.

Cover illustration/logo ® Zander Alex Garcez
Humans In Flow – Trade name ® Zander Alex Garcez

Zander's photograph by John Cassidy -
www.theheadshotguy.co.uk

ISBN 978-0-9932190-6-1

To my parents
Marly and Jayme

BECOME WEALTHIER

Your current knowledge combined with the flow state can bring you the prosperity you deserve. You can awaken the creative part of your brain to perform at your best while finding more satisfaction and rewards at work.

I will guide you to get in flow in many ways and a powerful way is to learn how to read in flow. You will read better and faster. You will also develop a passion for reading books and will read more books, just for fun.

Now, do rich people read more books because they are rich, or did they become rich because they read more books?

"According to the U.S. Labor Department, business people who read at least seven business books per year earn over 230 per cent more than people who read just one book per year." [4]

So, how about that for a challenge?

FAIR EXCHANGE

A lot of people have helped me countless times in my life, and I feel I am indebted to them because they showed me a better way to; read, work, think, have fun, love, learn, lead, be present, be grateful, focus and get into a flow state.

For this reason, I decided to pay it forward and to write this book, despite my invented limitations.

I have done a lot of research and experiments to create a quest that questions old believes and guides you towards improving your focus so you can get into a flow state fast.

This is my gift to you.

Refund

If for any reason you feel that the book was not worth

the price, you can reach out and I will personally send you the amount you paid for it, or the difference between what you paid and what you think it is worth. This way I aim for a fair exchange.

Pay it forward and make a global impact

On the other hand, if you received some value while reading this book or otherwise, I suggest you also pay it forward by sharing your wisdom.

I will show you how to have a global impact in this world after you have gone through the quests I have laid out for you. I will open new portals of perception so you can access new realms of possibilities that had been lying dormant inside you.

You will see by the end of the book that supporting someone on their way to growth and prosperity is the most powerful catalyst of flow because it holds meaning and purpose created by you and this is something to live for.

That said, you can get started by sharing the insights you will gain while reading this book, with your friends. Teaching something you have just learnt will intensify the learning process and you will reap the results.

As you will see later, paying forward is a great conduit for flow.

To your success,

CONTENTS

1.5.5 Create time blocks
1.5.6 Prioritise your actions
1.5.7 Take risks
1.5.8 Achieve any goal in an almost fool-proof way

Mental Quiet Flow

Flow reading
1.5.9 Read books to flow
1.5.10 Select authors that speak your kind of language
1.5.11 Finding your natural strength for mental flow
1.5.12 Book summaries can boost your confidence
1.5.13 Find a great place to trigger flow
1.5.14 Ergonomics and flow
1.5.15 Micro-movements and flow
1.5.16 Break the spine of your book

Flow writing
1.5.17 Write blogs, articles and books to flow

Flow drawing
1.5.18 I believe you can draw
1.5.19 The impact of the right side of the brain on finding flow
1.5.20 Drawing and the right side of your brain

Mental Loud Flow

Flow public speaking
1.5.21 Learn with the intention of sharing
1.5.22 Present and teach
1.5.23 Discuss projects and brainstorm

Creating a new project to flow
1.5.24 Pay attention and invent
1.5.25 Gamification of a project
1.5.26 Gaming industry
1.5.27 Gamification to achieve serious results
1.5.28 Focus on a project, not on the money
1.5.29 Game-like thinking to flow at work
1.5.30 Player types and context
1.5.31 Flowing down the rabbit hole

HORSES READ QUEST
Hack a smooth and simple way to read faster

Vision One – **Read faster without training**
2.1.1 How fast do you read?
2.1.2 Test yourself – measure your reading speed
2.1.3 Read faster without training
2.1.4 Preview and review
2.1.5 Secrets to guide your eyes
2.1.6 Become a maestro to read in style
2.1.7 Start reading with a pointer, and just let yourself flow
2.1.8 Skipping back to reread is a waste of time

Vison Two - **Experience four rhythms to read**
2.2.1 Easy practice with pointer and rhythm
2.2.2 On your mark
2.2.3 Get set
2.2.4 The secret sauce
2.2.5 BEBOP System
2.2.6 Go!
2.2.7 Raising your comprehension
2.2.8 Many subjects will not interest you, but
2.2.9 See your blind spot here. It exists
2.2.10 Developing your focus

Vison Three - **Achieve good comprehension**
2.3.1 Watch the eye tracker in action
2.3.2 More practice and the quantum leap
2.3.3 Important words can distract you
2.3.4 Getting ready to read really fast
2.3.5 BEBOP System
2.3.6 Karate Kid and you
2.3.7 Choose a rhythm to practise and get good at it
2.3.8 Expanding your peripheral vision
2.3.9 Computers can read and you can foresee the future
2.3.10 More practice using your awareness
2.3.11 Bounce around and be in charge
2.3.12 Reading with a pointer on your computer
2.3.13 Music sync
2.3.14 Set yourself a realistic routine and great goals

DRAGONS LIVE QUEST
Hack into the meaning of life and dare living forever

THE FUTURE TODAY

He stepped on stage slowly, with his red shoes, under an intense round of applause. I was about to be inspired by my idol, multimillionaire and famous star of the Dragon's Den series in the UK, Simon Woodroffe OBE.

Simon started talking about his vision to change the ancient art of serving sushi, even though he lacked any previous experience working in a restaurant. He wanted to open one that would have a conveyor belt to automatically deliver sushi to all tables and have waitresses in black PVC miniskirts serving drinks. The name chosen was "Yo! Sushi", which looks like a Japanese word, but Yo! is an English slang for Hey! that just sounded right. Twenty years later, his franchise has more than 100 branches and is worth millions.

Moments after the talk, my mentor Steve Bolton introduced me to Simon. We had a stimulating conversation about innovation and the future of reading and learning. At the end of our conversation, he looked me in the eye and asked me a question:

"Can you create a book that can be read faster automatically?"

I smiled, and almost without hesitation said:

"Yes, I can."

He left, but the question remained with me. This was a massive challenge, and many ideas expanded inside my mind until I found the first one, then many more solutions followed.

I'm happy to report that you are reading the first book in the world that makes you read faster while you read it automatically.

Read faster to enter the state of flow

I developed a method that will directly speed up your reading and once you are fast enough you will be able to drift into the flow state. Reading is the easiest way to get in flow so I will guide you to have more control to stay in flow for longer and this way enjoy reading books.

Flow will help you improve your focus and boost mental performance so you will make business decisions in less time with confidence. In flow, you will achieve excellence at extreme sports, play music better, be more inspired to make art, write original and inspiring content and much more.

Although flow can be reached while performing many activities I am aiming to support you to achieve intellectual flow and I am confident that you will be reading 100% to 300% faster by the end of the book.

Right now I'm working with technologies that can create new ways to deliver information faster and I am also developing a 3D movie to teach the ideas of this book in an immersive experience.

Humans of the future have new senses

Science fiction is becoming your new reality, as more than 70 million Americans have been implanted with medical devices, according to the documentary "The Bleeding Edge" on Netflix. We already have more than 60,000 implantable devices connected to the internet [5], and according to Deloitte's report [6] in 2018, the market for connected medical devices will grow from $15bn in 2017 to $52bn in 2022. Implanted medical devices account for one-third of this market.

The development of superpowers is just beginning, so I will give you a glimpse of what is in development right now.

We are visual beings, and we think that what we see is what is out there, but we can only see what is between the ultraviolet and infrared spectrum of electromagnetic waves, which is just a tiny fraction of the electromagnetic spectrum that vibrates around us. You probably think that you see with your eyes, but you don't, you actually see with your brain, that lives in complete darkness and your eyes are just the conduit for the visual information coming from the outside world, just in front of you. When you attach your brain to new devices, it will also adapt and learn how to see or interpret these waves vibrating faster, and you could be able to understand the world in X-Ray or Gama Ray frequencies. When you start seeing or absorbing the same waves vibrating slower, you would be able to see and perhaps understand the microwaves of phones around you, listen through radio waves or talk to another person without the need for using words.

Doctors are already helping those deaf from birth learn to hear from scratch by using an implant. This transforms sound waves into electric signals and transmits the information directly into a person's brain through tiny cables. The person will learn how to hear without any previous experience.

This implant implies that our brains can learn new senses and tasks faster in adulthood, so learning how to read at breakneck speeds and learning new skills, like getting into flow state, are more accessible than ever. I'm working on creating the future, and I'm researching new ways to contribute to this quantum leap.

Humans are already using a mechanical third arm with success, using their brain to move with precision a virtual arm that only exists in their mind. If you stretch your imagination a little further, you can see yourself learning how to flap beautifully designed artificial wings to make you fly like an eagle. You buy the suit, connect with it, and,

21

after learning the basics, you go for a trial and flap away until you fly just like a bird.

You would certainly need a few new senses, and the first is the sense of awareness to manage the response to go up and down, sensors to tell us the speed and the direction of the wind so we will instinctively know when to take off and fly.

To expand the scope of what it is possible to do with electricity in the brain, I want to share that scientists discovered you have about 14 to 20 senses, rather than 5, and animals have even more still. One sense that interests me a lot is chronoception, which dictates how we sense the passage of time. You can stretch the fabric of time by a flow state experience, speeding up your awareness of what is happening around you, which helps in giving you the best possible reaction to avoid an accident while practising a radical sport. What is also common is the perception of slowing down an exciting experience, like jumping out of a plane with parachutes for the first time and etching that memory very clearly in your brain, second by second.

Super soldiers will soon acquire exotic senses to use on the battlefield that only animals have. Some species of sharks can sense electrical fields to detect prey, bats navigate at night by detecting magnetic fields, and some birds and insects can steer their flight by polarised light.

So by learning how to amplify your perceptions of the world, you will start developing new superpowers.

These powers, when combined to achieve heightened levels of focus, will help you get into flow state to revolutionise radical sports and also boost creativity and intellectual performance. Perhaps what is called extrasensory perception will have a new interpretation too.

Flow implies doing something better and faster, so I'm interested in developing new ways to help you decode and transfer information to your brain at speed.

By reading this book and making small adjustments in many areas, you will experience flow more often, which will amplify your results to incredible levels.

Approaching the point of astonishingly fast change

We are living in exponential times, and we need to develop our reading skills to be able to thrive in this competitive world.

You probably heard about Virgin Galactic, Richard Branson's Space Tourism company, what you might not know is how this venture started.

Twelve American astronauts walked on the moon between 1969 and 1972, and I watched the moon landing on TV like millions of other boys. Like me, Peter Diamandis dreamed of becoming an astronaut and expected that NASA would start offering space travel to civilians, but they didn't so he decided to take matters into his own hands and create the X Prize Foundation. He offered US$10 million to the first team to build a new generation of private spaceships so he could go into orbit and beyond. The prize was won in 2004, Richard Branson bought the winning project rights and started selling tickets. Since then the X Prize has launched many other competitions to benefit humanity in a massive way. I support the X Prize initiative and I am looking forward to creating a prize to find extreme improvement in learning capacities for humans.

My big dream is to promote a significant increase in your learning speed to drive attention that will lead to flow. In flow you will increase your engagement and find more satisfaction in life.

We cannot wait for governments to solve our problems and my focus is to accelerate the speed at which we learn. Therefore, this book is just kickstarting the race to develop superfast learning and I am certain others will follow suit and develop even better ways to read, learn and win prizes.

A straightforward premise that predicts extraordinary breakthroughs in all sciences is the Law of Accelerating Returns. As we now use computers in virtually every area of life, instead of developing linearly over the next 30 years, we will be developing exponentially. This is hard to imagine, so let me give you an example:

We are used to linear thinking - if I give you one penny every single day, by the end of the month, you will have 30 pennies. Now, if you think exponentially, I will give you one penny on the first day of the month and will double the amount every single day. You will be surprised to know that, by the end of the month, you will have £5,368,709.12 instead of £0.30. Yes, it is incredible that one single penny can become five million pounds in just 30 days.

Similarly, Moore's law predicts that Information Technology doubles in power every one and a half year. Conversely, your laptop could be 536,870,912 times more potent in 45 years. Most fields of knowledge and sciences use IT and will also develop at a fantastic pace. As a result, you will have to learn massive amounts to make an impact within your area of work.

Don't you think that now is the right time to start improving the way you read?

Reading 100% faster will make a massive difference to your professional life, but what about being able to become more selective while focusing your attention? You could easily 3X or 5X your reading performance.

We have been taught how to read in the same linear way for hundreds of years, and I believe that it is about time to question and improve our learning skills and as well as our books.

Leading the reading revolution

We can go deeper into any area of knowledge to incredible levels of abstraction, but one common denominator that unites all human knowledge is that it has been written down into words and therefore, we must read to learn anything in depth.

What is surprising is that we learn how to read at five or six years of age, and then once we can read out loud – and at a good pace – our parents and teachers think that we have achieved what was expected from us. As teenagers, we can read at a level of speed that, for most of us, we will maintain for the rest of our lives.

Modernising literacy is long overdue

There is an ongoing debate about the best approach to teach reading. There are two main schools of thought. Synthetic phonics involves teaching the alphabet and then teaching children to read words, while analytic phonics teaches reading using flashcards with whole words and pictures depicting the meanings of the words.

The English language is very complex to learn because words are pronounced differently from how they are written. Synthetic phonics teaches children the sound of letters and then expects them to learn how to write the words correctly. This is not a good method because words do not sound as they are written. Teaching a strategy that has many exceptions to the rule can cause confusion, could contribute to the development of dyslexia, can cause spelling mistakes and can ultimately result in children feeling insecure in their ability to express their thoughts in writing.

I believe children should be encouraged to keep learning how to read using the whole-word approach or analytic phonics, even if they already know the alphabet.

To be able to read faster you need to see whole words, instead of trying to connect all the individual letters every time you read a word. If you teach children using analytic phonics, they will learn how to read words as if they are pictures or icons. They will naturally read faster and will be able to read aloud at a good pace. If they learn the principles described in the next chapters, they will ultimately be able to speed read and flow.

Expected results from reading this book

The easiest way to get into flow is by reading books so I will help you read faster to improve your focus and comprehension.

To illustrate, let's talk about Mark, an example of a typical adult, who speaks at 250 words per minute. While reading, his comprehension is best if he reads around 250 words per minute, too.

If Mark pushes to go faster, he can go up to 300 words per minute, but his comprehension will suffer a little. If he goes more quickly than that, his understanding of the text will plummet to deficient levels.

At 400 he is skimming the text and hardly learns anything from it. He can scan the text at around 500 words per minute and find a specific word or expression.

After reading this book, instead of scanning at 500 words per minute, Mark will be reading at this speed with a good level of attention and understanding. Mark's reading speed can go up to 600 words per minute, which is 140% faster. Over time his speed and comprehension will stabilise and adapt to each material and circumstance.

By observing the following graph, you can see how Mark can read at a more significant range of speeds.

Like Mark, most people read at the same speed they talk; therefore, similar results can be achieved by reading this book.

Mark's comprehension and reading speed before and after four hours of coaching.

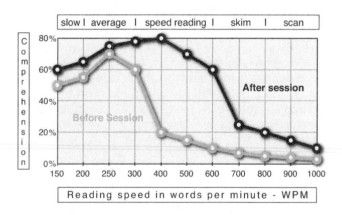

Before coaching - comprehension peaks at 250 WPM

After coaching - comprehension peaks at 400 WPM and is good at 500 WPM

Changing the time to read this book

Even if you think that you read quickly, you can improve your ability even further by accessing the flow state. The following chart shows how long it would take to read this book at different reading speeds and you will see the results you can achieve by the end of the book.

Reading Speed in Words Per Minute	TIME	Reading Speed in Words Per Minute	TIME
At 100 WPM	19.7 hours	At 600 WPM	3.3 hours
At 200 WPM	9.9 hours	At 800 WPM	2.5 hours
At 300 WPM	6.6 hours	At 1000 WPM	2.0 hours
At 400 WPM	4.9 hours	At 1200 WPM	1.6 hours
At 500 WPM	3.9 hours	At 1400 WPM	1.4 hours

Wherever you are is an excellent place to start

Keep reading, and you will gain insights, which will automatically take you out of your comfort zone.

Speed reading bridges the gap between reading and scanning by boosting comprehension.

You may be lucky enough to read faster than your peers, yet you probably can't explain to anyone else how to read more quickly.

The harsh reality is that you are on your own to develop this essential skill.

This is a real disaster. Any skill can be improved with further training, and reading is no different.

So, why is almost no one teaching young kids and adults to read faster? Perhaps because teachers are not aware that they can teach this subject matter.

I am here to inspire a revolution and help people read faster and more efficiently. It starts with a simple test that you can do at home. You can measure your reading speed in words per minute. Just time yourself to read for one minute and count the number of words you read in that time.

Reading at work

I believe that the success of a company is directly proportionate to the ability of a team to process information at speed so they can solve problems, promote innovation and increase productivity.

The good news is that I have discovered that the brain actually loves speed.

It thinks that fast is fun – slow is boring! If you think you have a short attention span when reading books, documents and emails, then you probably read slowly and carefully. Instead of understanding the text, you get bored and distracted. The main reason for this is that your brain is too powerful to go at such a slow pace and will drift off into something more interesting to think about.

You may be measuring the productivity output of your team, but what about their productivity input?

How fast are they taking information in?

Reading is essential in business. The amount of information available to us is doubling every year and information is getting out of date faster than ever. By learning how to read faster and smarter, you will be more focused; your mind will stop wandering, and you will have a better comprehension of any text. The result is that you will achieve peak performance the easy way and will become more productive.

Flow is not bliss

You can have a magical moment with your loved one watching the sunset, or while at a concert with your favourite artist. Yes, it feels fantastic, time flies, and you might think that you have achieved the flow state, but you have reached a bliss state instead.

Flow cannot be passive, as it requires engagement. Adventure and action athletes find flow accidentally out of intense practice and are more likely to get hooked on the feelings created by the flow state, to keep improving their game to levels that can surprise everyone around them.

You need to work hard, take risks and face struggle to achieve flow at action sports, but once you find it you will remember that moment and will try to figure out what the essential steps are to get there again.

Flow while thinking

You can physically induce flow in sports through continuous practice, and you can find evidence of the state with great detail in books from Mihaly Csikszentmihalyi [7] and Steven Kotler [8] [9], but the formula to find flow just by thinking is starting to be explored and explained.

The purpose of this book is to expose my research and experiments to scrutiny as a way to ignite the conversation around the magical powers of this elusive state. You will be faced with the choice of deciding what to change in your life to jump-start ultimate happiness and promote development in all the areas of knowledge. My intent is to show that you have what it takes to increase your capacity of being creative to find solutions to most problems you might face in your life.

Achieving flow state

In flow, you become highly focused and you merge with the experience at hand, time flies, you achieve the highest level of performance and feel your best self.

Although very desirable, this state is not easily transferable, so I'm breaking down the components of high performance for intellectual work to facilitate your quest for long-lasting success in your professional and personal life.

While practising radical sports you could get in and out of flow, but the metrics of intellectual performance and creativity are very different, and this is the starting point of your learning curve. At school and university you learn the lesson, and then you sit for an exam and test your knowledge, but to find the sources of flow, this premise needs to be turned upside down.

You will make the most out of this book if you decide to try the experiments and test my theories to promote flow. You might find that some of them will be just right for you, and other topics will not be relevant or make sense to you.

The important thing is to be open to new experiences, and you will undoubtedly learn your lessons from the results you achieve.

Flow is not for the timid

Flow state is the ideal mental state for high performance, and most of us can associate flow with radical sports where athletes achieve the impossible and take your breath away.

Psychology and science have contributed enormously to develop ultimate performance, especially in sports where a small mistake can unfold into a catastrophic event with multiple injuries or even death.

I will focus on finding the hacks to help you achieve flow while performing intellectual work, in the search for creative solutions to your challenges. In this case, you will not face death directly, but you will undoubtedly have to face risks while playing a high stakes game. You will be daring to expose yourself, by sharing your new ideas, and this way risk your reputation, relationships, career or even your wealth.

However, don't be discouraged as success will be more available to you as you understand all the factors that support flow.

HOW I SHIFTED MY MIND

It all started with my own frustration with reading. I found it hard to keep up and was much slower than my parents, friends and peers.

Learning to cheat

As a teenager, I would try to pay attention at school, so I would not have to study at home. Back then, I felt afraid of books and inadequate, but I developed coping mechanisms and managed to finish my basic education in Brazil. Even though I would study hard, I confess that, out of desperation, I had to deal with the moral dilemma of whether to cheat during my exams or not. After weeks of anxiety, I made my decision; I was ready to cheat. I developed a sophisticated way to cheat by writing information on the surface of a translucent BIC pen with a needle. I

31

could fit three lines of text on each side; my grades improved.

I was 17 when I had to decide my future by choosing which university degree to take. My grandfather was the chancellor of one of the most prestigious Agriculture universities in Brazil, and my uncle had just won a medal from the Brazilian president as his farm was considered to be the best modern farm in the country. I loved my holidays at the farm, and always had fun with horses, so I thought that becoming a farmer was meant to be my destiny and enrolled.

Cheating death to wake up

In June 1986, with the end of term approaching quickly, I became petrified because I had stopped attending classes a month earlier without telling my dad. While trying to figure out what to do next, I started hanging out with other dropouts. At first, I felt relief and inspired to find a new direction in life, but as the days passed, I found myself drinking during the day and becoming insecure and depressed.

I was driving back home after a disappointing party when I had my wake up call. While drunk, I looked at the red lights at the bottom of a hill and dared to cross them. Yes, I had lost my mind. I was alone in the car, daring myself to do something really stupid.

As I approached the point of no return at 70 miles per hour (113 Km/h), I saw a blue car zooming in front of me, then as I was almost inside the junction box a white car crossed in front of me like a dart.

As I looked to the right, I could see the headlights of a big car approaching really fast. I merged with the lights and couldn't look away, but suddenly, the connection was broken, and I was thrown back into reality.

I never felt more alive in my life, and I had to stop the car to catch my breath. Cheating death made me go from drunk to sober in a millisecond, and at that moment, I realised that I had to face my fears.

32

Facing my fears

My father was a serious man who worked as a Bank director during the day and as a teacher of Economics at a reputable university at night. The heavy frame of his bifocals made him look intimidating, and all of my friends were afraid of him. In fact, they gave him the sweet nickname of "Thunder Voice".

We had a library room at my house, and he would spend most of his free time there, reading. I approached him and asked sheepishly:

"Dad? Can we talk?"

He looked at me in dismay and said:

"Wait a moment."

He made me wait for a couple of minutes standing in front of him, while he finished reading an article in the paper.

Every second seemed to drag forever, and I started to sweat, as I was getting even more nervous. Finally, he looked at me and asked.

"What is the matter?"

"I've got a big problem. I've failed a few subjects at the university, even though I've studied hard, so I think I'm not cut out for it.

I want to open a shop to sell home appliances, and I can also fix them if I have a workshop at the back of the shop. I'm sure I can make good money if you help me get started. Would you like to become my business partner?"

He looked at me intrigued and didn't get angry, as I was expecting.

Instead, he stood up slowly and started browsing his books. He selected three books and handed them to me while staring at me with compassion and said:

"Read these business books. We will talk again after you have read them. If you want a business, you will have to take a Business degree."

I took the books and disappeared from his sight as quickly as I could. I was happy that I was brave enough to tell him about my ambitions, but I realised that books would be in my life forever, even if all I wanted was to become an entrepreneur and have a little shop.

Finding hope in an unexpected place

My friend Cid could read a book overnight, so I went to see him for advice.

"Cid, I'm in a pickle, and I need your help. I gave up my degree, and I want to become a businessman. The problem is that my dad wants me to take a Business degree. I think he'll support me, but he told me to read three business books before we talk again. Can you read the books and explain to me what they are about? I can't focus with all the stress."

He smiled and said:

"Zander, let's go for a ride."

Cid invited me to get inside of his beautiful convertible and told me that he wanted to show me something amazing. We were having fun until I saw the university gates approaching. He stopped the car, and we went inside the main building. He suddenly stopped in front of one of the notice boards, looked at me and said:

"This is the solution to your life."

I was looking at posters advertising dancing classes, a chess tournament, a talk about human rights, a garage band competition and a few other events, but I couldn't find the solution for my life there. I looked back at him puzzled, so he said:

"Can't you see that there is a speed reading demonstration on Thursday?"

"No, I don't."

I couldn't see it, just inches away from my nose.

I had disconnected from studying, and for this reason, I was blind to the speed reading ad.

While I was a little disappointed that I had to spend the money saved for my holidays on the course, I did it anyway. But I was excited to finally understand how successful readers read, and I knew I would not be the same after the course.

A new world of possibilities

It was money well spent because I discovered that I could actually read faster than before and, to my surprise, I started enjoying my father's business books; so much so that I started going to the university's library to read marketing books, just for fun. I was hooked and, without wasting any more time, started a Business Studies degree.

Soon after taking this speed reading course, I realised I was not struggling on my own. My friend, Marcelo, had a brother that was becoming very successful working at the Stock Exchange, and while having a conversation with him he opened up and said he didn't know how to go through all the information he had to read for work.

That was my opportunity to teach him some of what I had learnt and, for fair payment, I had a happy client. I was on my way to starting to help people to develop their potential and perform better at reading.

Not only was I able to complete a Business Study degree, but I then went on to complete a Masters in Marketing and Advertising.

After many years of learning, researching and subsequently teaching how to focus the mind, I discovered I was dyslexic with the additional challenge of suffering from Attention Deficit Disorder (ADD).

Moving to Europe

In a quest to expand my horizons, in 1999, I moved from Brazil to London.

At first, I struggled to communicate in English but managed to get a job in the kitchen of a Thai restaurant. Unfortunately, my co-workers spoke Thai all day long, so I resorted to learning English at night with a book and tapes, but with little motivation.

I discovered London's nightlife and, despite having some fun, felt lost and lonely in the big city. Without many friends, I was craving to belong to a community that would help me grow as a person. I knew that in London you could pretty much find whatever you wanted, but in those pre-Google days, who could you turn to?

I made a friend at a meditation course, who invited me to a meeting to learn about personal growth. At a beautiful hotel in London, I got a foretaste of Tony Robbins. The personal development meeting was run by the Yes Group - www.yesgroup.org - that my friend

Karl Pearsall had been inspired to create after a Tony Robbins workshop in 1993.

At the Yes Group event, someone offered me a ticket for the iconic Tony Robbins workshop, Unleash The Power Within, and I bought it without hesitation. It was a four-day workshop that prepared you to go on a fire-walk. That's right. You get so pumped up that you walk on red-hot coals with a smile on your face. When you get to the other side and look back at the glowing embers, you feel like you can move mountains.

In that workshop, Tony took my mind for a ride through the realm of possibilities. I was surprised to hear him recommending that everyone take a speed reading course to improve themselves. However, he didn't offer to teach us, nor did he recommend a teacher. I felt that he was talking directly to me, so I decided there and then to master the English language and teach speed reading in the UK. Some of my friends scoffed at my ambitions, but I found the means to pay for English lessons at the best and most expensive course in the capital.

Once I had mastered speed reading, the seminar promoters that booked Tony Robbins and other first-class speakers around the world, Success Resources - www.srglobal.com, invited me to attend a Gerry Robert presentation. Gerry is a renowned expert who helps people write and publish their book — fast. Ever since I had attended Tony's event, I had dreamt of being published, and Gerry explained to me how to make my book a reality. I wasted no time, started developing my speed reading methodology, and my book started taking shape.

Making a dent in the Universe

With my book proof in hand, I attended another Tony Robbins event, but this time, I was determined to talk to him and invite him to become my business partner. I could see it all in my mind's eye: I would give his books to my students to practice reading faster, and he would promote my speed reading workshops so people could develop themselves. A perfect partnership!

At the event, I asked many people from the crew to help me meet Tony, but the answer was always the same,

"No. No. No". I hoped that my friend Harry Singha, who was the MC of the event, would help me out, but he said, "No one talks to Tony privately, sorry Zander". That was a blow, so I went to the event's lobby to decide my next move. After a short while, I started talking to a woman called Lydia. What I didn't know was that she was the Personal Assistant to the CEO of Success Resources. I told her my journey, and she told me about new developments that were taking place to revolutionise education throughout the world. As I already knew, the education system moves too slowly and I doubled my attention when she said that we need to prepare our youth to find or create their own jobs. I agreed that the world is moving fast and everyone should be able to learn something practical and start earning good money, even without a degree.

I understand that in this ever-changing world, the power of anticipation is key to success. Having first-hand information about something that is going to become huge is giving me a major advantage; I want to pass that advantage on to you, to help you propel your business faster in the unchartered waters of the future.

I knew I was on the right track, but what happened next was just mind-blowing. A few minutes later, Lydia introduced me to the founder and CEO of Success Resources, Richard Tan.

We started talking and laughing; he wanted to know more about my courses, and I gave him the best answers and references. I was already having a great time, and then he told me that he needed me to speak from the big stage at National Achievers Congress events all over the world. He said that Tony Robbins keeps advertising speed reading and that he had finally found the person he was looking for. I was speechless - a nod of my head and a smile were enough to seal the deal. I was over the moon, but that was just the beginning of the adventure.

I didn't know at the time that Success Resources is the biggest seminar promoter in the world, organising 500 events a year in 30 countries.

Richard decided to introduce me to Tony Robbins because the synergy was there. Then, suddenly, against all the odds, moments later, I was in front of Tony Robbins, inviting him to become my business partner, just like in my dream!

I had now met Tony twice, and I thank him for the initial spark that gave me the confidence to try the impossible.

Zander with Tony Robbins and Richard Tan

Since then however, my life has taken yet another turn.

Richard Tan shared with me his most significant idea till date, that is using cutting-edge technology and ground-breaking content.

I've always wanted to help modernise the education system by showing people a better way to read and learn, and now I have found the platform from which I will be able to do it.

I was fascinated to learn that Success Resources is pioneering the use of holographic technology to project a fully formed 3D presenter on stage by partnering up with ARHT Media. They already had Tony Robbins presenting a workshop to an audience in Melbourne, Australia, but to everyone's surprise, Tony was not there. He was actually being streamed from Miami, Florida in real-time, and no one could tell the difference between the real Tony or his virtual reality projection. By the way, all of it happened without the need for wearing any special glasses.

Another innovative technology that is taking the world by storm is Virtual Reality. Tony Robbins is a partner of NextVR, and they are streaming one sports or music event per week in virtual reality. At the beginning of 2017, there were 10 million people with a VR headset, and in 2018 it is predicted that there will be 100 million. So, do you want to be one of the first people to experience and to create content for this new media?

I had the privilege of spending four days with Richard Tan in Bali in March 2017, and I can assure you that there is much more happening at Success Resources' headquarters.

If you want to succeed in this hyper-competitive world and learn essential skills that schools and universities are failing to deliver, please check out Success Resources events in your city because today might be your lucky day.

www.srglobal.com

Updating the education system

Much effort is made to teach young people to read, and most teachers believe that if you can read silently at the same speed that you talk, then you can read proficiently.

This is a real shame because your brain loves speed and reading slowly can leave you disengaged and much less motivated to read in your leisure time.

Research run by The Jenkins Group in the USA shows that 42% of college graduates never read another book after college.

If you read slowly and keep skipping back to re-read, you end up getting bored, and no one wants to get bored by choice, so they are wise enough to stop reading books or long texts.

My coaching career and flow

I have personally taught more than 3,600 people, and my clients are having a massive productivity boost by accessing flow at the office. In fact, after fifteen years of experience, I can say that I expect you to increase your mental performance between 100% and 1,000%.

I like working with smart minds; I have taught many people, including professionals from many high profile companies. However, when I ask them if they are slow or fast readers, their response is usually vague. Most suggest that they are not very fast and often compare themselves to someone else who can read material faster than they can.

You also know someone that reads faster than you, don't you? Don't worry, everybody does.

In my view, reading faster is as easy as learning to play a new video game. You might improve 62%, or even more than 112% in a matter of a few hours, and as a bonus, enter the flow state.

Change your life with flow

Getting into flow state is a natural ability that you have and, by developing it, you will be more willing to study, research and take more significant challenges in life. Taking more challenges that remove you from your comfort zone are essential for learning and growing.

I believe you can change this world in ways never thought of before. Education is a powerful way to help people innovate, improve the quality of life on our planet and promote peace in every country.

Be curious and do what you love. The possibilities are endless. Being able to learn to get in flow will help you progress in life at a higher speed and it will help you become more creative.

Through action, change can happen, and through passionate action, you can create flow, lead teams and leave a legacy.

The whole world is powered by imagination and the future is brighter for those who dare to flow.

HUMANS IN FLOW

This book will open a portal of access to altered states of consciousness by exploring one of the most challenging concepts that science has had to grapple with. An old technology that set the modern world in motion and is at the core of every disruptive innovation we will see in the future.

I'm talking about the power of storing and transmitting information outside the human brain. By translating sounds into symbols, we started to disseminate ideas, so I will let you discover how to see words in a new and better way. You will enter a process of discovery with four quests and will be guided on your journey by powerful creatures. By the end, you will acquire the power of developing more focus, getting into flow state and becoming more creative at work.

The easiest way to get into flow is by reading books. You've probably had the experience of enjoying a book so much that you immersed yourself into the experience, forgot to eat, and time just flew by.

This experience is undoubtedly a flow state, and most people wish they had access to it more often. The good news is that by learning how to enter the flow reading state, you will engage again with books and by having a bigger vision for your life, you will be entering the flow state while reading, thinking, talking, writing, exercising, performing, creating a big vision and committing to new levels of integrity.

The keys to intellectual flow

To build the expectation to the adventure you are about to embark on, I want to mention the keys that will unlock your flow. Although flow can be achieved while performing sports and exercising, you will be guided to achieve mental flow, so to unlock the highest level of flow you will need to open all the doors that will lead you to the big portal that is to create your legacy.

The five keys

- First key – Flow Reading State

- Second key – Flow Writing State

- Third key – Flow Drawing State

- Fourth key – Flow Speaking State

- Fifth key – Flow Vision State

Therefore this book will have an immediate impact in your life if you understand that by reading better you will be opening the portal that leads to the state of flow and, by applying the learning to your work and leisure, you will be able to take your performance to brand new levels.

I don't like reading

Many people approach me and share that they find it difficult to focus their mind long enough to enjoy reading books, and they ask me:

"Can you teach me how to enjoy reading books?"

I tell them that it's almost impossible to learn how to enjoy reading because reading is not an activity in itself.

People like entertaining themselves and they like learning new ideas or skills. They do so by reading because that's the way to access all that information.

The problem is that many people didn't achieve the minimum standards to read well enough to enjoy a good book as an adult. They might think fast like an adult, but they read slowly like a 13 years old with Attention Deficit Disorder (ADD).

Let me explain a bit further with the help of an example.

Almost nobody really likes flying and, though this statement may confuse you, I believe that you don't know anyone that likes entering into a big aeroplane and sitting for 17 hours on an uncomfortable chair and enduring turbulence, while being surrounded by people that they don't know. That's right, nobody likes that, but they love going on holidays, and if they need to sit down on a chair for 17 hours to get to Thailand and have lots of fun, laughter and incredible experiences with people they love, they will not blink an eyelid and will happily embark on the plane.

The plane is the best way to reach Thailand, and reading is the best way to access information.

Reading is the most common flow activity in the world but if a person reads slowly, the likelihood of finding flow and enjoyment while reading is small, making them associate reading with pain, not pleasure, and therefore they will not reach out and read a book for fun.

You can pay good money for a ticket and endure a long journey as long as you travel on a good plane, with a trained pilot, pleasant stewardesses, tasty food and a few good movies to watch. The problem is that you have learnt how to read as a child and never had further training on how to read efficiently as an adult.

To enjoy reading a book, you need to achieve good speed, but you think that you can go fast enough in the little aeroplane you built as a teenager. In fact, you need to upgrade the engine, smooth the bodywork and install a pair of turbines to replace old propellers so you can take off and enjoy the journey.

The problem is that you didn't prepare yourself enough for the journey and you burn rubber while you should be flying high.

Maybe, while under pressure, you learnt how to push harder and were able to fly in your old plane. The problem is that you are the pilot of a plane that could take you on the holiday of your life, but you are not a good pilot, and no one told you that.

You plan a new trip, have your bags carefully packed, your taxi come punctually at 8:00 am, and you endure extra stress as your driver dangerously ploughs along at rush hour. You are already tired from a restless night of sleep because you were so anxious to fall asleep, knowing you would be in charge of a huge plane.

You manage to take off after a lot of stress to find the right runway at Heathrow airport. You inspect all the instruments under pressure, while the countdown to take off is on. As you gain altitude, you feel relief and hope for a quiet flight but immediately the flight enters turbulence area. You were hoping to eat your breakfast, but you cannot even drink your coffee as the plane shakes badly and the last thing you want is a coffee stain on your pristine white shirt. So you are hungry, and the co-pilot starts screaming at you with a high pitch and irritating accent, telling you that there will be a lot of bad weather on the way to Thailand and that there are a few problems with the aeroplane that you were not aware of. He starts going through them point by point, and you feel like you are about to flip.

At this point, you realise that you would be better off at home. You could watch some of your usual TV programmes and perhaps try your luck watching a few movies, or going to the Pub on your holidays, as anything would be more pleasurable than this trip.

Figuratively speaking, you get to the end of your journey as you close your book on page 14, never to be opened again.

You know that many people had a blast in Thailand, but you decide that you don't like Asia anyways. You can have a good life without ever going to Japan, India,

Vietnam, Singapore or Bali. Perhaps the idea of going to Brazil lingered in your head for many years, but you will never manage to get there or anywhere in the Caribbean, and that's very sad.

Perhaps you had a good life and visited a few places that you could reach by car. You heard many stories about faraway lands and watched some videos about them, but never experienced going there.

I know that reading this book might fill you up with dread, but don't feel disheartened, because I'm here to help you learn how to be an excellent pilot, so you can go anywhere in the world and enjoy new adventures.

I will tell you a few stories because accelerated learning is all about storytelling, and you will entertain yourself as you embark on four quests. You will find many ideas that will help you relax and become in charge of your destiny.

I used the metaphor of flying to describe the enjoyment you can get in flow state while reading. You will understand that you can easily develop your reading skills and this way focus on reading subjects that will transform your life, without ever learning how to like reading.

You will feel confident enough to be a good pilot who trusts their skills while in charge of a new plane and focus your attention on enjoying incredible books and exotic holidays of the mind.

EAGLE HUNTER

In 2017, I was invited to present to a crowd of one thousand people from a big stage at the Global Business Forum in Kazakhstan. I went to one of the very last places on earth where men, horses, and eagles live a nomadic life and form a tight bond as a family unit. I met incredible people in Kyrgyzstan and Kazakhstan, learnt about their tradition of horse riding and was fascinated by the way they care for eagles like they were their own children. One person of the family will talk and sing to their eagle every day, hand feed the eagle for five years to develop a special bond, and train them to become a good eagle hunter.

It's very intriguing that horses were first domesticated in the Kazakhstan area 6,000 years ago and eagles were first trained to become eagle hunters also in the same area about 3,000 years ago.

For thousands of years, the tradition dictates that on a cold day when the Siberian winter starts to freeze the land they go out together on a horseback expedition for their first hunt, to bring food for the family, and they will keep risking their lives during all the harsh winter. They will hunt every winter until the eagle reaches puberty. They will talk to each other every day and stay best friends until the eagle's 15th anniversary. On this sad day, the hunter will cover the eagle's eyes with a leather hood for a long journey. He will release the eagle back into the wild and hide so it can find a mate to procreate with and live 50 more years enjoying the views and caring for its own family.

I like the way man, horse and eagle create synergy, so to make your learning experience more pleasurable, I will blend learning skills with stories that will involve these three as leading characters, and another two creatures will join them at later chapters for more excitement.

Your four quests and a prophecy

I predict that you will have a revelation when you discover your hidden powers, so you too will awaken to new possibilities to impact this world and leave a lasting legacy.

The quest to fulfil your prophecy will unfold as you read this book, and you will embark on an adventurous journey towards something difficult to find, but I assure you that your search will be full of worth. Your discoveries will change the way you see challenges in life, and you will be better equipped to have more fun at work and also during your free time, to have a level of enjoyment you never imagined possible.

Quests are often full of symbolic and mythological wisdom only achieved by the hero with full determination in finding a way to develop their higher self. The hero's journey brings great insight into your power to achieve your most wildest dreams.

You will have the opportunity to live a more adventurous life, test your skills and receive magical rewards. You will embark on your first quest and learn with the king of the skies how to experience the flow state.

The eagle will guide you to achieve ultimate performance and more pleasure in life. You will understand that all its power and control are at their peak when they do absolutely nothing, and soar above the

47

mountains by taking advantage of ascending currents of air.

You can also perform at your highest level by learning how to get in flow state and unlock your creativity with extreme focus so you can succeed and find your fortune.

Your second quest will start on horseback, and it will take you on a journey of discovery. You will learn how to be one with the horse to be able to ride it, and this way you will understand the principles of reading faster to eventually fall in love with books and transform your life.

Once you acquire this new power, you will travel into a different world for the third quest and will learn with the most terrifying creature of the seas. Some researchers say that humans might have evolved from prehistoric sharks as they were one of the very first vertebrates to inhabit the earth 450 million years ago. So I will expose some possible reasons for our distant cousins being on the very top of the food chain in the sea, and you will learn valuable lessons to position yourself at the apex in your field, build your reputation and accelerate your professional success.

You will enter the fourth dimension for the last quest and will be guided by a legendary creature.

The mythological dragon will help you question the basic notion that time ticks one second at the time. It will burn a hole in the fabric of time by showing you that its fire encompasses creation and destruction.

You will then be able to rethink Einstein's theory of relativity and gift yourself many more years to live a happy and fulfilling life.

I hope that these quests will inspire you to change the world and leave a lasting legacy.

So let the quest begin.

Hack your brain and find a new mind.

The *Eagles Flow Quest* has four insights to empower you to focus your mind, read faster, think smart and have more ideas.

F — **Feel** your body

L — **Look** and see

O — **Observe** your mind

W — **What** to focus on

Time to read the First Quest

Reading Speed in Words Per Minute	TIME
At 100 WPM	9.2 hours
At 200 WPM	4.6 hours
At 300 WPM	3.1 hours
At 400 WPM	2.3 hours
At 500 WPM	1.8 hours

Reading Speed in Words Per Minute	TIME
At 600 WPM	1.5 hours
At 800 WPM	1.1 hours
At 1000 WPM	55 minutes
At 1200 WPM	46 minutes
At 1400 WPM	39 minutes

To illustrate the process, I will compare the journey of finding deep focus and ultimate performance with the eagle's body and behaviour. Once you understand the links between the insights, you will be able to do new experiments and explore the possibility of entering a flow state at will.

The challenge

I will compare the effortless ways that eagles are able to fly for long periods during the day, while hardly flapping their wings, with creating flow states to help you improve mental and physical performance to optimal levels.

Eagles know how to flow because they have learnt how to take advantage of their body, environment, and circumstances and you will be able to do the same.

I will also explore the relationship between men and hunter eagles to explain how your mind works and how to increase awareness.

You will be surprised by all the ways you can channel your energy to tap into your highest potential to become more creative and productive.

You will learn how to focus and use many hacks to transform lost effort into energy that will be able to make you two, three or even five times more productive.

Hack into flow state and become the super version of yourself

I've chosen the eagle as an analogy to explain the flow state because no other bird symbolises majesty, strength, and courage as they do, and these are characteristics that needs to be developed to get in flow.

Eagles are at the top of their food chain, they hunt other animals, but nothing hunts them. Flow requires this relaxed confidence.

They are one of the only birds that love storms. Most birds fly away from the storm in fear and head for cover, but an eagle spreads its wings and uses ascending air currents to soar to greater heights. Flow demands significant challenges, too, and high stakes will help you get there.

Flow is an optimal state of consciousness where time flies. You merge with the task at hand, feel your best and achieve top performance in sports, working and thinking. You can prepare yourself to experience flow and excel in many areas, and I will guide you to get there again and again.

Four stages to achieve flow

Flow is not just one state that needs to be hacked. It is comprised of four stages that need to be understood to be accomplished.

Don't focus on flow; focus on the process of achieving it and flow will occur.

Surprisingly, the struggle is a part of the flow, don't resist or try to speed it up. You will find flow as the ultimate reward for your efforts.

So the first stage is the "struggle" where you can become overwhelmed and frustrated with a problem, or a big challenge you are working hard to achieve. For the eagle, the struggle would be flying under the storm.

The second stage is the "release", that could be moments of absolute relaxation and surrender to other activities, to entertain yourself and let your brain unwind. For the eagle this is achieving high altitude and flying above the storm with no hidden agenda but to enjoy the view.

Then you achieve the "flow" stage which will bless you with insights, breakthroughs and creative ideas if you are working with your mind, and precision of movement if you are practising extreme or radical sports. For the eagle, it would be to spot animals getting out of their shelter after the storm and hunting the best ones with precision.

The final stage is the "recovery" because you will need rest after using a lot of energy in a short space of time. For the eagle it is the time to have a deserved meal, go back to the nest, eat a bit more, relax and build up strength to the new cycle that starts with the "struggle" stage again, in order to achieve the "release" and then the desired "flow" state.

Almost no other bird can go to the height of the eagle, so they fly alone and not with pigeons or other small birds.

Results of a 10-year study by McKinsey & Company show that top executives increase productivity by up to 500% when in flow [2], which usually happens when they are alone. But as you raise your standards, you might be able to go down to the ground and motivate a whole group to find flow together, creating a team that bonds and develops synergy.

You can achieve different levels of flow, and the very high focused state can last around two or three hours. There is another level of flow called "helpers high" that can be achieved by altruism and can last two to three solid days.

Eagles create their nests at the top of tall trees or on the rock face of mountains, and every year they make them bigger, so an eagle's nest can weigh from 1-3 tons. Your insights while in flow will allow you to develop a new perspective on life to think big and also make your dreams a reality.

By hunting animals much bigger than themselves, an eagle never surrenders, and it is very strategic to win its prey or regain its territory. Over time you will also take challenges that others would be afraid to face, and you will keep winning as a true visionary.

Getting in flow state or in the zone is known to improve performance and produce intense feelings of enjoyment, which can lead to more significant achievements and enhanced creativity.

Radical and Olympic sports athletes are notorious for achieving flow to accomplish their feats that challenge gravity laws, endurance benchmarks and teams' synergy. It might take years of practice to achieve a level of effortless power to get in the zone, but you can get there much faster. For example, after a few lessons learning how to ski, someone could decide to go down the mountain and feel that invincible feeling of being one with their environment, and experience something they will never forget. Depending on the intensity of the experience, the person might be hooked forever on loving that sport, so they will be able to access that state more often.

Some people will endure hours on end in the ocean's freezing cold water, risking the possibility of an encounter with a hungry shark for the chance of catching another wave and tube riding. It can be even more exhilarating if the risk of injury is higher, by surfing over a seabed with sharp coral reefs. The circumstances can change a lot, but the chemistry created by the body will induce a highly addictive feeling.

Many scientists are researching the best ways to achieve flow while practising sports, and results can be measured by the number of broken records and gold medals won.

I'm more interested in the achievement of flow while performing intellectual work, and you will understand the similarities between mental and physical flow throughout the book.

Gold medallists

What thrills me the most is that I decided to start working with gold medallists to research more about how they find flow during training and competition, I was doing this so I could carry on my experiments about intellectual flow.

I have met gymnast Steve Frew, gold medal at Commonwealth Olympics on the still rings. We have been talking about flow and ultimate performance. I spoke to cyclist Matthew Walls moments after receiving three medals, including a gold medal at the Track Cycling World Cup in London 2019, and I have many more athletes lined up for interviews and mental training.

I'm certain that my research with gold medallists will help me discover many more secrets to unlock this elusive state and let others learn how to find pleasure in achieving their challenges.

This intellectual quest will help you focus on the present moment so you will be deeply involved in your projects and visions. Even though you might be delaying immediate gratification, you will be immersed into a feeling of personal growth and happiness.

A great benefit of flow is that you will have a sharp focus and will be able to make decisions faster with confidence.

53

EAGLES FLOW QUEST

Vision One

FEEL YOUR BODY

"Once we accept our limits, we go beyond them."

Albert Einstein

Awareness is key

The first area to pay attention, to get in flow state, is your body. Eagles are one of the fastest birds in the world, flying at the incredible speed of up to 200 miles per hour (320 Km/h) so you can imagine the awareness they have about their body to stay in control.

They are powerful beyond measure, and they can fly for hours on end without flapping their wings. They are so fine-tuned with the environment that they identify the geology of the area and predict air currents of ascending hot air that are known as the thermals. They enter into this uplifting zones, and they fly to go higher and higher.

I flew gliders many times, and we looked for eagles to find these ascending air currents because gliders are slim aeroplanes with long wings, but without an engine. By spotting these air currents, the pilot can soar and gain many extra hours of flight that will enable them to cover greater distances.

So you will start your quest by analysing the impact that your body can have on your intellectual performance.

1.1.1 I don't want to be normal

I want to be an inspiration in some way, and I found out that researching, thinking, and teaching fulfil my highest value to be able to contribute to this world. Perhaps you want to become super smart, strong, fast, rich, happy, famous or attractive, and these desires are shifting the way we eat, take legal and illegal drugs, build relationships, have fun, rest and work.

I don't want a tablet to cure a headache and be normal, I want to feel limitless, and keep pushing my mental capacity to produce excellent results.

I don't want a dose of an illegal drug to go crazy; I want a mystical experience to feel connected.

I don't want to take a pill every day to help me handle depression; I want to be robust to stay motivated.

When you learn how to get into flow state, you will be able to create happiness out of nothing.

Instead of achieving immediate gratification by buying something you desire, you can choose to focus on a challenge and create enjoyment while accomplishing the desired outcome. As a welcoming side effect, your body will produce a powerful combination of the most pleasurable chemicals, and you will feel happy, inspired and fulfilled. Happiness is a mental state, and your body chemistry is deeply involved in the production of a cocktail of six neurotransmitters and hormones. The only time your body release all these compounds at once is when you enter the flow state. The exact dosage will make you enter the desired flow state, so take a look at the ingredients of your happiness potion as they will give you the best high in the world.

- Serotonin regulates your feelings of well-being, happiness, mood, social behaviour, appetite, digestion, sleep, memory and sexual desire.
- Dopamine is the main chemical responsible for motivating you into action by making you recognise the value of a particular reward. It makes you engage and keeps you excited on your quest for your perceived reward.
- Oxytocin is the hormone released in childbirth and breastfeeding. It is also called the love hormone as it is produced while you develop trust and bond with your friends, and also during sexual intercourse.

- Norepinephrine is released in fight-or-flight situations, so it mobilises you for action. It increases focused attention, memory and arousal.
- Anandamide brings you a state of joy or delight as it brings balance to your body and mind. It regulates your ability to endure stress, inhibits your sense of fear and improves lateral thinking.
- Endorphins reduce pain sensations and trigger a positive feeling in the body, similar to that of morphine. They also reduce stress, boost self-esteem and inhibit anxiety and depression.

Illicit drugs and flow

Neurochemical changes can be triggered by very powerful illicit or legal drugs and it gives you a glimpse of flow and other altered states of consciousness, like profound meditative states, but the feel-good factor can result in addiction, and the low after the high can be very depressing.

The aftereffect of flow can leave you with a long-lasting creative afterglow, and it will not give you any hang-over, even though the change on your neurochemistry would be the equivalent of taking Ritalin, cannabis, cocaine, MDMA and heroin together at the same time.

If you have some knowledge about these drugs, you probably think that they don't mix together, and you are right. But somehow in flow, your body becomes the alchemist that creates something unexpected and magical.

Notice below the correlation between the ingredient of your flow potion and the effects of very different drugs.

- Serotonin – MDMA, Ecstasy, LSD and Prozac
- Dopamine – Cocaine
- Oxytocin – MDMA and GHB
- Norepinephrine – Speed, Adderall and Ritalin
- Anandamide – Cannabis
- Endorphins – Heroin and other Opiates

Adrenaline and flow

Your heart probably missed a beat or two while watching thrill seekers and adrenaline junkies risking their lives while performing incredible stunts. For you, they might seem all crazy people, but a big distinction needs to be made between two separate categories of people that enjoy chasing excitement by risking an early encounter with death.

It will surprise you that people that have been achieving the biggest feats in radical sports and have been breaking records in surfing, skiing, skating, parachuting, biking and many more sports, are actually averse to the adrenaline rush. They might have an adrenaline build-up as their turn to perform approaches, but nothing compared with the adrenaline rush you would expect.

If you release adrenaline, you get a boost of power and your heart races like in situations of fight and flight. Contrary to popular belief, the record-breakers don't want to get too excited in a competition or performance, but they want to be in total control.

Being in a state of flow will give them the ability to notice every single nuance in their performance and peace of mind to act wisely in case things don't go according to plan.

The adrenaline rush is for the amateur or inexperienced thrill-seeker, not for the professional daredevil who builds a career out of perfecting their skills to very high standards.

On the other hand, adrenaline can have exceptional effects when triggered as a preparation stimuli for flow. I've learnt with daredevil Wim Hof, AKA The Ice Man, that you can fight disease and boost your mental balance by doing his breathing technique. It combines deep breathing, breath-holding, physical exercise, visualisation and cold showers. I have been following his protocol for more than two years, and it is surprising that I feel calm and relaxed after the practice, even though my body releases large quantities of adrenaline in my system.

I've been taking only cold showers for the last two years because I understood the power of his technique and I invite you to look at his work by visiting his website or watching some of his videos.

www.wimhofmethod.com

Download his app to be guided in his method and decide for yourself if all the new science validating his method is something you want to play with.

1.1.2 Legal and illegal drugs are good and evil

Not many people realise that nicotine is a drug that can be used to enhance performance on cognition, but I steer clear from it. Some people take advantage of nicotine patches, gums, vaping, or even snuff tobacco instead of smoking it, to diminish the cancer risks.

Alcohol is hardly ever considered to be a drug just because it is legal, but alcohol is the drug that kills more than all the other drugs combined. It's good, it's evil, and it can cause dependency.

According to Steven Kotler [9] more Americans are dying from prescription drugs than car accidents. Ten per cent are taking antidepressants, and one in four kids are taking drugs to control their attention deficit hyperactive disorder (ADHD). So the scary figure is that 22 per cent of Americans have an illicit drug problem to achieve a state of mind that can be achieved by someone in flow. What is surprising is that their body will release the same chemicals in the body as illicit drugs would, but without any side effect, on the contrary, the person will know they have to focus hard to get in flow instead of relying on the short term gratification of drugs.

You can find anything on the internet that can be delivered to you, virtually any drug you might want to try is within your reach, but would you dare taking something that comes in an envelope from someone you don't know, or handed to you from unknown sources?

Although, even if you use a drugs test kit to find out more about the purity of your drugs, there are risks on taking them.

Some people take drugs because of curiosity or peer pressure, and some are taking a blind risk to find relief from post-traumatic stress disorder (PTSD), depression or mental and physical abuse.

59

Painkillers prescribed by doctors or bought in the black market, especially opioids – painkillers, heroin or fentanyl - are responsible for the biggest number of overdoses in the US, representing two-thirds of all drug overdose deaths. These drugs can be very addictive, and a doctor can do a lot of harm, even with the best possible intentions.

I've suffered from depression for a significant part of my life, and I'm fortunate that I never tried heroin or strong painkillers recreationally. But to fight anxiety and depression, I abused alcohol, tried a few drugs, did therapy, and experimented with many mystical practices in the search for relief, for more years than I can remember. From time to time, I would feel like isolating myself, not wanting to look for work, clients or even make friends. I can tell you that sometimes the situation was incredibly lonely, hopeless and dire, but I found flow and it was worth it.

In this quest for flow, your first step might be to look for what makes your heart sing. Most people I talk to don't have the faintest idea of what they love doing and feel disengaged at work. From a meaningless life, someone can start drinking too much and perhaps get into depression. My work here is to help prevent that, but if you go into depression and anxiety like I did, you might be happy to know about new treatments using psychedelic drugs and following a strict protocol that includes therapy, is taking the world by storm. They can also help you find the flow state, or a clear mind, to create more possibilities for your future; it all depends on where you are and what you want.

I'm not a physician, and I don't recommend any drugs or treatments, I'm just sharing my findings and experiences. As you know, everything has a risk and reward ratio, so it's your job to consult with a medical doctor and research further before making any decision. A comprehensive website about legal and illegal drugs that I find very useful and can be worth looking at is called Erowid.

www.erowid.org

1.1.3 New technologies to achieve flow

I will start by pointing out that technology is achieving better results than many antidepressants by using something called transcranial magnetic stimulation, and this is an area of high interest to me. Many studies are measuring the effect of this technology on the brain, and some early adopters are stockbrokers as they are always in search of new ways to be sharper and spot opportunities.

A company called Halo has been using transcranial direct current stimulation to enhance sports performance and to create flow with incredible results. I've never tried it as I'm not into sports performance myself, but if you are, you can find out more about it by visiting their website.

www.haloneuro.com

I experimented with neurofeedback for the first time about ten years ago at the HearthMath office in London, and you can learn more about the benefits of creating coherence between heart and brain by measuring your heart rate variability (HRV). You can visit their website and do your research.

www.heartmath.com

Another company that developed a smart way to measure heart rate variability (HRV) is called Oura Ring. Their ring measures many vital functions to help you get in flow, so I will go into more detail later on.

www.ouraring.com

Research shows that soldiers were able to master new skills five times faster than normal using new technologies to stimulate the brain. Smart sensors and wearables like Fitbit and the Apple watch are tracking the unimaginable paths, and more sophisticated devices are entering the market to help you track and enhance your mental and physical states to improve performance. For example, Navy SEALs are cutting down the time to learn a foreign language by 75 per cent of the usual time by using sensory deprivation tanks combined with brain entrainment and heart rate frequency regulation.

Transient Hypofrontality leads to flow

Biotech is doubling in power every four months, or five times faster than Moore's law, and it is revealing that the extremely powerful portion of your brain, responsible for processing logical decisions, planning and exercising will power, called the prefrontal cortex, shuts down and redirects all that processing power to other parts of the brain responsible for boosting lateral and creative thinking at incredible speeds. The technical term for this surprising effect in the brain while in flow is called Transient Hypofrontality, and it means a temporary slowing of activity of the prefrontal cortex.

As a side effect of this abnormal brain activity, you will plunge into the deep now, where most of your fears and anxieties wither. Therefore your inner critic gets smothered, risk-taking goes up, and you will have more ideas.

Many brain and biohacks are available, and you can test some equipment that can have an impact on creating flow for sports and brain functions.

Biohacking

Author and biohacker Dave Asprey created something for which I have been a great fan of, called the Bulletproof coffee, and it consists of having a cup of coffee and replacing milk with a spoon of coconut oil and a spoon of butter. To homogenise the fat in the drink you need to use a blender, and you will create a tasty drink that will give you a constant level of energy. It works very well for me, and you can learn more by searching about him on YouTube or by visiting his website.

www.bulletproof.com

Dave is the creator of the word biohacking, and he has the best facilities to try many ways to supercharge your body and upgrade your brain. Visit his website below to understand what each equipment will help you with. I also recommend his books if you want to understand more about biohacks.

www.bulletprooflabs.com

You can find the equipment described below at his lab in Santa Monica, California.

- Virtual Float Tank – virtual float tank without getting wet and use brainwaves entrainment.
- EEG Brain Trainer – neurofeedback to make your brain more focused and creative
- Brain Charger – light therapy that promotes creativity and mitochondria function.
- Cryotherapy – spend 3 minutes in a -184°F (-120°C) chamber.
- Redcharger – expose your body to red and infrared light.
- Atmospheric Cell Trainer – a futuristic pod that uses changes in air pressure to create a workout for your cellular energy system.
- Oxygen Trainer – supplies oxygen at various concentrations and tracks your heart rate and oxygen saturation.

Below are a few other technologies that you might want to take a look at. Research the net to learn more and find out if you can try some equipment near where you live.

- Floatation Tank – total darkness and dense water at body temperature will set your mind free.
- Pandora Star – synchronised flashing lights and gongs that promote different levels of consciousness.
- Sound technologies – Everything is vibrating, so are we, and I had incredible experiences while relaxing and listening to planetary gongs, Tibetan singing bowls and crystal singing bowls.
- Transcranial electrical stimulation – constant electric current delivered via electrodes on the head.
- Transcranial magnetic stimulation - brain stimulation by changing magnetic fields.
- Vagus nerve stimulation - treatment that delivers electrical impulses to the vagus nerve.
- Gyroscope – spin your body in all directions by moving your body's gravity centre.

- Brainwaves Entrainment – listen to designed sounds to help you change brainwaves.

I'm researching further and applying what I learn to coach my clients to achieve the flow state faster. You can start researching science before experimenting with whatever feels right for you.

1.1.4 Psychedelic drugs to treat war veterans

A serious institution called Multidisciplinary Association for Psychedelic Studies (MAPS) - www.maps.org - has been studying the application of some compounds, normally used as recreational drugs, to treat and also cure mental diseases that traditional medicine can't seem to find a good solution for. Substances such as LSD, psilocybin or magic mushrooms, MDMA, ayahuasca and marijuana once combined with assisted psychotherapy sessions can achieve incredible results to treat Post Traumatic Stress Disorder (PTSD) on war veterans and people that were sexually abused with fast and profound transformations. Some of the substances also have been helpful to treat alcohol addiction, drug addiction and depression.

Another surprising application for psychedelics is that they can apparently help you find solutions for complicated problems at work.

If taken under specific protocols, psychedelics can reveal surprising insights, and practical solutions have been achieved by respected professionals while under its influence. The potential for transformation can also be enhanced if combined with the practice of meditation or mindfulness.

Research conducted by James Fadiman, using psychedelics in microdoses, can have significant results for intellectual workers. They will not experience a trip or any of the symptoms usually associated with taking psychedelic drugs because the dosage is rather small. Subjects that take these microdoses claim that it can improve lateral thinking, enhance mental performance and promote the flow state bringing more creativity to their work.

1.1.5 Power drugs for kids and flow

A new category of drugs and supplements has been hitting the markets hard, giving the edge to many students and professionals, as they are cognitive enhancers. They are called nootropics or smart drugs, and this market is growing fast, even though the efficacy of these drugs is not totally understood.

Drugs like Ritalin, originally prescribed to treat children and teenagers diagnosed with ADD (Attention Deficit Disorder), and ADHD (Attention Deficit Hyperactive Disorder), have been proven to help them to focus their mind better, even though the diagnosis of these conditions is still very controversial.

What is interesting is that people that don't struggle to focus will show remarkable improvements in their mental capacities if they take the same drugs, which brings to light a puzzling question. Would the use of these drugs be seen as a way to cheat in school?

Other prescription drugs, supplements and natural compounds make wild promises, but their efficacy can vary from person to person, as the placebo effect can be the only reason someone will think that they work.

If a person finds a smart drug that suits them, their capacity to achieve flow can also be enhanced.

1.1.6 Mindfulness is better than meditation

Mindfulness is the modern version of ancient meditation practices, and its scientific approach is motivating people to learn how to relax and focus their mind in order to reduce stress and improve productivity.

According to Dr Michael Gervais in 1980, there were only three research articles about mindfulness. In 2008 a couple of hundred articles were published, and in 2017 you will find thousands of research articles from scholarly universities.

The word mindfulness is more business-friendly than meditation, so much so that 35 per cent of American companies are offering some sort of mindfulness training to their employees, and this is just the beginning of a revolution.

Different states of mind produce particular brainwaves, so now you also have apps that produce sound waves that entrain your brain into the brainwaves of highly successful meditators. You will also find other apps with guided meditations and an array of shortcuts that can help anyone progress with their practice in a fraction of the usual time.

Yoga, Qigong and Tai Chi are also on the rise, and all of these practices can help you relax and focus your mind, giving you the head start to achieve flow.

1.1.7 Abstain from addictions and flow

Sex can be an immersive flow experience, but if you want to experience flow in other activities you can experiment cutting down the number of times you have sex by half, have a period of abstinence or avoid the orgasm, and pay attention if you can improve flow in other areas, especially reading and working. A high number of athletes abstain from sexual activities a few days/weeks before important tournaments to stay more focused and have more energy and stamina.

For most men, masturbation is an addiction and it can be related to flow state. So, if you deprive your senses of the empty pleasure of masturbation you will have more energy stored, and an extra drive to find pleasure in reading, learning or daring to try brand new experiences and adventures.

Other addictions that can be curbed to create time, mental space and enthusiasm to get into flow state include; drinking, gambling, playing video games, watching TV, exercising, eating sugar or sweeteners, sleeping too much, smoking tobacco or dope and using drugs.

1.1.8 Group flow

Navy SEALs

Navy SEALs are trained to get into flow individually, but their best achievements can only be reached by teams, so if they can achieve group flow, their efficacy will be extremely high.

According to Steven Kotler, the cost of training one Navy SEAL is US$3.5 million. About US$1.5 million is spent on skills acquisition, and US$2 million is used to train them on group flow.

Many methods and technologies have been used to help them move and make decisions like a single unit, which reminds me of a school of fish changing direction simultaneously, without the need for a leader.

Group flow is required in companies to create teams that work in sync, and extensive studies by Google were not able to find out why some groups have synergy and others don't. So, more research is required to understand why some groups can really perform optimally, and other groups with high calibre individuals don't seem to work well together.

Formal education

I believe that schools and universities should be places to learn how to work as a team. However teachers and administrators insist in making students work as individuals, by learning subjects that some students are not good at and testing them. I believe that exams should be taken in groups of two or more students, so they can learn how to trust others and focus more on their higher abilities and help their peers. This way, they might be able to develop group flow not only academically but also participating as an essential team member of a company or sports team and develop group flow.

Montessori method

The Montessori method of education believes that we are naturally eager for learning, and we can initiate activities by engaging the senses and doing things, instead of just listening to instructions. This way they can create uninterrupted three-hour blocks of learning time, and children develop their focused attention by being able to choose the activity they want to be a part of. This results in developing flow, which spikes learning and engagement.

There is not such a thing as a self-made millionaire; anyone that became rich from scratch had to assemble a team and create a group flow. So there is nothing better than learning how to be part of or lead a team from school years.

Group flow triggers stretch their impact when there are shared goals, a sense of control, open communication and, with a bit of luck, a unification of egos will create a new identity. For example, you could experience group flow playing in a band, contributing to a brainstorming session or playing basketball.

Google 20%

Google is in the forefront of hacking flow, starting with their popular 20% time policy, where employees are paid to work on whatever they want, and this can promote flow a lot more than the other 80% of work time.

What everybody doesn't know is that the 20% informal projects will end up creating teams that will have to be assembled organically, by enrolling people voluntarily to work in the new project, or else the idea will die.

Mastermind

Whatever is your profession, you will benefit from being part of a mastermind group.

It is fundamental to have a great facilitator that can promote a combination of goal setting, brainstorming, education and accountability.

Some of the principles that can help you find flow during the meeting are honesty, respect and confidentiality. As you experience flow during your mastermind session, you will increase the possibility of creating the same kind of environment at your workplace and also to create group flow.

Talent Dynamics profiling test

To accelerate trust and promote flow in companies, I am particularly a fan of the Talent Dynamics profiling system from Roger James Hamilton. He shows that by discovering what your profile is, you will understand what kind of people should be the next ones to join your team to create flow.

It makes a lot of sense to me, and you should visit the link below to understand a bit more about this incredible system.

Download his book for free or take the profiling test that suits you best. Start learning how to make the most of your talents to leverage other peoples' power and create more flow in the organisation you work for.

www.humansinflow.global/wealth-dynamics

1.1.9 Hydration and water mysteries

If you drink a lot of coffee, tea, energy drinks or alcoholic drinks, and not enough water, then you might become dehydrated. Bear in mind that if you are dehydrated, you can lose a lot of your focus and comprehension while performing intellectual work. The best drink is still pure water; you can't beat H_2O, because one-third of it is oxygen, which is the fuel for your brain.

You might forget eating and drinking while in flow, but being hydrated is essential to prepare yourself to get there.

The easy way to know if you need to drink more water is by looking at the colour of your urine. If it is strong yellow, you are very dehydrated; if it is clear or slightly yellow, you are hydrated.

Exact numbers can vary from person to person; however, if you are 4% dehydrated, your performance can drop 10 to 15%. The same number works for intellectual or physical work.

So, to keep yourself focused, you should always have a glass of water handy, don't wait until you are very thirsty to reach out for a glass of water. If your tongue feels dry, this is one of the last symptoms of dehydration.

Many studies say that the ideal pH for our bodies to stay healthy is slightly alkaline, but a diet that includes meat, processed food, sugar, coffee and soft drinks tends to make our body acidic.

Some studies advocate that alkaline water can neutralize the acidity in your body. So, if you decide that alkaline water is a better option, you can buy test paper strips that will show you the pH of your tap water and also of your saliva and urine.

You can choose to drink mineral water with pH above 7, or if the pH is below 7, you can squeeze a lime or lemon in your water to turn it alkaline. I know it is strange, but even though limes and lemons are acidic, they have an alkalising effect on your body. An alternative is to buy alkalising drops to add to your water.

Another curiosity about water comes from research done by Dr Masaru Emoto. He has conducted experiments freezing water that has been exposed to classical music and heavy metal music. The crystals formed by the water were really intricate and beautiful for classical music, and malformed for the heavy metal. The experiment went even further. The crystals would be different if he would label the water bottles with words like love, peace, harmony, hate or war. I believe that there is an energetic field around everything and, if words can impregnate water, everything we say and read is somehow stored in our body, which is composed of about 80% water. If you want to see some examples of his work and gather your own conclusions, google him.

Other studies say that water has a memory and it holds the secrets of the creation of life, just like it has the DNA information of all life on Earth and beyond.

John Kanzius claim to have discovered that radio frequencies can split saltwater into Hydrogen and Oxygen which can burn and could be used as a clean and abundant source of energy.

Water is the only substance that expands when frozen, and an incredible fourth state of the water, which is viscose like honey, has been discovered.

In nature, it's common to say that you should not drink stagnated water and instead look for running water to fill your flask. So, what about the mineral water bottles that hold stagnated water for months on end?

To make my mineral water more similar to its natural state, I have been doing something that seems quite sensible to me. For many years I have been drinking water that I vigorously steer into a vortex to revitalize it like it was running down the stream. I also insert a metal rod connected to the earth outlet of my power socket, into

70

a storing glass container, to ground my water like you can find it in nature.

I believe there is a lot about water that cannot be explained yet, so I will keep studying and experimenting with it.

1.1.10 Breathe deeply to ease stress

There are numerous ways to control your state by manipulating your breathing patterns, and you can research them. I will recommend you take a few deep breaths if you are feeling anxious or unfocused. It helps to ease stress and gives you more oxygen, which is essential for good focus, which can lead to flow.

1.1.11 Box breathing

Flow demands focus and controlling the way you breathe can develop your focus and poise.

An interesting way to do it is by holding your breath twice on every cycle while sitting down.

You can try it right now by breathing from one to five minutes to start feeling the effects.

Let's start with the cycle of four. This means that you will be breathing in for four seconds, holding at the top for four seconds, breathing out evenly for four seconds and hold again for four seconds after exhaling, just to start it all over again.

Your deep instincts will want you to grasp for air before it's due especially when you start raising the cycle to six, eight or ten seconds. Observing and controlling this rhythmic cycle prevents your immediate panic response taking place by making you relax into it while raising the and developing more balance to be in control of your breath and your life.

If you face a negative incidents your breath is affected, so if you learn how to control the way you breath you regain focus and control faster. Stay cool and find the solution to your challenges with box breathing.

Research on the net where to find guidance to learn more about Box breathing if you are interested.

This practice can help you feel control which might induce flow.

1.1.12 Be warm to concentrate

Our comprehension while reading and learning are linked to the amount of energy we use. If you feel cold, a lot of your energy and focus will be dissipated, and your mental power will suffer. Turn the thermostat to a warmer setting, or dress accordingly to avoid feeling cold. But be aware that if you make it too hot, you might feel sluggish and lazy.

Get comfortable and warm; your performance will be enhanced.

1.1.13 Brain nutrients and gut health

Many people that are following a diet plan to lose weight decide to avoid oils and fat. I am certain that even if you are dieting you need some oils/fats to keep your body in balance. I believe omega oils, olive oil, avocados, nuts and butter are essential, so they are on my diet, and whenever I want to pan fry I use coconut oil as the healthier option amongst all the oils.

Micronutrients deficiency can have a massive impact in your brain health and performance, so I recommend you consult a doctor and take a test to find out if you need any supplements, and take an allergy test to make sure you do not have foods that you are intolerant to. This way, your body will be working optimally, and you will be more likely to find your flow.

As I've been doing research to find the best brain foods, I found out that our gut can reveal a lot about our health.

Gut microbiome

New discoveries are revealing that by identifying and quantifying all of the living microorganisms in your gut you can find out how to improve your health.

The microbes in your gut include bacteria, viruses, bacteriophages, archaea, fungi, yeast and parasites, so they produce thousands of chemicals that affect your overall wellness. Your microbiome controls your immune system and plays an important role to treat diabetes, mental health, Parkinson's disease, heart disease,

Alzheimer's disease, colorectal cancer and many more health issues. So if you want to lose weight, are concerned with your health or have food allergies, you can research the net and find a company to analyse your gut flora. I've done some research, and I found a very reputable laboratory in the market. It is an American company called Viome, and you can find more information by going to their website.

www.viome.com

1.1.14 Exercise your body

It's good to remind you here that exercising can have a massive impact on your mental performance. Many studies show that if you exercise, you become more alert with a sharper mind. Just going for a walk in the park can help you relax and give you the mental space to think up some great new ideas.

Sitting is the new smoking, so I have my exercise routine in the morning, and I also do a headstand to give me strength on my neck muscles and also bring extra blood flow and oxygen to my brain.

Perhaps going for a walk or a run can take your mind away from intellectual work for a while, and you will feel much more productive whenever you get back to work.

One important tip to help you have insights and new ideas is to keep yourself focused on yourself, so while walking or running, don't look at other people, just look ahead. Don't pay attention to people's clothes and don't get distracted by moving objects. This way you stay focused and more likely to get in the zone, especially if you have an inspiring electronic or classical music playlist.

Whenever I'm too busy and don't have the time to go for a long walk, I bounce on a little trampoline for a few minutes, and I feel refreshed enough to keep working.

If you are at your workplace, a great way to release the tension that keeps building up in your shoulders and neck is to put your right hand over your head and slowly pull your head to the right. Do it really slowly because you might hold a lot of tension there and you don't want to hurt yourself. Then put your left hand over your head and pull it to the left even slower. You will stretch many muscles and will relieve tension. Move your shoulders up and down to feel more relaxed without having to leave your workstation. If you can stand up, you will feel even better, and your mental focus will strengthen automatically. It might also help to ease headaches and neck pain. Give it a try.

To really help you relax your body, you can have a sauna to detoxify and also have a massage with an expert to reinvigorate your system. Perhaps an adjustment with a chiropractor can also align your body and give you more energy to get into flow state.

To develop both sides of your brain, you could learn how to play a musical instrument or learn how to juggle. They require eye-hand coordination, making both sides of the brain work together. You can also try using your non-dominant hand to brush your teeth or use the mouse, and you will be developing part of your brain that is not usually stimulated.

1.1.15 Sleep enough to have the energy to flow

Even though getting in flow is a pleasurable experience and it feels effortless, you will spend high amounts of energy during the process. After a great flow experience, you should remember to rest well, maybe six, seven or eight hours to be able to get in flow state again. Remember that you integrate memory during your sleep, so the following day might bring you useful insights.

To get in flow, you need to train yourself, so stay rested by taking short breaks or a nap whenever you feel tired.

1.1.16 Understand your circadian rhythm

The flow state can be experienced more easily if you are in good health, so understanding your "body clock" will have incredible implications on your health and on your performance on a short and long-term basis.

It was thought that our "body clock" was influenced only by external factors like light and temperature to function on a 24-hour cycle, but new discoveries can help your body have a more harmonious cycle. So you will rest better and have more mental and physical energy to get into flow. It makes so much sense that you will not believe that somebody didn't think of it before.

The circadian rhythm regulates all our bodily functions on a cycle of 24 hours, and it can be profoundly disrupted if you work a night shift, or when you travel into another time zone and go into jet lag. Your body might take time to adapt to the new conditions, but I have great news for you.

Every morning your body will have a sharp rise in temperature and blood pressure, many hormones will be secreted, and you wake up. This cycle is observed in plants and animals, and it varies with the seasons. Every day your "body clock" resets because of external cues as light and temperature, but our modern lifestyles have been disrupting this cycle with the use of full-spectrum light, heating and air conditioning during the night. To avoid making my body confused about day and night and have it functioning optimally, I use a dimmer to turn down the brightness of the lightbulbs at night. Energy-saving LED bulbs can wreck your sleep because they emit more of the dreadful blue light spectrum than traditional lighting. You can also find blue-light-blocking bulbs, or check the incredible lights called Philips Hue, which you can control the colour of automatically and filter the blue light, or change to any shade from your phone.

I close the blackout curtains or use an eye mask in bed to help my body rest deeply. If I am traveling, I need to deal with light sources in my hotel room, so I carry with me a roll of aluminium foil to cover the window and block any light from entering the room. Just sprinkle the glass with water and the aluminium foil will easily attach to the window for a few days without damaging anything. Now, if you have those small LED lights on your TV, AC or other appliance, that cannot be turned off, you can use electricity tape or Blue Tack to cover them and sleep in complete darkness.

My phone and computer screens switch automatically into night time mode at 7 pm, and they don't emit blue light until it is 7 am. You can change your screen settings or install F.lux on your computer or phone. I also wear yellow glasses that filter blue light after 7 pm, so my body starts producing melatonin to prepare it to feel sleepy at the right time, make me rest well, and my body is able to repair itself the way nature intended.

Glasses that filter blue light are also called gaming glasses or computer glasses, because they create a better contrast on-screen, avoiding fatigue and eye strain. An excellent alternative for these glasses are the contact lenses that filter blue light, but be aware that you should wear them only after 7 pm, and wear a clear set during the day, because you should be exposed to blue light during the daytime to help you boost alertness, memory, cognitive function and elevate your mood.

London is one of the top 10 cloudiest big cities in the world, so we have people suffering from a type of depression called seasonal affective disorder (SAD) and the treatment to it is being exposed to some special bright light to make the person feel well again.

If you understand your circadian clock you will help your body work optimally, and be able to get into flow, by identifying the best times for specific activities, as you will be hardwired to perform at a higher level. For example, you might be highly alert in the early morning, so you should use this time to focus on pro-active and high productivity activities. Avoid checking your phone messages and emails in the morning as you would engage your brain in re-active activities, and would be wasting the best time of the day to get into flow and do your most productive and creative work.

Most of us keep working through the evening or just stay entertained by reading or watching TV until late, so it's understandable that we can get peckish and have a few snacks to keep us going.

New discoveries show that this indulgent behaviour impacts our natural cycle and have damaging effects like making us put on weight, and perhaps developing autoimmune diseases. Our internal organs also follow the circadian rhythm, our pancreas is lazy at night, and it does not release enough insulin to break the fat and sugar molecules of a big meal after 8 pm, so our body will store fat cells instead of burning them. If you were to eat the same fat and sugary snacks during the day, your body would break them down, and you would not put any weight on. This is fantastic news for those people that want to lose weight because this is a diet that doesn't restrict any calories but makes you lose weight by restricting the eating period into a 10-hour window during the day.

I know this is hard to believe, but I'm sure that you will have a go at it once you understand the science behind this simple idea. Research shows that it can also help you revert chronic diseases, make you sleep better and also give you much more mental and physical energy.

The research

According to research done by Dr Satchidananda (Satchin) Panda at The Salk Institute for Biological Studies in California, eating at night has a terrible effect on our body and mind.

His discoveries are based on an experiment that has been repeated more than 10,000 times in many labs around the world. If you give mice high fat and sugar diet (60% calories from fat and 40% calories from pure sucrose) they will become obese very quickly if they can eat any time of the day. Within ten weeks they will be overweight, and in 16 weeks they will be morbidly obese.

The revolutionary experiment uses two groups of mice. One has free access to a high fat, high sucrose diet, and they can eat whenever they want. The other group has the same number of calories from the same high fat, high sucrose diet, but they have to eat all their food within nine hours at night time, which is the time their circadian clock tells them to eat.

Surprisingly, after 16 weeks, these mice that were eating the same bad food within nine hours window were completely healthy, were not overweight, were not obese, had utterly normal liver function, normal cholesterol, normal glucose control, and they actually stayed on the treadmill twice as long as mice that ate the same food whenever they wanted.

The good news is that if you have morbidly obese mice and give them the same food, but they have to eat it within nine hours, they will lose weight and reverse their diseases.

This is incredible because humans have been losing weight and reversing chronic diseases by following this straightforward rule,   eating during a 10-hour window during the daytime and having their last meal before eight at night. I've been following this recommendation and making some adjustments like reducing the window to 7 hours, and also spent two weeks eating just one meal a day. All I can say is that once you understand the benefits of it, you will quickly adapt to this new habit and will not have food cravings at night because this is a more natural way to live.

If you want to learn more about this study, you can watch a few videos on YouTube or listen to podcasts by searching "Satchin Panda circadian rhythm." If you want to participate in this study, you can go to his website and download their free app to help you track the time of your meals and start benefiting from living in sync with your circadian clock.

www.mycircadianclock.org

1.1.17 Wake up at 5 am

If you feel like you don't have enough time in your day to accomplish your targets, I suggest you read a book called *The Miracle Morning* by Hal Elrod. He might be able to help you understand how waking up at 5 am, or a little earlier than normal, you can create more quality time in your day, as mornings are especially good for the mental flow state.

www.miraclemorning.com

Be aware that waking up at the right time during your sleeping cycle can make you feel more rested than sleeping more hours. I use an app called "Sleep Cycle" that wakes me up within a window of time to coincide with the time when I'm dreaming, and the transition into an awakened state is easier and natural. If you just set your alarm clock for a random time in the morning, you might wake up while in a deep sleep and will stay groggy for a while until you gradually wake up fully. I will explain the technology that these apps are using, and how to benefit from using them, later on in the book when looking at how to remember your dreams.

1.1.18 Go to bed at 5 am

From time to time, I've been experimenting waking up early, as part of challenges I introduce into my life.

My normal body clock likes staying up late at night, and my writing seems to be more inspired, as I enter in flow much more often late at night than during the day.

One of the reasons I believe that night time can be so inspiring to read and write is that, beyond not being interrupted, our cortisol levels go very low, late at night. So, I write happily, without much of the stress and judgement that cortisol triggers, especially in the morning. This is my window of opportunity to enjoy my own company and think deeper.

Many people say they don't want to read because they want to relax after a day's work, but this idea can be overcome if you try different times of the day with a different state of mind.

1.1.19 Stable level of energy

To be able to get into flow it is preferable if you have a diet that gives you a more stable level of energy for longer, so you don't have to break the state to snack.

A great deal of our energy comes from carbohydrates and refined sugars which give you a boost on your energy levels, but after burning the calories, you crash and need to refuel to keep functioning.

I'm not a doctor, but I've been following many types of research that say that a ketogenic diet can help you have a more stable energy supply, as this diet is based on vegetables, proteins and fats with very low intake of carbohydrates and refined sugars.

Unlike common belief, once you settle into a ketogenic diet, you will burn the fat as the first source of energy, instead of burning energy from carbs and sugars. This way, you will swiftly transition to burning your own fat reserves once your fat intake is used up, therefore will have fewer food cravings and will be able to lose weight.

Do your research and find the best way to keep your body with a stable level of energy to get into flow.

Please remember that you should give yourself a break and perhaps go for a walk after eating a heavy meal. Don't try to get in flow just after your main meal because your blood will migrate from your brain to your gut to process your digestion and trying to think will not be so easy.

1.1.20 Use peppermint oil

It is not by chance that one of the only things discovered inside the great pyramids in Egypt was peppermint oil.

Peppermint has excellent properties that can help you develop your focus before an examination or simply when you want to read a book or feel tired and want to carry on working. It's like having a strong coffee, and it works if you want to improve concentration, focus, memory, alertness, energy, and wakefulness. You can place a couple of drops on the palm of your hand, rub them together and smell them. You can also rub a drop of the oil under the nose, or put a drop on the tongue for an instant boost.

Alternatively, you can have the traditional peppermint tea, or mix one or two drops of oil in a hot cup of water and drink it. You can mix a few drops with water and spray it on your clothes or in the air. Another way of enjoying the smell and benefits of peppermint oil is to use it on an oil burner.

EAGLES FLOW QUEST

Vision Two

LOOK AND SEE

"The only thing worse than being blind is having sight but no vision."

Hellen Keller

See further than ever

I have a great friend that has a factory producing acrobatic aeroplanes and gliders in Brazil. His nickname is Mini as he is 6'7" (1.95m) tall and I flew many times with him. The best memory I have from our flights is of soaring a glider about two miles high on an ascending thermal, when an eagle appeared on my side just a few feet away. I felt like I was a bird too, then suddenly it turned its head and looked me straight in the eyes. I smiled, and we kept staring at each other, creating a unique and unforgettable connection.

An eagle's eyeball is the same size as a human eye, but it is eight times stronger, making them able to spot a rabbit three miles away.

I'm sharing this information with you because I'm about to tell some surprising things about your eyes.

Your eyes are the most critical interface you have to communicate with the world, and there are many ways to help you get in flow state that are hidden from the ordinary person's knowledge.

You can see beyond your field of vision

There is the visible field of vision, and there is the world that can only be seen through your mind's eye. As you see clearly you will be closer to getting into flow, so I will explain topics connected with your vision.

1.2.1 Your eyes are the window to your world

I've learnt Neuro-Linguistic Programming (NLP), with its co-creator Richard Bandler. It is a fascinating field that studies human behaviour by observing all the different ways we communicate with ourselves and with others. I believe it's been helping me in the process of change towards excellence. I'm always studying human behaviour, and I want to share with you a discovery. Taking into consideration the ergonomics and eyes movement, I've noticed that whenever I read a text from a monitor immediately in front of me, I perform better than reading from an iPad flat on the table. I believe that you will read faster if your eyes are looking straight forward or slightly looking up, and you will read slower if you are looking down to read like someone using bifocals. I would recommend you to try it for yourself after you understand the science behind this theory. It all starts by analysing the position of the eyes in their orbit while we access internal information.

Many studies have shown there is a pattern in the way most of us move our eyes while accessing our memory banks. We hardly notice, but whenever someone asks us a question, we need to find the answer inside our minds, and as a result, we move our eyes around in search of the answer. The fascinating thing is to know that it's possible to see where you're accessing that information from, if you understand the underlying patterns. Once you know the basics, you might even be able to tell with high accuracy if the person you are talking to was being truthful or not.

For example, if I ask you the colour of the front door of your house, what would you say? Pause for a second to see your front door with your mind's eye and answer the question.

Now focus your attention for a few seconds to remember the front door of a house you used to live when you were a teenager.

Perhaps you've moved your eyes up and to the left, or just looked straight ahead to be able to see the door and recognise the colour. Most of us do it even though we are not aware of it, mainly because we might see images inside our mind in a flash, perhaps at one-hundredth of a second or even faster.

Can you imagine yourself sitting on a sandy beach you've been to before, with your favourite drink in your right hand and enjoying the heat of the sun?

Feel comfortable in your chair and imagine feeling the sun on your bare skin. Connect with this feeling for a moment before you carry on reading. You can close your eyes if it helps.

I bet your eyes were looking down. This is because we move our eyes down whenever we connect with our body and feelings. If you didn't look down, it was because you probably imagined, with your mind's eye, the sandy beach and the people around you, and in this case, you probably looked straight ahead or slightly up and to the left.

Eye Movement Chart
for most right-handed people
(flip image for most left-handed people)

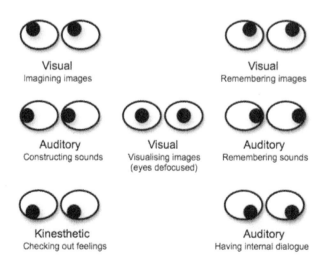

| Visual | | Visual |
| Imagining images | | Remembering images |

| Auditory | Visual | Auditory |
| Constructing sounds | Visualising images (eyes defocused) | Remembering sounds |

| Kinesthetic | | Auditory |
| Checking out feelings | | Having internal dialogue |

If you see someone crying, I bet you that they will be looking down; if you entertain them and make them look up, their tears will start to dry up because the body

83

connection that kept the person feeling the pain was severed the moment they looked up. As a man, I had to learn about this interesting connection; however, women already know that.

Let's say that a girlfriend of yours went to a party. She is all dressed up and has her make-up on. She is having a good time, but someone says something to her, and for some strange reason, she suddenly feels all emotional. She panics because she thinks that if she starts crying, she will ruin her beautiful, smoky eye make-up. What she does is not surprising, I've seen it countless times. She will use her hands and shake them in front of her eyes like a fan. She will look right up like she was staring at the ceiling and will try to contain the tears by tilting her head up. In an instant, she will stop feeling emotional because she will sever the connection with her feelings and emotions by keeping her gaze high. She will stay connected to the visual and functional world until the emotion subsides. The message to the body is evident. If you've ever met someone who is sad or depressed, where do they usually look at? Yes, that's it! They typically look down or at the floor! They can't appreciate the environment or their surroundings too well. They don't look at the sky because they are concerned with their feelings. So, now you've learnt that you can also manage your state according to the way you move your eyes.

If you can't sleep at night, it is very likely that, even with your eyes closed, your eyes will be looking above the imaginary horizon line. This means that you are dealing with images that are very exciting to the brain, and you can't stop thinking. To have a good night's sleep, try to look below the imaginary horizon line by looking down, and you will start getting connected with your body, and you start feeling your legs and feet. Once you have achieved the connection with the body, you will begin drifting into sleep very quickly, without the need for any sleeping pills. Just try, and if it works, tell your friends.

Just by looking above the imaginary horizon line, you will be dealing with images. You can remember images by looking up to the left, which is the past, and you can create new images by looking up to the right.

Learning NLP I've noticed that most people would move their eyes horizontally whenever trying to remember or humming a song. Just try to hum a song you like, and you will recognise what I'm saying.

So, if you are trying to remember a song you will tend to look to the left, which is the past; if you are trying to create a rhyme or a song, you will be looking horizontally to the right.

If you start talking to yourself, you are very likely to look down to the left. This is just the general idea, and each one of us has a pattern that always repeats. Try asking your friends some questions and be aware of the patterns that people make with their eyes.

You can use some of these questions with your friends but try to answer them yourself first, and pay attention to where you are looking as you answer them.

- Can you describe your favourite childhood toy?
- How does it feel to relax in a warm bath?
- What would your name look like in bright red neon lights above your front door?
- How does your doorbell sound?

Now that you know that your eyes are the window to your private world, I want to ask you a question.

What would happen if your head was looking down while you read?

Well, the answer is that you are probably more connected to your feelings and the sound of your voice than the images of the world.

If you want to perform better while reading, just lift your book. By looking above the horizon line, you disconnect with the sound of words and therefore, do not rely on your own voice to understand what is written in the text. This way, you will learn the information visually because the visual channel will be open and the auditory channel closed.

By doing that, you will be playing with more images, and you will be able to do whatever is visualised in this book. You can become more creative with your writing, and I believe it can also help people with writer's block.

Learn more about reading further down in the book.

Prism glasses

I use prism glasses to read in bed, and they are great. I can lie flat on the bed, and the glasses work like a periscope. It also works well to read a book or tablet flat on the table or use your mobile phone close to your waistline, because you don't need to bend your neck down to read the pages or play with your phone. They are very comfortable, and you can find them on Google under "prism glasses."

Prism glasses work like a periscope.

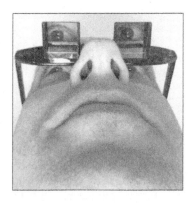

Keep your gaze high to look straight down.

Using prism glasses to read a book flat on the table, while keeping good posture.

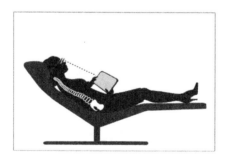

Using prism glasses to read on a chaise lounge. The neck is relaxed, and you save energy.

By keeping a high gaze, you are more likely to speed read with greater confidence because your eyes will be in a much better place. You will also be able to imagine all the action and details of the book as if you are watching a real film.

Now, if I ask you which one is better, the book or the film of the same title, most people would think the book is usually better than the film. This means that you can create better movies than Hollywood can. Look at the book, document or screen the right way, and you will develop the ability to imagine more while reading. This is a very useful tip, and it will aid your memory, too.

If you feel sleepy while reading in bed, it is because you keep the book close to your chest and you gaze at the book by looking down. You connect with your body, and it's exhausted, so then proceed to fall asleep. If you want to read for longer, raise the book or use the prism glasses.

Try to lift the book, Kindle or iPad, and you are more likely to be alert. If you don't buy the prism glasses, at least you know how to look at things to be more awake and perform better while reading.

Bifocal glasses

If you use bifocal or varifocal glasses, I would suggest you have an extra pair of single vision lenses only for reading or for working on your computer, because this way you can look straight ahead, while with bifocal or multifocal glasses you always need to look down.

Computer glasses

The so-called computer glasses with anti-reflective coating and blue-light filter reduce the risk of developing digital eye strain and this way you will stay focused for longer and more likely to get into flow.

I advise you to try it for yourself and do what you feel is comfortable.

1.2.2 Visualisation and flow

Any creation of the mankind requires visualisation.

If you ever had a great idea or desperately wanted to have something, and that thought haunted you until you got it done or bought the object of desire, without realising, you had a very clear visualisation that compelled you into action, and you got the results you wanted.

This book is a by-product of an exercise of visualisation I did while at Tony Robbins' Unleash the

Power Within event. He invited us to dream our future, and I imagined myself on his stage teaching people how to read faster and better. That vision gave me the inspiration to start studying English, develop my method and write this book. I kept that desire alive because I could see it. I ended up meeting Tony. I was invited to speak from the big stage already. If I did it, you can do it too.

As you are searching for flow, I will guide you towards it by quoting Einstein. He said:

"Imagination is more important than knowledge. For knowledge is limited, whereas imagination embraces the entire world, stimulating progress, giving birth to evolution."

Having a stable job might be a great thing, but soon enough people settle down and keep repeating a recipe that works, and forget to imagine new possibilities for their lives. Some might be adventurous and book their holidays in an exotic country, but most end up going to the same holiday places year after year.

To get in flow you need a dream, and the bigger the vision, the better the chances that you stay in flow for longer, and the frequency of flow will also increase.

If you visualise something, you want to have, realise, or create you are one step closer than wishing that something would happen because visualisation is active and wishing is passive.

You can visualise something privately, with your family, with your work team, or mobilise like-minded people in your community to achieve a common goal.

Many times, dissatisfaction in your life can fuel your creativity, and propel you on a quest to have a better life, creating the possibility to get in flow and achieve great transformation.

If you don't like your boss or the company you work for, stop complaining and start visualising a career move. By having a clear idea or a desire to change, you will stop watching the news and movies on TV and start doing something towards a more fulfilling life.

I recommend a fantastic book by Shakti Gawain called *Creative Visualization,* because she explains all the steps to gain clarity and use visualisation to change any area of your life, from losing weight, gaining muscle, finding a partner, increasing prosperity, solving problems, or anything you might want to create in your life.

So, go ahead and search on YouTube for "creative visualisation", and you will find many guided meditations that might take just ten minutes. Choose one that you resonate with, close your eyes and start imagining something you desire with more details; it will be fun. The more you practice focusing on what you want, the more likely you will be to start moving towards it, and even start bringing serendipity and coincidences to your life, because somehow you will begin changing the energy around you, and you will attract new circumstances into your life, increasing your probability of success.

Once you get started, you can add a vision board with cut-outs from magazines, or create a digital one that you can print and look at often to reignite that desire every single day. One other thing that you can add to your vision board is written affirmations; they work well as they work on your belief system. You can also find videos with guided meditations that use affirmations to help you focus your mind.

Another inspiring book that can expand your understanding of visualisations was written by Hal Elrod, which I've mentioned before, and it's called *The Miracle Morning*. He describes six habits that can inspire you to visualise a new future to transform your life.

Anyway, your chances to get in flow will grow every time you connect with your vision so I suggest you stop reading, connect to your dreams and start writing down some goals that you know you can accomplish if you decide to. Maybe something you have been postponing, like taking an online course to learn how to code, or anything you want.

Choose something reasonably simple to start with, schedule the task in your diary, and work on it for 30 to 90 minutes of uninterrupted time without any phone alerts to distract you, and you will be on your way to get in flow. Consistently work on it until you reach your goal, then choose something else to focus on and keep expanding your world.

1.2.3 Image streaming

Win Wenger has done a lot of work to help us increase our intelligence, and he created a method to improve people's ability to visualise called *Image Streaming*.

He believes that many discoveries have been made through daydreaming. Einstein used to daydream to develop his work, so Wenger decided to make daydreaming a technique that combines left and right brain functions by letting a person describe out loud the images that come to their mind. By doing so, people will create links between visual and verbal thinking, which he believes can increase creativity and intelligence.

I think this method can actually help people develop their visualisation skills and also help to generate more focus and flow.

1.2.4 Your eyes need to be checked regularly

It is essential to check your eyesight from time to time, mainly if you don't use glasses. You might find that you start to underperform or get tired for no reason if you need glasses.

I've heard there is an alternative to wearing glasses, which is an eye exercise to strengthen the eye muscles to get in focus. You can google "eye exercise," and you will find a few options for programmes and books that you can purchase.

Can you read the sentence below? If you can't read it from two feet away (60 centimetres), then the time has come for you to have your eyes checked and buy some glasses.

People tend to get tired quickly while reading if they need glasses but don't use them.

Have a good reading light

Good light is essential for good reading performance.
The light coming from over your shoulders can also be a good option if you are sitting on an armchair or even at your table.

91

Look for options on the Internet to suit your needs and find some inspiration at the website below:
www.seriousreaders.com

1.2.5 Tinted glasses create a new dimension

It's surprising the number of people that tell me they think they are a bit dyslexic when in fact they avoid reading books by being a slow reader.

If in fact, you are dyslexic to some degree there is a quick fix that works for a lot of people.

Something astonishing is that many people with dyslexia or diagnosed as having the Irlen Syndrome can instantly read well if they start wearing tinted glasses. For some reason, the black and white contrast between the letters and paper is not the right combination for many people. Some people will find pink, green or purple as the best shade to help them read better and stay focused, so you can also try reading with tinted glasses or book a consultation with an optometrist to understand if they can be helpful to you.

If you are reading an eBook, you can adjust the colour of the page to sepia for a similar effect, and some apps will make your browser change the background colour and improve readability. For paper books, you can also use a translucent sheet of plastic in yellow, blue or any colour you decide to experiment, to adjust the contrast and improve your reading experience.

1.2.6. Expose yourself and get feedback

Taking risks amplifies the incidence of flow, and these risks can be physical, psychological, mental, mystical or anything you want to experiment with.

I would recommend you search for a Toastmasters meeting and visit them to practice public speaking, start a conversation with a stranger, join an improv comedy class, put your name down on an open mic night, sing in a Karaoke or go on a dance class.

Be seen, take risks and learn faster with immediate feedback. Feedback is a great teacher and flow inducer.

EAGLES FLOW QUEST

Vision Three

OBSERVE YOUR MIND

"If you feel like an outsider, you tend to observe things a lot more."

Anderson Cooper

Finding mental flow

I found a mention about eagle hunters during the height of Genghis Khan's empire, and Marco Polo wrote about his travels, in the 13th century, of "a great number of eagles, all trained to catch wolves, foxes, deer and wild goats," indicating that this tradition probably started before Jesus Christ was alive.

I found in the British museum a Roman sculpture from the 2nd century AD depicting what looks like a great friendship between an eagle and a man.

So the big question is: Why didn't the eagles fly away to freedom?

For the same reason, a well-trained dog never goes astray, always returning to their owners' house. The hunters spent so much time with their eagles that they created a dialect of words and whistles between themselves, eagles end up feeling part of the family and never think of running away.

To keep the birds relaxed during their travels on horseback, the birds stay perched on their owners' arms at all times, and they fit a leather hood on the eagle's head, keeping the bird in the dark.

Humans change their brainwaves from wide-awake beta wave to meditative alpha waves just by closing their eyes, so the same kind of change of state might be present with eagles [10]. The birds would travel great distances in a meditative state, trusting that their dear friend would protect them from predators and extreme cold by tucking them inside blankets at night. They would also know they would feed them and a few times a day they would see the daylight and would be free to fly, catch prey and be rewarded for that.

Brainwaves affect the way we see and perceive the world, so I understand that a great number of people don't like reading books because they are not creating the right frequency of brainwaves that will bring engagement with the narrative of the text to make them enjoy reading books.

Until now you have been kept in the dark, like the eagles, about your true potential to engage in intellectual work, and I will invite you to do some experiments to raise your brainwaves to a higher frequency, which is the right frequency to enjoy reading books. Once you understand how to control your mental state and also start producing theta waves, you will be more likely to get in the flow and be rewarded with the knowledge that can be used for creative work and will also increase your power of recall.

Every year in Kyrgyzstan and in Mongolia there is an ancient festival dedicated to birds of prey, especially the golden eagle. It's an incredible vision to see the eagle trainers come from far away on horseback with their eagles perched on their arms.

They compete to find the best eagle at hunting prey, and the best eagle at locating its owner.

There is an incredible movie about a girl that decided to become an eagle trainer in a male-dominated activity. Against the odds, she becomes the only female eagle trainer to compete with old and experienced male trainers and ends up winning the yearly eagle training competition in Kyrgyzstan, to the amazement of the elders. The movie is available on YouTube, it is called *The Eagle Huntress*, and I recommend it dearly.

While hunting on horseback, once the trainer spots a prey, he lifts the leather hood that covers the eagle's eyes, so the eagle flies and grabs the prey with precision without damaging the valuable fur, and waits for the trainer.

The eagle is kept in the dark most of the day and always performs once prompted. Routine makes us blind to reality, and if we had just a few moments of clarity during the day it would make us become aware of new talents. We can fly high with our imagination, and I will share some new possibilities to make you connect with parts of your brain that you've been keeping in the dark. The right side of your brain will give you more freedom to expand and fly into flow.

As the eagles travel on horseback, standing on the trainer's arm, they are awake, but without being able to see they go into a trance or in alpha, much like humans would go while meditating or watching TV.

I will share with you some research and practical ways to produce the right brainwave for flow state, and will show you some shortcuts for a panoramic view as you read book summaries before reading the book. I will also discuss that time constraints will help you develop flow and finally a simple technique based on alternative medicine, including the 2,000-year-old acupuncture treatment and NLP, which can unlock your potential to overcome your limitations.

By analysing your brain performance, you will be able to harness your hidden power.

1.3.1 The focus paradox

In this information overloaded world, many people think they get easily distracted and identify themselves with the label of having, or suffering, from Attention Deficit Disorder (ADD) or Attention Deficit Hyperactive Disorder (ADHD), so let's get a bit clear on focus.

The big misconception with this label is that people with ADD or ADHD are actually able to focus their attention for long periods of time if they identify a subject or activity that interests them.

So the real challenge is not to make them pay attention to every subject they have to study, but identify the subjects they are really curious about to keep the interest high, which will evoke the necessary focus to perform very well in that particular subject.

The danger is to surrender to the label and think that everything will be difficult to focus on.

Your values system

Nothing could be further from the truth. If they can focus their mind on a video game for hours, they can also focus on tasks that are high up in their values system. In the same way, they will easily disengage if the task at hand is very low on their values system. Now, for how long can you hold your attention?

The simple truth is that you have the focus to study or research about something that is important to you. You can also find time to dedicate to that task, have money to buy whatever is needed to accomplish your purpose, and develop an excellent memory to learn what is essential to excel in this new activity or endeavour, if you really think that activity is high up on your value system. But there is a caveat.

Your mental state and your focus will have a direct correlation between the challenge level and your skills level, and I will explain this in detail later on.

Most of us used to like reading books as a child, but fell out of love with them as we grew up, due to a mismatch between challenge and skill levels. By reading slowly, you can quickly disengage from the text as your brain is too powerful to learn at such a slow pace.

By applying the techniques described in this book, you will be able to sustain focused attention while reading books, but some extra factors will help you get in flow state so you will really get immersed in the experience of reading and learning. Once you get there, you will become more creative and will also be able to transition into an active state of inspired writing.

You can benefit from entering flow state not only for reading, but on a wide range of activities.

While in flow, you can make decisions faster with confidence as you can process much more information per second, and develop creative thinking.

People with the most flow in their lives develop the highest satisfaction in life.

Gold medalists have an intimate relationship with flow, and great paradigm shifts have been achieved by people in flow, especially in business.

McKenzie & Company, the biggest management consultancy in the world, conducted a 10-year study and found out that top executives have reported being 500% more productive while in flow [2].

So let's explore the environment to get in flow.

1.3.2 More flow at work than at leisure time

People that experienced more flow during the week felt strong, active, creative and motivated. What is surprising is that people were experiencing flow often while at work and rarely in leisure.

One of the experiments presented in the book *Flow* by Csikszentmihalyi [7] showed that people were experiencing flow 54 per cent of the time spent at work, and only 18 per cent of the time while watching TV, reading or going out with friends as a result of underusing their skills while in their free time, making them feel dissatisfied, sad and weak.

Jobs induce more flow because they are structured with goals and challenges, whilst free time demands choices, planning, discipline and goals to become enjoyable.

Did you ever plan to sleep all day on your weekend? What a horrible way to waste a day. The body doesn't need that much sleep, and if you ever slept too much you feel even more tired, your body aches, and you got frustrated that you wasted a whole day. People do that because they have no challenge to wake up for.

The paradox here lies in the idea that people want to work less and have more free time to get bored.

The solution is to change jobs or challenge yourself more at work, and also find challenging hobbies or activities to develop new skills and have more fun in life.

What is also observed is the attitude of the person performing their work. Even for seemingly repetitive work, the more a job can be performed as a game, with clear goals, challenges, variety and immediate feedback, the more enjoyable it will be perceived.

Workaholics can have a new perspective on the reason they enjoy working so much, and use this knowledge to structure new hobbies or activities that can create flow and enjoyment with family and friends during their free time.

1.3.3 The flow of money

People spend time and money to watch others practice sports, play music and create art, instead of taking risks and putting the effort to learn or experience a rewarding activity themselves. Rather than accomplishing something worthwhile, they will focus on paying more for new experiences that will leave them empty again.

The leisure industry keeps growing as a result of people not tapping into their mental and physical resources to experience flow.

Entrepreneurship and flow

I was bitten by the bug of entrepreneurship very early in life, and started working with power tools in my dad's workshop unsupervised at the age of 11 because one day I saw a big pile of perfectly treated bamboo offcuts that were going to be used as fuel at a bamboo furniture factory. I asked the owner of the factory if I could take some offcuts with me and he told me to help myself. With free material, I ended up making beautiful decorative wind chimes inspired by Japanese design, and a few months later I was selling them to a fancy interior design shop. At

98

14 years old, I opened a sweet shop and hired my first employee.

I understand the thrill of making money, and I can see that society is now valuing entrepreneurship to higher levels. This is good news for everyone that wants to find flow because work and leisure can blend with incredible results.

Entrepreneurial grit and flow

At least 65 per cent of the work force is not engaged at their jobs, which makes getting into flow very difficult for them, but the good news is that the other 35 per cent might have a high incidence of flow moments. So I will investigate how to increase the frequency of flow while at work.

Starting a company demands a great deal of grit as you invest time and money on a completely unproven idea.

By taking risks in every level of a start-up, combined with determination and ingenuity, you are cooking up a recipe for the state of flow. A clear vision motivates people to engage in their work and also promote group flow, as everyone feels they are essential in the organisation.

Responsible employees of big corporations can be easily replaced, so they try to avoid mistakes, don't take as many risks, become more passive in their role, and flow becomes harder to achieve. Open-plan offices are not good to induce flow, as uninterrupted attention for more extended periods of time is critical to achieve consistent flow.

1.3.4 Flow accepted as money

Most underestimate that we all have a hunger and desire to be helpful. People love to help and sometimes all you need to do is to ask.

Volunteers work for flow

A pool of 400 volunteers managers wanted to know if volunteers could be pushed to work harder, so they asked the managers if they ever heard a volunteer say:

"You are asking too much of me." Only 11 per cent of managers ever heard that, which is really an insignificant percentage. The most surprising was that 70 per cent of managers said they could ask much more from the volunteers.

Mozilla's open-source web browser Firefox is an example of organised volunteer work in a competitive environment. They are the third most popular browser in the world, and it is run almost entirely by volunteers. They work on coding, translating, marketing, and so on.

Amateurs and volunteers can be more powerful than paid employees because they do it for a deep sense of commitment, and they find pleasure and enjoyment by achieving flow state at work. War veterans, hard of hearing, and mums, can work very hard as volunteers if they decide to be part of a worthy cause.

A few years ago, I spent three weeks at an ashram in India run by the followers of a guru called Osho, and was surprised to know that this meditation retreat is run mostly by volunteers. Most of them actually pay a certain amount to work seven days a week for a set number of months, and be part of a programme to learn how to enjoy working, so they will never need another day off in their lives.

I thought that was very strange and only now I understand that people will be happier working instead of drinking margaritas on an idyllic beach, because just enjoying free time leads to boredom. Volunteering makes the person more authentic, builds real connections and helps them develop a deep interest in other people's lives, which can promote the beginning of genuine friendships.

If a volunteer at the restaurant strikes a conversation with a guest at the ashram, they can plan to meet up later for a drink because the volunteer creates an aura around themselves that is related to abundance. They might even be seen as a wealthy person giving back. This kind of circumstance rarely happens in a normal restaurant, as the waiters are working because they need the money and the tips to survive, and they cannot be spontaneous as they need to perform a role that can numb their personality and real energy.

So if you don't have much money and want to make friends with rich people and perhaps find a good-paying job, think about working for free. Do your research and volunteer at a place that suits your skills and your needs.

An incredible place to look for placements is a website that matches volunteers and organisations called Volunteer Match, so follow the link below to volunteer one or two hours a week and get started on this new adventure to have more fun and create flow in your life.

www.volunteermatch.org

My volunteering work

I have the firm belief that the ultimate reason we came to this world is to serve each other.

We all have different talents to contribute, and even if the task at hand is menial, I focus on doing it better each and every time.

Money is great, but I have dedicated more than seven years of my life to work hard on this book while earning negative wages.

I wrote it with you in mind, and I was rewarded with intense feelings of satisfaction and insight.

I volunteered to write this book, no one asked me to do it, and I know that to be committed to writing something meaningful is very difficult but I took the challenge and worked silently in my little world, avoiding parties and interactions with friends.

This book now is my platform to reach out to more people, do more work and eventually enjoy the smile of gratitude from those I could help find pleasure in learning and serving others to create lasting happiness in their lives.

So I hope I work to fulfil my mission until the day I die.

Don't ever retire

Many people become financially free at 30 or 40 years of age and can retire. The danger for them is that they only take significant challenges and grow as a person until they find a way to keep reaping the results of their previous efforts, and then start coasting. They keep enough discipline to stay afloat, and then start spending more of their time and money on entertainment, alcohol, drugs, or anything else that doesn't seem to be hard work.

One of the great traps that can lead to an early grave is thinking that retirement will be a great time to relax and do nothing.

I saw my father giving up life the moment he retired, because instead of solving problems and having discussions about work or politics, he started wasting time in front of the TV and had very little interaction with the real world.

Many people dream of pottering in the garden and relaxing, but without challenges or contribution, the enjoyment will be short-lived.

If you want to slow time down, find something to fight for and get out of your comfort zone. Read the Fourth Vision of the Dragons Live Quest, at the end of the book, to understand how time passes and how to bring more pleasure into your life.

Don't focus on all those things you can't have, or on the pains and restrictions of your older life, and instead find problems to solve.

Be aware that many people use their children as a distraction to occupy their free time, and instead of giving the example of having the discipline to pursue knowledge or develop other skills, they put their effort in controlling their kids, expecting them to learn and grow, but not doing that themselves.

Teaching youngsters about flow

Learning how to enjoy activities for their own sake is also referred to as autotelic personality, and according to Csikszentmihalyi [7] the relationship between teenagers and their parents can influence the way they will learn how to entertain themselves, and therefore have better chances to make flow possible as they grow.

The five characteristics that promote the autotelic personality are:

Clarity regarding parents' expectations with clear goals, which centres on the perception that teenagers have that their parents are interested in what they do.

Freedom of choice, including breaking rules and knowing that there will be consequences.

Commitment to be open and get fully involved in any activity they choose.

The ability of parents to create increasingly more complex challenges to their children.

I would suggest that parents could direct some of their kids' effort into volunteering to get experiences without having to spend money, or towards experiencing the thrill of becoming an entrepreneur and investing their money.

Being alone at home with nothing to do can make people start worrying about trivialities, so they empower themselves by having the remote control and actively choosing something on TV to watch, to mask that bad feeling. They might find something structured that will give them a break, but the emptiness is there waiting for them to switch the TV off. Many people have their TV inside the bedroom to transition smoothly into sleep, and suffer less with their predicament.

There are other alternatives to television that some will use to help them numb the anxiety of doing something meaningful with their free time, such as going to the pub for a drink, gambling, having sex, pornography and even masochism.

A few people might try reading, but as they read slowly, they will disengage quickly and feel bored again. Learning how to read faster usually helps to motivate a person to learn something that can be used to improve their performance at work, expand their horizons and create flow.

Ultimately, the learning experience is a lonely one, and each one of us needs to find a purpose to keep studying in a disciplined way, choosing the direction they want to expand, instead of waiting for someone telling them what to do. The transition from school or university into their professional capacity can be difficult, as many will keep the mentality of waiting to be told what to do by their teacher or superiors, and this habit will undermine people's capacity of choosing challenges that will bring out their power to explore their potential to grow.

1.3.5 The challenge and skill ratio

The first thing to start paying attention to is that your mental state is dependent on the ratio between the challenge level and the skill level for a particular task or activity.

According to the Flow Model by Mihaly Csikszentmihalyi [7], depicted below, you can enter eight emotional states of mind while engaged in any task.

Flow Model
by Mihály Csíkszentmihályi

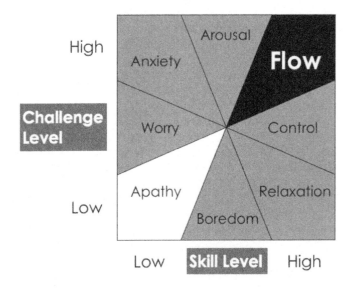

As you can see, you will feel:

- Apathy if you lack interest in the task
- Boredom if you are fatigued or dull
- Relaxation if you are calm and lacking excitement

- Worry if your attention is directed toward negativity where your problems seem to get bigger and solutions do not appear to exist
- Control if you have developed your skills so well that the task makes you go on autopilot
- Anxiety if the work is too challenging and it may cause you to freeze or stagnate
- Arousal if you feel stimulated and attentive while developing your skills
- Flow if you are focused entirely on the activity or task by succeeding or achieving excellence

The 4% challenge target

A very delicate balance between challenge and skill needs to be achieved to facilitate flow, and the sweet spot is just outside your comfort zone.

A common way of achieving flow is by playing video games. Behaviour psychologists and other scientists work hard to create a game that follows the 4% ratio. Games should be difficult enough to hold your attention, but not too difficult that you feel you are not progressing. They have many levels to keep you motivated, you gain bonuses and work hard to score to go onto another even more difficult level, but as games raise the difficulty by on average 4%, you will keep playing it, and easily enter the flow state. You can even become addicted to the games by releasing many feel-good chemicals in your bloodstream.

Many high achievers, type A personalities, would reach out and aim to tackle a challenge that is 20, 30 or even 50% higher than their current skillset, as they aim high. An enormous challenge can be very unsettling, and make flow not easily accessible. Flow happens in a moment of control, so if you are aiming too high, you need to learn how to create a steady pace to work that is not stressful.

The use of meditation or mindfulness will have to be explored and experimented with, to give you more balance and control, even though a certain dose of risk during your endeavours will be necessary to achieve flow. Risks can be your reputation, physical, emotional, spiritual, financial or any other kind.

Research conducted by Steven Kotler at Google Headquarters found out that 4% is the increment for the challenge ratio, so understanding the compounding effect of this small number can bring you great insight. For example, an athlete could practice for many months to shave 4% off of their time. Then it's time to enter a competition, say the Olympics, and the athlete can expect to perform their best ever by achieving 4% better performance, from one day to the next and break their own record. Records are broken during competitions and not during training, because a bigger challenge will promote flow and ultimate performance as a result.

You will be surprised that radical sports athletes are progressing in their achievements faster now than ever before. You can see the details of this explosion in performance by reading Steven Kotler's book, *The Rise of Superman [9]*.

Reaching the sweet spot

For intellectual work, the 4% challenge still applies, and it represents a continuous effort to achieve an outcome and the discipline necessary to stay focused on an objective.

An easy way to create more flow at the office, or while doing tasks usually performed on auto-pilot, is by aiming to execute the activity 4% faster. This tiny increase in speed is enough to awaken you from mindless action and it's almost impossible to hate an activity if you are trying to perform it faster, better or putting the effort to delegate the activity in a way that will minimise disruption and eventually gift you with extra time for creative work.

Transforming 4% into 700%

While working diligently to find a way to progress in your career, 4% doesn't appear to be a substantial increase in your productivity.

In fact, 5-10% increase in productivity can be the result of self-help or regular training.

As flow is a heightened state of awareness, your 4% challenge target can have a massive impact on your productivity, by triggering your creativity.

Believing you will find a great solution for your work problems will lead to developing the confidence of having a series of minor ideas that can eventually reveal an idea that could really change paradigms to seriously impact your career.

Although measuring creativity can be very difficult, flow is considered to be a near-perfect decision-making state, so much so that Steven Kotler and Harvard studies estimate that you can boost creativity by 400-700% while in flow [1].

Creativity is the most sought-after skill in the market today, and being capable of harnessing this state will prove that people don't really know what is possible for them.

Motivation to become more creative

Perhaps seeing the competition creeping in your market will give you great motivation that will lead to a sudden realisation or idea that can totally change your predicament and transform you into a superstar in your field.

What is important is to have, in the back of your mind, the motivation to keep looking for new ways to improve your work and look at problems as opportunities in disguise.

Author James Altucher recommends everyone have a little notepad in their pocket, exclusively to take notes of new ideas, and this is really a brilliant idea in itself.

He challenges himself to come up with ten new ideas every day, and he writes them down on his notepad. Most ideas will be useless or impractical or expensive to implement or downright crazy.

But if you end up having one great idea after one whole month of note-taking, you have the upper hand of having something new to implement and also discovered that you have the ability to cultivate your creativity.

The chicken-and-egg conundrum

It is hard to define where the cycle starts, because flow promotes creativity and creativity promotes flow.

Creativity is crucial in business, but I don't see many courses teaching how to be creative, apart from creative writing courses. On the contrary, the great majority of people learn skills and feel they are not creative at all; therefore their belief will undermine any effort to have new ideas.

If you get enrolled in flow training with me, you will receive a pocket notepad that you will have the responsibility to use, I will check on you to motivate your creative muscles to work hard for you, and the big ideas will come just as a gift. You could use your mobile phone and an app for this task, but the notepad is more memorable and effective.

Another way to motivate creativity is to decide to write your book. You will start seeing the information that relates to your subject, and in order to fit into your model of the world you will adapt it to the subject of your book, and as you have the discipline to write a little every day, new connections will be available to you.

I will discuss the idea of writing your book during the third quest, and this is a key element of creating flow in your life.

1.3.6 Strengths of a flow experience

Now it is time to understand how powerful a flow state experience can be.

Duration of the flow experience

It can go from a microflow moment to a few days long, so I created and analogy between flow and air to describe four possible durations of your flow experience.

- Skirt lifting
- Riding with the wind
- Hang gliding
- Parachute jumping

Skirt lifting

You were walking around in a big city, and suddenly the wind passing by the skyscrapers gathers speed and hits a girl at once, messing up her hair and lifting up her skirt. The girl was surprised and for a moment, felt like she was the centre of attention. The boys around her might have had an intense and memorable moment, too. This circumstance may be comparable to being in a microflow by shifting a person's mind into a brief pleasurable experience.

This microflow state could last a few minutes of focused attention, and an example of it could be an engaging talk about work with a colleague, or an inspiring moment while writing an important email.

Riding with the wind

You were enjoying a bicycle ride when you looked at the horizon and saw a storm approaching, so you decided to ride back home. The strong wind hit you hard, and you struggled, but you made a left turn, and the wind now worked as a propeller, making you go 30 per cent faster and with less effort.

This experience would be comparable to being in flow while writing a blog entry. No one asked you to write it, you desire to share ideas that can help others, so you struggle to organise your thoughts, and put the effort on something that doesn't have an immediate payoff, just the satisfaction of being creative and experience the timelessness of flow.

Hang gliding

The sun was shining bright, so you decided to go to the top of a mountain and open the flimsy frame to stretch the fabric of your wings. You attached your harness to the frame and ran towards the abyss. It was exhilarating to feel free like a bird, and you scanned the sky looking for eagles or big birds flying in circles to join the flock. They were gathering together to take advantage of ascending currents of air that would take them higher and higher, without having to flap their wings.

This experience would represent a deep state of flow where you have a new perspective of your normal landscape, and an example of it could be to spend two hours putting together a PowerPoint presentation to raise money for your dream project. Your creativity is heightened and time flies while you choose pictures to depict your project, and you get surprised with the results.

Parachute jumping

The ultimate flow experience is represented by a parachute jump, but this in no ordinary jump as it took three years to prepare and 250 tests.

In 2014, Alan Eustace jumped in freefall from the artificial satellite belt to break the sound barrier and go straight into the Guinness Book of Records.

This is what going into deep flow state would look like for the experienced radical sports enthusiast. His mind was relaxed, heart rate under control, and he was breathing calmly during this exhilarating experience.

The bodysuit technology, used for the dive, can improve the safety of space hotels under construction and enable a millionaire to opt for a faster check out. Instead of taking the shuttle they could put their suit on, open the hatch and jump into the void, travel at 820mph (1,320 Km/h), break the sound barrier and touch down safely on earth after 4.5 minutes.

In the same way, a skiing champion knows that their body armour is the flow state. It will give them protection from harm by having their whole body working in synergy, secreting the right hormones and making all the micromovements that will grant them an Olympic medal or a viral video on YouTube.

I experienced the long haul effects of flow while writing this book, as I saw complex problems unfold into simplicity. I would write for three hours, go for a walk, have another breakthrough and get back inspired to write for three more hours to transcribe the insight into a brand new topic.

Altruistic endeavours can also bring two or three days' worth of flow experience. This state is called the "helpers high" which can sometimes be achieved when a person engages in something much bigger than themselves to impact humanity, creating great accomplishments from a deep purpose.

Intensity of a flow experience

The other dimension of flow is related to the level of commitment to the activity and therefore the satisfaction generated by the experience.

You will find three levels of intensity and they are:

- Pleasure loaded flow
- Task accomplished flow
- Purpose driven flow

Pleasure loaded flow

At this level you accidentally fall into flow, which is the most common occurrence of flow as there not seem to have a real cause and the duration of the experience is arbitrary and not easily repeatable.

Having a long conversation with a friend and finding a solution for a working challenge they might be facing would fit here. Start reading a business book, loose the track of time and having a brilliant idea to grow your business would also be generating pleasure that might be worth celebrating.

Task accomplished flow

This second level is mostly related to work endeavours or home related tasks that might or might not be totally pleasant, but are necessary to achieving targets and deadlines on time.

You might be propelled into action to avoid the discomfort that could be created by failing the task and a good example here would be to do my accounts. It's hard to get started but when I do I immerse myself into the task and suddenly the work is all done and I feel very proud of myself. Another experience would be to organise my house, workflow and other commitments just before I go on holidays. I get impressed on how efficient I become while making important decisions and getting all done fast to have a deserved break.

Neither of the activities described are intrinsically pleasant but accomplishing them by deciding to get them done quickly and efficiently can drive flow and satisfaction.

Purpose driven flow

These are the most relevant of all and they can give you the best highs in the world. They relate to having a purpose in life as a driving force or by giving meaning to the work you do. It is vital to understand the importance of your work as we live to serve others and any action can be noble if done with love in your heart.

Many people will find their purpose at work, on a hobby or by engaging in a project or cause that benefit a specific communities they belong to.

My one to one clients go through a process of selecting a purpose laden project and we converge the theory into practice by getting serious about using the triggers and conditions for flow with discernment and discipline. I recommend they choose or create a project that can be accomplished from three to twelve months and we break it down into weeks to select activities and daily targets.

The results achieved are simply fantastic because they discover the power of creating new possibilities out of nothing and as we structure their projects they become so passionate about them that they start enrolling others to achieve their desired outcomes. They develop their leadership and also create group flow by impacting their communities in ways that will surprise them.

By reading this book you can also learn the fundamentals to prepare your environment and routines to make flow happen in a continuum basis. You will achieve a new level of satisfaction that will be responsible for igniting creativity to create breakthroughs, making you break records in any field and inevitably generating great wealth as a result.

1.3.7 Fourteen supporting conditions to get into an intellectual flow

Enhance your chances to get into flow for longer by understanding the supporting conditions. Use the information below to start a discussion about promoting flow at work with your boss, business partner, colleague, teacher, coach, tutor, parents, or anyone that could help you gauge your progress and keep you motivated. It is possible that around five per cent of the time you spend at work you get into flow, but you don't even realise it because you don't know how you got there in the first place.

Notice that the topics below could be descriptive of parameters to create a new and exciting game. If you put an effort to transform tasks into games, you will increase the satisfaction of executing activities.

- Aim for being world-class
- Creativity and constraints
- Clear goals
- Projects should be sufficiently challenging
- Visualise the outcome
- Mental highlight reel
- Decide to focus your attention
- Avoid distractions
- Work during your peak time
- Enhance heart coherence
- Focus on the task for at least 30 minutes
- Risk taking
- Question your interest and performance
- Intense feedback

Aim for being world-class

You've heard successful people saying that you should work on something you would love to be successful, but this is easier said than done. I had many jobs and created many business ventures in my life, and there is a way to find fulfilment at work to create your dream job.

Look at your work as an opportunity to play different games with struggles and rewards.

If you think that at least seventy per cent of people are disengaged with their job or study path, understand that it is a choice to start loving the work you do. If you decide to be world-class at work and put your heart into the activity you do, trying to improve by doing more than what is expected from you, you will connect with the primordial idea that you are using your free will to find something in your job to be happy about. If you are doing photocopying, make it neat and aligned, not sloppy, pay attention to the details and stay interested in finding what are the problems in your job. Most of the best ideas for businesses started once someone decided to scratch their own itch and find a solution to a problem they had. If they find the solution, they will probably find a lot of people that had the same problem they had, and a new and profitable company can be founded there and then.

I started putting this book together out of the frustration that I was dyslexic and had to put real effort to start reading a book. I wanted to find a way to make reading books more pleasurable for myself, and it was more than a decade ago that I started researching and questioning everything because I wanted it to be not only world-class but the best book about flow in the whole world. I am happy that I had this mentality to keep working and perfecting it until publishing my work of art.

If you focus on doing things better each time, someone will notice your efforts, opportunities will open up, and you will find out what you love and then dedicate your life to it.

Establish rewards to motivate performance, and give rewards for suggestions or innovations if you have people working under you. Be grateful that you have a job that gives you money to live and enjoy life.

Learn about your strengths by taking the Talent Dynamics test and find your wealth profile.

www.humansinflow.global/wealth-dynamics

Once you understand this clever way to leverage your potential you can start thinking of all those other professions you could do and start learning how to prepare yourself to do something that might be more rewarding than the work you are doing right now.

Some people are more likely to achieve flow if they already have an autotelic personality, which is characterized by them being curious, persistent and self-centred, as they enjoy performing activities for their own sake.

They are individuals that naturally search for action and feel stimulated by any sort of achievement, even without direct expectation of future benefits.

You can keep learning how to play the guitar, how to sing, work on a business startup idea or, like me, keep researching and writing my book, even when I considered it finished. Yes, I confess, I can't stop! This is my autotelic activity. For me, writing will lead to more writing, more ideas, more teaching and lots of travel, so I keep doing it.

Getting into flow will require risk-taking and struggle, so if you decide to love your job and become world-class, synchronicities and serendipity will appear in your life. If you decide to try a new career path, start reading or taking online courses to expand your awareness and perhaps take the plunge and find the work that you will really love. So, stop complaining, smile and say yes to life.

Creativity and constraints

The highlight is that motivation leads to creativity, and constraints play a big role in promoting the most important trait one needs to prosper today.

Being more creative implies taking more risks, so to become more creative you need to learn how to fail easily and use the experience as a motivator to come up with even better ideas. This is the constraint of a reality check, and knowing that a creative solution is achievable will demand perseverance and grit.

So, you will be developing your creativity by learning through failure, which is a constraint that most people avoid. They want to do the right thing, all the time, especially if they are a student or they work for a big organization with a precise job description. So finding a subject that you are interested or curious about and starting to study it will create the space for creativity to unfold. Have one or two friends that you can exchange new ideas with to keep it going. What is crucial is that you are aware that you can pivot to another subject if you feel the need to stay focused and strengthen your grit, which is one of the top predictors of success.

As you become constrained by your field of interest you will expand and discover your true talents and skills. Remember that speed and pressure will contribute to developing your creative mind. The principle of doing something 4% more challenging than usual or 4% faster will bring you more flow, as faster decision making usually makes people happier.

Contrary to common belief, you shouldn't have the aspiration of finding yourself. Creativity is in everything you can see or imagine so the true quest is not to find yourself but to create a new self. If you think that is possible, perhaps you will like reading a fascinating book by Joe Dispenza called "Breaking the habit of being yourself" to understand the psychology and science of daring to reinvent yourself and becoming more creative.

Creativity appears to be one of the most important skills for office workers, and Steven Kotler mentions in some interviews that studies show that flow can also spike creativity from 400% up to 700% [1].

He also mentions that the defence department in the US found an increase of up to 490% in learning speed [3], and I'm certain that creativity will spike if you start learning any subject.

So, individuals and companies that understand the concept of flow and apply it will have an unfair advantage from their investment in training.

Stay motivated with a project or a vision that you move towards, and you will find your way into flow and will become more creative. The good news is that creativity can outlast the flow state by a day, two or more days. Teach your brain to become more creative, this is a crucial ability in today's world. Start by taking a new route to work today?

Start changing and the world will change with you.

Clear goals

Games help you focus because you understand exactly what you should do at each stage. This is critical to achieving flow, so creating a plan that goes from short to medium and long term can help you establish clarity.

116

Only then you can decide what to do, believe that you can accomplish it, and you know why you are spending time on that activity. The result of making your goals clear is that you will immediately improve your attention and cut down the noise from your life. For example, you will stop watching too much TV/YouTube, or spending time in the pub, because you know you have important stuff to do and you also have a deadline to achieve.

Projects should be sufficiently challenging

To illustrate degrees of a challenge, I will elaborate on developing your abilities while practising the martial arts. They require focused attention on the learning process and ultimate control during competitions. The coloured belts system utilised in martial arts helps understand all the levels that can be achieved, and the limitations expected on each level. The intellectual improvement I'm interested in helping you develop goes beyond the academic system of grades and credentials like Degree, Masters or PhD. Information is readily available to everyone, and you could benefit from the guidance of a more experienced professional, but your aim should be to transcend the system and come up with new ideas to attract a team that can implement them. Knowing that you are reading or studying something that you don't grasp completely, is a sign that you are on the right path. So keep pushing the boundaries.

Visualise the outcome

As you set your goals, visualise the steps and final accomplishment to give your unconscious brain a pathway to follow. The more you practice in your mind, the more likely you will achieve your desired outcome. If you decided to write your book as a major motivator to read more and position yourself as an expert, you could choose a graphic designer and order the cover design for your book. Print and glue it on the cover of an ordinary book. Place it on a good spot in your office, where others can see what you are up to, and you will stay motivated. Spending some time creating your "Goal Map" (**1.4.6 Create a Goal Map, prioritise and plan your diary hour**

by hour) or a vision board can also help you create a mental picture to guide your actions.

Mental highlight reel

Another visualisation that most people ignore and I find very powerful is the mental highlight reel, where you write down the best ten flow moments of your life and the build-up for them in detail, especially the emotional state you were in before the grand finale. This practice will guide you in finding the pattern that is more likely to bring you flow, as we can accomplish a lot by connecting with a high state of mind before performing. After writing down the ten moments, close your eyes to think and feel connected with each one of the accomplishments to hardwire that mental pathway that will lead you to flow.

I also advise you to start a journal to track down all the activities and insights that lead you to flow, by looking back and talking about them so you can repeat those patterns.

Decide to focus your attention

As you have established your goals, you need to choose your most important task to focus your attention. As you have learnt about brain waves, start experimenting with different programmes and keep track of your progress so you will be able to refine your choice for superior performance. Read books actively and always be on the lookout for the big idea, not worrying too much if you skip parts of the book that do not resonate with you.

Having challenges will help you pay attention and engage in the process of creating novelty out of complexity. Dealing with unpredictability requires courage, and it will stretch your skills and raise your standards.

Avoid distractions

Clear your desk, switch your phone to airplane mode and choose the right environment to attract flow.

Work during your peak time

Monitor the time of the day that you are more alert and productive and use this time to engage in creative work and achieve flow.

Enhance heart coherence

According to Jamie Wheal, when you are in high cardiac coherence, you tend to harmonise the function of the vagus nerve. The vagus nerve goes from the top to the bottom of your body and controls a lot of your organs, but scientists are just figuring out this area of study.

To enhance coherence, you need to learn about the biofeedback devices that can show how to reach this favourable state that influences your body and mind.

Learn more about it by Googling "cardiac coherence," or visit the Heartmath Institute.

www.heartmath.org

Focus on the task for at least 30 minutes

A continuous period of uninterrupted time builds momentum. If you are interrupted in your train of thought, you can take from one to ten minutes to get back to the mental place you were in, if you can get back there at all. If you work at an open-plan office, you might benefit from wearing big headphones as they help you create an invisible bubble around you and other people will think twice before interrupting you. It's also helpful to avoid the temptation of checking out who passes by your desk. By resisting the temptation of getting distracted, even for a couple of seconds, you will train your brain to focus deeper in less time, so avoid eye contact with any passer-by if you want to get into flow. Multitasking might be useful in certain circumstances, but it is definitely detrimental to the achievement of flow.

You can try a great way to stop thinking about other things you have to do while reading, thinking or working. To focus, set a timer for 30, 60, 120 minutes or more of uninterrupted reading or thinking time. Just allow that break in your day. It will give you more discipline to focus, and you will get more consistent in establishing a new routine. You can use the timer for any other activity you want to introduce.

Risk taking

An essential thing to know is that if you are taking a risk, you are much more likely to focus and get into flow.

It can be a physical risk, emotional risk, creative risk, intellectual risk, psychological risk, spiritual, or social risk when your reputation is at stake.

A great way to learn how to get into flow is by practising public speaking. Fear of embarrassing yourself in public, while being the centre of attention, is enormous in the world. On the other hand, being good at communicating your ideas under pressure might change the course of your career very quickly, and presenting in public can be learnt.

As one of the main objectives of this book is to motivate you to read more books and learn faster, you will have the opportunity to share the ideas you learn in public and reinforce the learning by sharing the knowledge. Visit a Toastmasters group in your city and see for yourself that if someone messes up, the group will be there to give them immediate feedback and support for continuous growth. Another place to practise exposing yourself and taking social risks is the infamous karaoke.

Remember that too much nor-epinephrine and cortisol in the system is a recipe for anxiety that will block creativity and flow.

So it is necessary to develop emotional control and you will benefit by having some level of a working agreement with fear.

Mindfulness breathwork practice is beneficial because it gives you a little distance from your emotions.

High flow organisations are the ones that promote fail forward and fail faster mentality, so the taking of risk is encouraged more than you might be used to. Excellent company culture requires safety, and not being fired for taking risks, can promote creativity and innovation.

Question your interest and performance

The point here is to question yourself if the material you are reading or studying is exciting, unusual, challenging, entertaining or useful at all. If the text you are reading is not interesting enough, you can skip a paragraph, page, chapter or close the book and move on to a better topic or author.

Having a purpose will help focus your attention.

Sometimes I feel guilty that I'm not doing something else more useful than reading a book; it feels like a very egocentric habit, but if you think that you can share the knowledge you have gained, you will feel like you are sharing that time you spend reading with a lot of your friends. I believe that knowing more will help you develop a great career and amazing friendships.

Intense feedback

Having feedback while practicing sports seems to be easier than performing intellectual work. For this reason you need to be willing to ask for feedback from a trusted advisor that will read what you write, and listen to your rehearsals for any presentation. If you are reading a book you could ask yourself if this book is worth reading any further or not.

Whatever you do, look for new ways to get feedback, either asking others, yourself or even recording video or audio while you perform or interact in social or professional settings.

An enlightened request I've done a few times, to receive invaluable feedback, is to ask a work colleague, a friend or an acquaintance the following question:

"Hi, you've been a good friend for two years, and I appreciate the way you opened my eyes to new ways of seeing the reality around me… (you can praise them for what they are in your life)

I'm in a quest to be able to get into flow state to have a more fulfilling life, and I want to ask you a few questions to know myself better.

Can you help me?

Yes/No answer.

Can I ask you what our friends think of me? (Replace friends with colleagues, clients, family or whatever is relevant but don't ask what they think of you as it is too confrontational to start with.)

What are my weaknesses?

What are my strengths?

What can you count of me for?

What does everyone know about me?

What would people talk about me if I'm not around?

Is there anything incomplete that you want to open your heart and share so we can become better friends?"

This interaction will open your mind to a new you and will bring the other person much closer. These questions can bring brothers and sisters to a place never experimented before, and the risk will be rewarded with profound feedback that can be followed by a supportive person to help you become a better version of yourself.

Start the intense feedback conversation with someone you think you know well and see your relationship go deeper than you've ever thought it could be, then keep exploring or not, you are in charge.

Don't say "I'm scared of asking someone about myself."

Say, "I'm excited to ask someone about myself."

You will be aroused by this affirmation and will end up enjoying the experience.

1.3.8 The flow triggers in action

Writing this book was the most challenging adventure of my entire life. As I decided to write in English, I would feel insecure, rewrite a paragraph 5-10 times and still not be satisfied with the results, wishing that I could convey the message in a better way.

What was surprising was that, from time to time, I would immerse myself in a state of flow that would allow me to write for uninterrupted periods of time with very focused attention, and a strange feeling that I was not writing my own thoughts, but downloading new ideas from a different dimension. Surprisingly enough, the ideas were clear and also gave me my best breakthroughs.

As I started exploring the state of flow, I was intrigued to know how to develop these feelings of concentration and deep enjoyment that can be achieved while writing, playing chess, surfing a wave, playing music, having sex or practising radical sports to a high level.

STER flow

I found explanations about flow while reading the works of Mihaly Csikszentmihalyi but who is really revolutionising this field is Steven Kotler and Jamie Wheal. They are the founders of the Flow Genome Project, and they identified four signature characteristics of flow.

The acronym STER will remind you the basic characteristics of being in flow.

STER stands for:

- Selflessness
- Timelessness
- Effortlessness
- Richness

Identify your flow style

Flow can be experienced in many ways, so I developed a profile test where you can identify your flow style preferences to improve your flow superpowers.

You can experience flow in your mind or with your body so you will have mental or active flow.

Mental flow can be achieved while being quiet or loud, and active flow while being quiet or loud.

Rate the incidence of flow for all the following activities in the last year to understand where you can expand or start applying the concepts to achieve flow.

Mental Quiet Flow	Incidence of flow
	Rate from zero to 10
Read	
Write	
Draw	
Think & Plan	
Solve problems	
Work	
Study	
Play video games	
Other activity	
Mental Quiet Flow (Average rate)	

Mental Loud Flow	Incidence of flow
	Rate from zero to 10
Present/teach	
Coach	
Learn	
Discuss project	
Brainstorm	
Other activity	
Mental Loud Flow (Average rate)	

Active Quiet Flow	Incidence of flow
	Rate from zero to 10
Religious & Mystic	
Help others	
Yoga, Tai Chi	
Meditations	
Martial arts	
Create art	
Other activity	
Active Quiet Flow (Average rate)	

Active Loud Flow	Incidence of flow
	Rate from zero to 10
Hair & Beauty	
Romance	
Travel	
Exercise	
Party & Play	
Gamble	
Adventure	
Volunteer	
Other activity	
Active Loud Flow (Average rate)	

Flow Summary	Incidence
	Rate from zero to 10
Mental Quiet Flow	
Mental Loud Flow	
Active Quiet Flow	
Active Loud Flow	

Flow unfolding

In practical terms for reading, working or studying, you will have profound clarity about the subject and things make more sense to you. You will have the ability to detach yourself from preconceived ideas and dive into the author's perspective, or view the core of the problem you are trying to solve. You enhance your power of pattern recognition to find new connections or have new ideas. As a result, you will feel in control knowing that you will make the right decisions as the activity unfolds. For example, you could decide to skip ahead on the book, stop to reread and highlight a few passages, or start writing a new topic triggered by a hunch. The beauty is that you keep moving forward at speed without questioning the change of direction, as you feel assertive at every step you take.

Transient hypofrontality

Flow is an altered state of consciousness where you get so focused at the task at hand, that everything else disappears and you perform as your super self.

It would be just natural to expect that you would be switching your turbo power on, to use more of your brain while heightening your senses, but the opposite is true.

Your prefrontal cortex is your rational thinking brain, and it is in charge of your higher cognitive functions. It calculates time and gives you your sense of self, which makes you judge what is moral and helps you make decisions.

While in flow, this part of the brain goes into transient hypofrontality, which means that the prefrontal cortex slows down or shuts down to save energy to more critical functions, and the result is unexpected and magical.

Perceived effects of transient hypofrontality

Your sense of time gets distorted as you plunge into the deep now. In this place, you might feel the experience unfolding in slow motion.

Your sense of self, self-doubt and your inner critic disappear, and you become more creative and confident.

Being in flow is hard to describe, and some people dare to say that they feel like they can see their reality two seconds ahead of time. This means that they can observe new possibilities and accelerate without having to work harder for it.

If you are reading a book, you can notice the mind of the author thinking and guiding you towards a goal, and you integrate their thought process. You can also feel free to speed up or even skip ahead to find the information you are after. If you are searching for a solution to a challenge, you are open to new creative insights.

The feelings created by the flow state were first described by Csikszentmihalyi, and I highlight the following:

- Vanishing the sense of self – It's like watching yourself perform where your inner critic disappears, and you take more risks by feeling free and creativity blossoms as you don't doubt and analyse every idea.
- Distorted sense of time – You connect deeply with the present moment, and you make contact with the deep now. Time can run faster or slower than normal. You might see things happening in slow motion, but a session of one hour in flow might be perceived as happening in just ten minutes.
- Sense of control – You do or think with total knowingness over the situation even if you have never experienced it before. You could write a

127

profound poem or explain a new idea precisely and elegantly.

- The activity is intrinsically rewarding – You don't focus on achieving an objective as you do it for its own sake and action becomes effortless.
- Loss of bodily awareness – While immersed in flow you might forget to eat or go to the bathroom, and any pain can subside into non-existence.
- Absorption – Awareness narrows down to the activity itself, and they both merge. The writer becomes the text, and the surfer becomes the wave.

Altered states encompass flow states, states of awe, psychedelic states, meditative states, dreaming, trance states, mystical states, orgasmic states and more. Neurobiologically they are very similar, and flow is just one of the states where there is loss of time, loss of self, information richness, creativity and so on, but flow demands action, so mental states of ecstasis need to be translated into the world by some kind of action.

Flow is always a positive experience, and it follows focus. One interesting factor is that creativity triggers flow, then flow enhances creativity.

1.3.9 The four stages to achieve flow

While pursuing the flow state for mental or physical activities, you will need to understand that flow doesn't really happen by chance, and it is comprised of four stages.

Although getting into flow state can last two or three hours, I want to highlight the flow state achieved by altruism. As you get involved in a project to help others, you can enter a state of flow that can last two or three days, and this state is commonly called "helpers high."

Flow follows challenges

You probably expect to get into flow state as a way to stimulate your creativity, so a great surprise is to know that by being creative you will also enhance and prolong the flow experience, but there is a caveat.

128

Steven Kotler mentions four stages one typically needs to pass in order to achieve flow, and they are:

- Struggle
- Release
- Flow
- Recovery

As I'm focusing on getting into flow to produce intellectual work, I will give examples that concern this way of achieving mental results. If you practice radical sports, perform on stage or entertain an audience, your four stages might be quite different from what I describe below, but the principle is the same.

Struggle

So be prepared to overwhelm yourself with new information; read books, reports and research on the net. As you start reading with a purpose, notice that if the text is not nourishing you with the relevant information you should be brave to skip a few paragraphs, sub-chapters or even jump ahead to a chapter that resonates with you.

Watch videos and listen to podcasts in search for the big idea. The secret here is not to become frustrated or anxious. You know that this stage is necessary for the process, so do your job and look for connections.

Release

After all the hard work to collect data working through the night, it is time to change focus and entertain yourself with sports, playing or listening to music or any other activity that is not connected to the activity you've been involved with, so meeting your friends and having fun is a step in the right direction.

Flow

As you set up a date and time for productive work, you might achieve the flow state or not. You will need at least one or two hours of uninterrupted time to focus on your creative work and let your mind give you the direction to work your way to extreme focus that can bring new and surprising outcomes.

Recovery

If you succeeded in achieving the flow state you had an intense mental workout, releasing many chemicals into your bloodstream and depleting yourself of vital energy in a short period of time. So the following day you might start the day on a high note, but you may fall from grace and feel like you have a slight hangover. If that's the case, you should not hang on to that feeling of frustration because the next stage will be the struggle again.

I had to create more discipline in my life to force myself to endure this last stage by not celebrating the achievements of my flow state with alcohol. If I drink to celebrate, I will feel bad the next day, and will keep celebrating for a feel for more days, and instead of re-entering the four stages to achieve flow again I can get stuck on an alcoholic loop that can side-track my progress and jeopardise the overall development of my projects.

So I recommend you have a team or accountability buddies and deadlines to keep moving forward and not be too isolated like I was while writing this book.

1.3.10 Parkinson's Law to create flow

Now you will understand the variables that will impact your flow experience while reading, working, studying and writing.

This law states that any activity will be accomplished within the time frame you have pre-determined for. For example, if you have the entire afternoon to write a report, you will spend the whole afternoon fiddling with it and will finish by your 6 pm deadline. But if you only have one hour to write the same report, you will magically accomplish your task in that amount of time and are more likely to ignore distractions and get in flow.

If you want something to be done quickly and want to delegate the task, ask a busy person to do it, not a person with a lot of time on their hands, because they will fit the task into their schedule and get it done by the deadline.

130

If you are the person responsible for accomplishing something, you need to establish a deadline, make it public and be certain that not achieving the deadline would have serious consequences.

So if you are planning to read books as part of your continuing education, you should be comfortable with deciding what time of the day you will start and finish your reading habit. Set the alarm on your phone and get used to it. I recommend that you have at least 30 minutes to focus on the task, so a wise thing to do is to set your mobile phone on airplane mode or night time mode. I only have notifications on my phone to alert me of appointments from my calendar, and I recommend you do the same to focus for longer, and this way have more flow experiences.

Another extension of this same idea is that you can give yourself a certain amount of time to read a whole book. For example, you could give yourself two hours to read an entire book. This way, you will be highly selective and skip or skim the text, while looking for something that will be important enough to grab your attention and make you read it through. You will not read entire chapters but will develop your confidence to tackle a book and achieve fulfilment at the end of the book, instead of frustration by reading just half of the book and never opening it again. I'm sure you know the feeling, don't you?

I've done it, and you can do it, too.

1.3.11 Emotional Freedom Technique can help you learn faster

If you feel that you are not progressing at the expected speed by using the techniques described in this book, it is possible that you might have an emotional blockage, or some limiting beliefs about your power of reading faster, learning, or remembering what you read.

I'm a practitioner of EFT, which is short for Emotional Freedom Technique. This is a technique developed by Gary Craig, and it has the power of releasing you from limiting beliefs. It works by tapping with your fingertips the ancient meridians of Chinese medicine that have been used for acupuncture. Paul McKenna is well-known for using this technique mixed with NLP, and he is famous for achieving incredible results. Deepak Chopra also recommends it.

The EFT has been used to cure phobias, allergies, anxiety, traumas, and also addictions.

If you want to try it out, you can take a course or even learn it online. The basics of the technique are described below:

Step 1 – Get connected with your limiting belief. Think about one particular area that you are frustrated with like: "I'm a slow reader," "I'm not very clever" or even "I don't have a good memory." Connect with that feeling.

Step 2 – Rate the intensity of the feeling on a scale of 0–10. Have a guess and write the number down so later on, you can compare it with your new rating after the practice.

Step 3 – Say: "Even though I feel this frustration of... (Add here your own limiting belief, tension or trauma)... I deeply and completely accept myself."

While saying it out loud three times, keep tapping the karate chop point continually. It is vital to feel and mean it when you say the statement. Accept yourself for having these feelings.

Step 4 – Tap the sequence of points on your body you find in the drawing below. You will be tapping from 5 to 7 times on each point and you will be saying the remainder of the full statement. For example, say "slow reader" or "bad memory." Make it a two- or three-word statement and keep tapping as you say this keyword in your mind.

After you finish the sequence, take a deep breath, gently stretch your neck and roll your shoulders. At this point, many people yawn, sigh or feel a shift.

Step 5 – Continue tapping on your karate chop point and look down to the left and right while keeping your head still. Move your eyes round to complete a circle in a clockwise and then in an anti-clockwise direction.

Now count from one to ten and then hum the "Happy Birthday" song. Look down and look from right to left three times and you are done.

The last thing to do is to check on the scale from 0–10 how you would rate the feeling you had before.

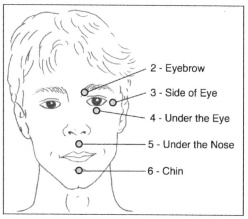

2 - Eyebrow
3 - Side of Eye
4 - Under the Eye
5 - Under the Nose
6 - Chin

The majority of people feel very different and empowered after doing this sequence, which takes only two or three minutes to complete. I believe that it removes blockages by connecting the left and right side of the brain and by releasing unconscious tension or traumas.

For a more detailed explanation or for an introduction with videos, go to this website:

www.emofree.com

1.3.12 Brainwaves and flow

Now you will understand your brainwaves and how to take advantage of them.

Brainwaves affect your performance

Your brains represent just 2% of your body mass, but they use 20–25% of your energy, creating brainwaves while they are working. Normal waking consciousness is associated with beta brainwaves, but if you close your eyes, your brain will not have to process visual information, and will be changing automatically to alpha brainwaves that are slower. If you start meditating, you will go into deep alpha, which operates at very slow brainwaves. Different outcomes become more natural to reach whenever you are producing the right brainwaves for the task. The brainwaves give you the background to play different life games.

If you are fully alert driving a car, your mind produces certain beta brainwaves; however, if you are sleeping, you will produce more alpha brainwaves. If you are trying to concentrate, you need to change the brainwaves to high beta brainwaves for optimal performance.

Alpha waves are slow and go from 8–12 cycles per second. Beta waves go from 12–35 cycles per second.

Beta waves are split into three sections:

Low beta waves (12–17 cycles) are present if you are talking to a friend or start reading a book without much focus.

Medium beta waves (17–25 cycles) are present when you are worried about something, or when you get more focused while reading or studying.

High beta waves (25–35 cycles) are present if you are focused and doing complex, intellectual work.

The challenge is this:

You are going about doing your daily chores in low beta waves, and everything is all OK, but then you pick up a book to read. You are distracted and start reading using low beta waves, then your mind wanders, and from time to time you skip back and re-read a paragraph or two and keep moving forward without much focus.

By deciding to avoid going back to re-read as much as you can, you end up paying more attention, even if you miss a detail from the text. Your brain will naturally start to go to medium beta waves that are the optimum ones to boost your performance while reading.

But if instead, you keep going back to re-read the text, your brainwaves will tend to go back to low beta waves, because somehow you will be reading something that you already know and you don't need a lot of brain activity for that. So instead of raising your brainwaves, they will tend to go up and down, and will not give you the best performance. Reading and keeping medium beta waves is like burning the right fuel for your mind. If you end up going to high beta waves, you will be in flow and will really understand the core message of the text with less effort.

So, by forcing yourself not to go back and re-read, your brainwave will raise to medium or high beta, and you will start to get immersed in the text with better comprehension while you read faster.

An easy way to resist the temptation of going back to reread unnecessarily, or control involuntary eye movements that make you skip one or two lines, is to commit to reading the page of your book or document until the end, before going back to reread. This way you will see that you will end up not going back so often, because you are not on default mode, and you catch up on the message as the following paragraphs usually help you to get back on track.

Around 30 per cent of the time you spend reading you are actually rereading, so by making a conscious decision to reread only after reaching the end of the page you might start going back only ten per cent of the time, which makes you read 20 per cent faster.

Brain entrainment will help you to get focused

If we can measure our brainwaves, we can also create them. So many companies are selling CDs, downloads, software, and apps that help your brain get entrained with different frequencies. If you want to work and achieve better focus, you will find particular sound or music that plays specific frequencies and your brain follows it. To help you unwind at the end of the day, there are specific sounds, too, so I also like using some of them to help me meditate deeper and faster.

I've been using different brainwave software over the past nine years to help me focus, and I think they are beneficial. You can make your own mind up if you Google "brain harmonics," "brain entrainment" or "binaural beats." Many years ago, I bought the Neuro-Programmer from Transparent Corp, and I think this is great software if you want to create and record your own personalised tracks.

The Brainwave App for Apple

I've been achieving great results with an App called Brainwave from Banzai Labs because it helps me get focused while reading, thinking hard or even meditating. Below is the icon of the app for the iPhone.

The version I recommend is "BrainWave: 35 Binaural Programs." It has the tools to help you get more focused while reading. You can choose many options, and I recommend you start your journey by using the tracks that play medium and high beta brain waves.

Firstly select a track like "Concentration" that plays constant mid beta frequency, to help you keep a consistent, focused cognitive state. To know what kind of frequency is played with your selection, just tap on the "i" inside a circle at the bottom of the screen to read about the track. At the top of the screen, you will see the minimum time that the track should be played to achieve all the stages it's programmed to play. You can select a longer time for it to play, like one or two hours, and this way make you focus for a longer stretch.

You will also notice that you have two big dots on a sliding scale to control the volume of the brain wave, and also the "Ambience" which has a selection of different kinds of white noise to be played in conjunction with the brain wave. You can also select a music track from your library to play simultaneously with the brain wave by adding it to the library. I like to make a small selection of electronic house music and let it play over and over again.

Be aware that just by playing a white noise sound like the rain falling or waves crashing, you will be improving your focus, especially if you are wearing earphones. So if you listen to white noise in conjunction with brainwaves the results will increase even further. If you have children and don't want to make them use brainwaves, you can at least play some white noise like forest sounds, and they are very likely to feel relaxed and focused. Give it a try.

The Brainwave App for Android

There are many apps to choose from, and I recommend Brain Wave Therapy (Binaural) from Black Coffee Programming. It has similar features from the app for IOS described above.

Mozart Effect

There is a Bulgarian psychotherapist called Georgi Lozanov, who developed a teaching method to learn languages where classical Baroque music is played while you learn. This method can accelerate the speed of learning by two or three times. The point I'm making is that from this study, many researchers found that a selection of tracks from Mozart has a relaxing effect that can aid the brain to study and learn. It is now very common to talk about the Mozart Effect, which is the result of research that suggests that a selection of Mozart's music can, in fact, improve mental performance. You can find more information about it and download the music if you Google it. Try it for yourself and see the results.

Some people can also read while the TV is on, and it can work if you use it as a background or white noise. I like listening to the same track or playlist over and over like a mantra to focus my mind while reading or writing. Maybe you can give it a proper trial.

I think that developing attention while under noise pollution is a great skill to master. It will help you build your focus.

Theta brain waves that help you with flow

I always associated beta brain waves with heightened states of focus, but after learning about flow with Steven Kotler, from the Flow Genome Project, I understood that when you get into flow your prefrontal cortex shuts down, and instead of creating mostly beta waves, the brain starts creating theta waves. This is something technically called transient hypofrontality, and it is astonishing because theta waves are associated with deep sleep.

So if you are choosing a track to assist you while you aim to find creative solutions to a project, or deep understanding of a new subject, you can choose tracks like "Problem Solving" or "Critical Thinking" which include theta frequencies, and therefore they are more likely to induce a flow state while you read or study.

1.3.13 Remember your dreams to find solutions for your challenges

Most people say they can't remember their dreams, but if they start Freudian therapy sessions, they start remembering their dreams just because they can see the importance of the messages their dreams can bring to them. This door of perception will stay open if you take the time to create a Dream Journal, or start trusting and using the information you receive in your dreams.

You probably noticed that you could have an eight-hour night of sleep and wake up fresh, and certain other nights you sleep the same number of hours but wake up groggy with very little energy and a foggy head.

I've learnt that you will wake up energised if your alarm clock goes off while you are in REM sleep, which is when you are in "Rapid Eye Movement" state and are dreaming. This is the closest state to awaken consciousness, your brainwaves will easily switch into the beta frequency, and you will get your day started naturally. On the other hand, if you awaken when you are in a deep sleep, your brainwaves will jolt you, and you don't get into beta wave easily, needing a strong coffee, a cold shower and an hour or two to feel alive and ready to start thinking straight.

And guess what? If you wake up while having a dream, you can remember your dreams much more easily, and these dreams might have the answer to your problems or challenges. As you get into flow and acquire information, you will integrate memories and do important intellectual work while sleeping.

Therefore using an app to help you wake up while in REM sleep might bring you the best insights from what you read, otherwise much of what you've learnt will be stored at a deeper level of your consciousness and not so available. I recommend the app called "Sleep Cycle" which is free for the first month, so you can try it out and use the basic version for free, or pay $29.99 per year if you like all the sophisticated functions.

Remember that books can be perceived as great books if the timing for reading them is right, and the second reason a book can be perceived as a great book is that it actually has great content that was written in a way that resonates with you. So make the most out of reading a book at the right timing to use that information creatively to your advantage.

Most people think they only process information and come up with creative ideas while awake, but the brain never sleeps, and you can peer into your dreams to find many useful insights to your profession and to your life.

You can also direct your intention before going to bed, that you will find the answer for a specific problem in your dreams, and just by giving yourself a suggestion you might direct your dreams to find what you are looking for. There is also the possibility of waking up inside the dream and finding the freedom to do whatever you want, including conscious solutions to real problems using tools that are not available while awake. This is called "lucid dreaming," and I had the privilege of having a few of these. If you are interested in learning the process of waking up in your dream, just Google lucid dreaming to find workshops and courses that might give you the answer to your prayers.

If you want to wake up while in REM sleep, there are a few apps that can track your sleeping pattern during the night. Set the alarm clock for a specific time, and the app will listen to every sound in the room, so it will know when you are dreaming, because you move your body while in REM sleep and stay still while in a deep sleep. Therefore, if you put your alarm to go off at 7 am, the app might go off at 6:45 am to catch you in REM sleep, so you will sleep less than you planned but will feel in high spirits and ready to rock. I use the app called "Sleep Cycle" mentioned before, but you can choose from a selection of apps if you search for "alarm clock rem."

To illustrate the creative power of the dream state, I want to share with you that Thomas Edison used to sit down on a chair for a nap when very tired, focus on a problem and let himself drift into sleep. But what makes his strategy very powerful was that he would hold some marbles in his hand. Knowing that he could catch his subconscious mind at work, when he would loosen his grip and the marbles would slip from his hands and hit the wooden floor with a bang, he would suddenly wake up. He would focus on remembering his dreams or use that moment to stay calm with his eyes closed, and while maintaining alpha and theta brain waves would be able to keep thinking half-sleep to find solutions for his challenges in the realms of dreams. Salvador Dali used the same technique, and other geniuses, including Albert Einstein, are known power nappers that used their dreams to create solutions in our real world.

1.3.14 Jump from dream straight into work

If you wake up fresh, you might even want to do something I like doing, which is to start writing on my computer within one or two minutes of awakening. This way, my brain is still producing alpha and theta brainwaves and I can jump into this daydreaming state and translate my creative thoughts into words before they vanish. I confess it's quite strange to write for one hour straight even before washing my face or have a good cup of coffee.

Now that you know some of the theory concerning brain waves, perhaps you will decide to do some experiments like focusing on finding a solution to a problem, taking a nap in the middle of the day, and waking up with a new solution. Many times I like to keep working through the night until seven in the morning and have lots done so I recommend you keep experimenting and reap the rewards.

EAGLES FLOW QUEST

Vision Four

WHAT TO FOCUS ON

"You can't depend on your eyes when your imagination is out of focus."

Mark Twain

Cultivate a reason to enhance your focus

Eagles change their focus according to their developmental growth, the seasons of the year, and special conditions that demand a quick response.

Starting their adventure into our world requires extreme focus. Breaking an egg from the outside couldn't be easier, but the eagle chick has to break free by itself from the inside. For this task, it has developed a strong muscle and a sharp egg tooth. The muscle is on its neck, and is called a hatching muscle. Since its beak is pointing inwards, it grows a small and sharp egg tooth on its upper beak to puncture the eggshell. When it does, the air will enter the egg, and the chick will breathe air for the first time, gaining the energy to work hard for a few days to break out of the shell.

An eagle will develop many skills in its life. After hatching from the egg, it will learn how to fly, it will start hunting, and when it is mature enough, it will find a mate. They will build their love nest, and will develop patience by incubating their eggs. They will feed and protect their family. And throughout each cycle they will enjoy life by flying higher than any other animals, and by staying in flow even under stormy weather.

I will now compare the development of the eagle with new possibilities, to increase your power to focus and to make decisions faster and with confidence.

Your interest will open your perception to new dimensions, and by focusing your attention, you can merge into the experience and get into flow.

1.4.1 You are at least three times more focused than a goldfish!

The golden eagle chick takes many hours to hatch, and usually breaks totally free from its egg in two to four days. If there are two eaglets in the nest, there might be aggression between them. If the weaker sibling retreats under pressure and stops screaming for food, the parent eagles will not feed them unless they start screaming again. Similarly, I will discuss your talent to get in flow, so you can focus your efforts to break free from your limiting boundaries, voice what you want clearly, and get what you deserve.

Attention is a cognitive process of ignoring part of the environment to concentrate selectively on just one aspect of it. We change our focus or move our eyes, on average, once every second. This constantly shifting focus has implications on our attention span. Some studies say that a goldfish holds its attention for three seconds, while the average attention span for web browsing is around ten seconds. Therefore, you are definitely at least three times more focused than the goldfish!

The general attention span of a literate person is ten to 25 minutes. This means that you will miss specific details in a movie, book or conversation because your attention goes up and down all the time. So, it's no wonder that you get distracted. Did you just fidget? This is a distraction for sure.

We can focus our attention just by having an intention. A good example is listening carefully to what someone is saying while ignoring other conversations at a noisy party. This is called the "Cocktail Party Effect," which is an excellent example of "focused" attention. You can have "sustained" attention where you are able to sustain a consistent response to repetitive activity. The "selective" attention frees you from distraction by being

144

selective. There is "alternating" attention, which is the capacity to move between different tasks and "divided" attention, which helps people to multi-task.

US snipers and radar operators observed a 490% increase in their learning rate when learning took place in flow [3].

It is clear to me that we keep getting distracted for various reasons, so it is therefore essential for us to re-focus and be persistent. We all lose track from time to time, however, with sheer determination, we can focus on the very thing that we want to focus on. Some people find it challenging to remain persistent throughout their endeavours, so I will explain a few more hacks to help their performance. In his book, *Outliers*, Malcolm Gladwell said that it takes at least 10,000 hours of hard work to become a genius. This is relevant to any area of human expression. So, achieving the flow state will be a persistent search for improvement.

I've done a lot of meditation, and I'm sure it was this practice that helped me focus my mind and be assertive, because meditation exercises the mind to focus. Once you learn how to become more focused, you will apply that quality to everything you do, and achieve outstanding results. That's also my aspiration - to get even more focused.

1.4.2 Attention Deficit Disorder and your power to get into a flow state

Eagles grow quickly. They start flapping their wings at 20 days old. Two months later fledging occurs, and on an inspiring day they will attempt to fly from their high nests, and will survive a crash landing if they are lucky. Three weeks later they make successful flying attempts, and after another month they will excel at flying high. In the same way, you can develop new skills if you value the skills highly enough, and even flying is possible if you want it badly enough.

As I kept researching new learning techniques to help myself, I started to hear about a condition that has been of great concern in the educational sector. This condition is usually called ADD, which is short for

Attention Deficit Disorder, and it is also known as ADHD or Attention Deficit Hyperactivity Disorder.

I didn't think these labels suited me well; having a creative mind, I thought I was experiencing a lack of focus because creativity is fluid. With the overload of information available to us, our attention span is getting shorter. In spite of that, many people can develop exceptional power to focus their attention, but like any skill, focusing your mind can be developed in various ways.

Reading slowly can make you think you have ADD

Many people who don't like reading books, label themselves ADD or ADHD, and this becomes the reason for not being able to concentrate. I think they find that reading slowly is frustrating, and that's the real reason they avoid books. Now, teach them how to speed read, and they will be more likely to read a book, because by going faster they naturally develop their focus, and engage with the message. Simple, isn't it?

To enjoy reading books, you need to have the confidence that you can hold your attention to finish the book, otherwise, you will not even start it. To empower you to read more books, and get into flow, it is essential to understand if you have ADD or not, and what to do about it.

Most people diagnosed with ADD will be prescribed the famous Ritalin, Adderall or other drug, but there are many ways to understand and treat this condition, so I will analyse and suggest new ways to see the ADD condition. This wider perspective will give you tools and resources to focus better, and to get into the flow state more often.

Cognitive Bias

I have a more holistic approach, and I believe there is harmony in the apparent chaos. The polar opposites exist inside each one of us, even if we can't clearly see them. Studying Dr John Demartini's work, I understood that if you have Attention Deficit Disorder in one area, it is because the subject you want to focus on is not high up enough in your values system. But there will be areas of your life that rank very highly in your value system, and therefore you will develop the opposing and complementary Attention Surplus Order, or ASO, to counterbalance the ADD or ADHD.

You see, we are all balanced. The important thing is to direct your attention to something that is meaningful to you, so if you find your passion in life, you will have all the attention that you are craving. The problem will arise if you have to study or work on subjects that you do not like.

If you want to improve your focus on areas that you give low value to, you can read Dr Demartini's book *Inspired Destiny* or *The Breakthrough Experience*, and you will learn more about supporting your dreams by aligning your values with your vision. Then, you will have time, money, focus, and memory to pursue your wildest dreams.

For example, you might have a hard time focusing on doing your accounts, but that doesn't mean you have Attention Deficit Disorder.

If you look carefully, you will see that you are highly focused in other areas of your life. You may have Attention Surplus Order when you are cooking, playing Sudoku, reading your favourite magazine, or choosing your next holiday.

Attending the Breakthrough Experience workshop from Dr Demartini equipped me with awareness about my values and how to link activities that are rated low, to others that are rated high on my values system. In this way, my low values will support my top values. Dr Demartini created a free test to determine your values system, and he can help you or your children by linking values to develop instant motivation. Follow the link below to have a look at it.

www.drdemartini.com/values

Misdiagnosis and alternative treatments

Dr Richard Saul, a behavioural neurologist, based in Chicago, wrote a controversial book called ADHD Does Not Exist. He thinks treatment will vary from case to case. What he revealed is surprising. He found that many people were anaemic from eating too much junk food, so they only needed a more balanced diet to raise iron levels in the blood, and the symptoms would disappear. Others needed glasses because of short-sightedness, or hearing aids to hear what a teacher was communicating during a lesson. Some children have learning difficulties, but instead of focusing on this, their parents try to treat ADHD with medication, and as a result, things go from bad to worse.

Likewise, children that are gifted and creative can become distracted and disruptive if they are not sufficiently challenged. Dr Saul also mentions that sometimes depression can be misdiagnosed as ADHD. Well, if you are interested in the subject, google him and buy his book.

It's essential to understand the mind and body, and I believe that just having a better diet can alleviate or even cure countless diseases. The medical profession, perhaps with the best intentions, has led us to believe that there is a pill for every ailment – but you are what you eat. If even diabetes can be reversed with a change of diet, what do you think would happen to your focus if you drastically reduce the amount of sugar and processed food you eat?

The seven types of ADD

The explanation about ADD that makes sense to me is from controversial Dr Daniel Amen. He looks at the actual brain with sophisticated technology that shows a 3D image of the brain while performing different tasks.

To get acquainted with his theory, you can visit his website.

www.amenclinics.com

And if you want to find out if you have ADD you can take the free online ADD assessment at Dr Amen's website.

https://addtypetest.com

While reading his book, I was shocked to discover that ADD could have many different symptoms and treatments.

There are excellent doctors treating ADD around the world, each one having a particular way to deal with

148

diagnosis and treatment, so you should do your research before deciding to follow any advice or treatment.

I don't believe that medicine alone can treat ADD effectively, and I like Dr Amen's holistic approach.

He had five books on the New York Times bestsellers list. He is controversial for using the SPECT brain scan to see the brain of his patient while focusing and while relaxing. This is done in order to diagnose his patients more accurately. For example, many patients show a decrease in blood flow in the pre-frontal cortex when trying to focus, which means that the harder they try to focus the more their brain shuts down.

Google "SPECT scan ADD", and you will see intriguing things like a scan showing a healthy brain verses an ADD brain while focusing.

In some cases, certain areas of the brain might not be functioning well, and specific treatment will be prescribed. What I like the most is that he treats the biological body as well as the psychological, social, and spiritual aspects.

So, he could help the patient find out if they have any food allergies or intolerances, and prescribe a change of diet to boost energy by restricting processed sugar and simple carbs. Once you understand the impact that your body has on your mind, you will follow his recommendation to exercise, take supplements or meds, and also use neurofeedback, which is a tool to train the brain. The psychological support would help to heal family dynamics, past hurts, and automatic negative thoughts. Social interaction and stress would also be assessed, and the spiritual approach would support the patient to find meaning and purpose in life.

Dr Amen found that while some people developed the condition after a brain injury, most were born with it or developed it over time. Many will never outgrow their ADD, but can become very successful adults if they have people to help them organize their lives and keep them accountable. Treatment would bring many benefits for their overall life satisfaction and development, even if they are older and retired.

People with ADD can be hyperactive, but that is not the norm, so the label ADHD is very misleading.

149

Dr Amen found a way to differentiate ADD patients into seven types that share the most common symptoms of this condition, which are short attention span, distractibility, disorganisation, procrastination, and poor internal supervision.

Below I describe the main characteristics of each of the seven types of ADD as Dr Amen described in his book *Healing ADD*.

- Classic ADD – This is the ADHD which is hyperactive, restless, and impulsive.
- Inattentive ADD – This is the space cadet, daydreamer, and quiet type or couch potato.
- Overfocused ADD – This type can focus on one particular subject like an obsession, and can become inflexible. They can also feed their imagination with negative and repetitive thoughts, and can become very argumentative. They may or may not be hyperactive.
- Temporal Lobe ADD – This is the dark thoughts type that has a short fuse and may have other learning disabilities. They may or may not be hyperactive.
- Limbic ADD – Their symptoms are similar to mild depression, they tend to have low energy, and they isolate themselves. In some cases they can also be hyperactive.
- Ring of Fire ADD – This type is very sensitive and can get easily moody, irritable, and oppositional. May or may not be hyperactive.
- Anxious ADD – As you can imagine, they are tense and predict the worst. They get very nervous with standardised tests, and are socially awkward. Their symptoms can present as headaches and gastrointestinal problems. May or may not be hyperactive.

Facing my ADD condition

It took me very long to realise that I had ADD, because I could get highly focused on my book project or another exciting idea. Even though I felt I was constantly distracted, I thought that ADD was mostly associated with people that can almost never get focused, and that are also hyperactive, so I dismissed the condition.

In fact, people with ADD can be highly focused and engaged with interesting, stimulating, new or scary subjects. Dr Amen mentions a study – it found that without external stimulation, children don't produce enough adrenaline, and as a result they don't get motivated or interested. This explains why people with ADD like scary movies and risky activities like action sports where brain injuries can occur, and worsen the ADD symptoms. For those that are not hyperactive, a good discussion or argument will fill them with joy and energy.

Thanks to Dr Amen's book *Healing ADD*, I realised that I could improve in many areas of my life, so I took the online assessment, followed the recommendations that resonated with me, and I am really impressed with the results and boost on my self-esteem. Follow the link below to take the assessment for free.

https://addtypetest.com

After taking the test, I found out that I have a combination of Overfocused ADD and Anxious ADD, and by reading all the stories of people like me I realised that being an introvert was good, but I could face my anxiety and have a more adventurous life.

I am experimenting with supplements, and I am receiving psychological support to come out of my shell, to become more sociable, and to trust people more. I am fighting against my perfectionism to eventually publish this book that has been more than seven years in the making. In this way, I want to expose my ideas and create the impact I want to make in the world.

Without the insights from Dr Amen I could have stayed in a loop, feeding my anxiety and negative thoughts. Being depressed was helpless, and now I am sure I can keep a much more positive outlook in life, by using visualizations, meditating and also planning my days in advance to get organised and achieve more with less effort.

I've started to exercise more, and I do headstands at the end of my workout to increase blood flow to my brain. I also go to dancing classes to interact with more people, and to improve cross coordination which stimulates brain growth. I've eliminated most sugar and simple carbohydrates from my diet, and I feel more energetic with my cold showers every morning.

Some of the recommendations for all people with ADD to improve their focus, include the following.

Take Omega 3 fish oil (higher in EPA than DHA) every day – 2,000 to 6,000mg for adults, and 1,000 to 2,000mg for children

Take a multivitamin and mineral supplements every day. It is important to take vitamin B6, B12, folic acid, zinc, magnesium and vitamin D, so read the label to make sure you cover all bases.

And, remember to spend some time in the sun for vitamin D absorption.

Limit the time you spend watching TV and engaging on social media. The more children can limit that, the less likely they are to develop ADD.

Use the Sleep Cycle app to measure the quality of your night sleep and also to record if you are snoring. Listen to the recording to verify if you have sleep apnea which is correlated with ADD as it diminishes oxygenation to the brain.

Do some exercise to boost dopamine availability and to help with focus. Table tennis is the fastest response sport, and it can help develop parts of the brain responsible for focused attention. Avoid sports that can cause brain injury, and use a helmet for safety.

It is interesting to note that people with ADD can search for conflict to turn their brains on, so avoid engaging in arguments with them, because although this kind of stimulation can work like medicine for them, it doesn't bring any good results.

Dangers of having ADD

Knowing that people with ADD can represent ten to 20 percent of the population, it is important to highlight that untreated ADD can increase the incidence of depression, drug and alcohol abuse, obesity, and smoking. So be on the lookout to recognise the symptoms, because the probability that someone with ADD is at arm's length is very high, and a little help from you might be highly appreciated by them. I just wish I knew I had ADD when I was a child, but it is never too late to look for help and treatment.

People with ADD have many strengths

Remember that if you have ADD, you can also be gifted with great memory and intelligence that can be applied to many areas, including creativity at visual arts, design, and the written word. Other qualities can be present in individuals that become great negotiators and entertainers.

I am excited to have discovered that I have new superpowers. I will develop and expand my creativity and productivity while dedicating more of my time to deliver my workshops, train other coaches, and give consultancy to schools, universities, companies and professionals.

1.4.3 Mindfulness and meditation options

Eagles do not eat breadcrumbs, peanuts or dead things; they feed only on fresh prey. They will develop extreme focus while in flow to be able to spot a rabbit a couple of miles away. And I will show you how to harness your power to achieve extreme focus and flow with meditation.

We all have thoughts that spin in our heads, and when you want to focus, it is difficult to pay full attention to the subject. To concentrate more doesn't mean extra effort; it is the opposite. If you relax, you learn more, and the act of reading becomes more comfortable.

A lot of people think that to meditate you need to sit down on the floor with your legs crossed, and think of fluffy clouds. That's not true.

To meditate, you will learn how to focus your mind.

You can learn how to focus your mind on real or imaginary things. You can practice focusing your attention by staring at candlelight, looking at a picture of a mandala, or by repeating a sacred word like a mantra if you are practising Transcendental Meditation. The idea is to focus for a period of time, so you start to be in charge of your

153

thoughts, and become able to notice whenever your mind starts drifting away. Exercising your mind in this way, you will become more aware that you have the option of changing the direction of your thoughts at will. If you meditate, you feel more alive; you have a glimpse of your thoughts, are able to focus with more clarity, and for longer too. You will be able to stretch your mind a few steps ahead of yourself.

Do you want to look into the future? Well, I do, and meditation to me is about being able to connect with the right side of the brain, which gives me lots of ideas and possibilities for my life.

Imagine you are in a fast sailing boat in a storm bobbing up and down. But this storm would be of thoughts, not heavy rain. The sea is rough, which gives you limited visibility, because you are always going up or down on a wave. You are busy and tense, checking if everything is in order, and you cannot see far ahead.

Now imagine sailing on a sunny day; the sea intense and blue, and the wind building up in intensity. In the distance, you can see the coastline of France, and you can even hear the sound of seagulls as they fly above in their search for food. This is the clarity I'm talking about.

My quest is to have fun even if I'm all by myself. Since I've started to close my eyes without the intention of falling asleep, a lot began to change in my life.

Think about good things, and you will see more of the good stuff. Do you remember that I've been talking about the RAS?

Meditation will not only help you to relax – it is a means of creation and making fundamental changes in your life.

Dynamic meditations

For all those people that find it challenging to sit down quietly and practice meditation, I've got great news.

There are many styles of dynamic meditation that might be more attractive to the western way of life. I've practised many of them, and experienced various degrees of integration and liberation while keeping my eyes wide open.

154

A very uplifting meditation is commonly called Laughter Yoga. Participants learn various ways to initiate laughing, and as they start doing it a little awkwardly, they begin to feel good as the body starts releasing endorphins that make them feel good. Then they keep laughing more naturally and the intensity grows in the room, as laughing is contagious. You will find yourself laughing for five or even ten minutes to brighten up your day.

My favourite active meditation has been practised by the Sufis since the 12th century. Perhaps you've seen a group of men wearing long conical hats, and plain long dresses that start to lift off as they start spinning together in the same direction, while immersed in intense music. Search on YouTube for Whirling Dervishes to get a glimpse of it. I've practised it in Brazil, UK, India, and Bali on sessions that go from 30 minutes to one hour of uninterrupted spinning. Well trained Sufis can spin for more than four hours while entering into an ecstatic trance.

As the time passed, I was going round and round, faster and faster, until I stopped noticing that I was moving my legs, and instead of feeling dizzy I had the unusual sensation of having eyes on the back of my head, as I could see 360 degrees around me on a continuous stream. I felt like I was floating just above the ground, and had the vivid sensorial perception that I was standing on the Earth that is actually floating and spinning in the sky at a tremendous speed.

Another dynamic meditation I've practised many times is called Humaniversity AUM meditation. It lasts about two hours and 30 minutes, and it has 14 stages. Every stage is designed to awaken and rebalance many emotions that surface, can give you great insight about yourself, and also about the way you interact with others. You will embark on a journey that will help you express repressed sadness, anger, love, laughter, forgiveness, sensuality, madness, peace, and many other facets of yourself, to promote insight and freedom of expression. The environment is supportive, and the music makes the shifts between stages smooth.

Find an active meditation near you, or learn and practice by watching it online. There are many ways to get into a meditative state, and you can start with something as simple as colouring an intricate drawing, like children do, to focus your attention and release stress. Try the Osho Dynamic Meditation that has five stages or choose something you identify with.

If the idea of meditating while sitting down in silence is too overwhelming to you, you could also experiment with guided meditations. I have been listening to the meditations from Joe Dispenza; you can have a go at them by searching on Apple Music, Spotify, or YouTube. Sit down, close your eyes, and use your imagination to find a place inside yourself where all possibilities for your life are created.

So now you know that you can practice alternate states of consciousness even if you cannot sit still. I invite you to talk to people, who can guide you on this path, or simply try what feels right for you.

1.4.4 Decision making to attract flow

When eagles decide to catch prey, they don't care if the animal is much bigger than them, or if it has sharp teeth like a grown-up wolf. When the decision is made, they attack with the certainty of victory.

Better quality input will help you make decisions faster and with confidence, so I want to open your eyes to new ways of making decisions. I want to empower you to really take advantage of your free will. As you make more decisions faster and commit to action, you will be getting out of your comfort zone. By taking more risks, the possibility of getting into flow will grow, and you will enhance the quality of your execution naturally. Remember that immediate feedback is a key element of flow so by making more decisions you build a faster feedback system to help you get into deeper flow.

Decision making advisors

Some people question if we are alone in the universe, but not me because I've already seen Unidentified Flying Objects and I'm certain that there is extraterrestrial life out there. So, for me, the big question is to understand if we are alone inside our own mind.

156

If you walk by an ice cream parlour, you might get the impulse of buying a cone, but suddenly a voice whispers in your ear, "You need to lose weight, and you should not have it." Then the other voice replies, "I've worked very hard today, and I deserve a treat."

So this is a "split personality" that you might recognise in yourself when moments of doubt arise.

Now, what about having new points of view connected to strong identities to win the battle of choice?

According to Carl Jung, as you develop yourself from childhood, you manifest different personalities or archetypes that will be part of yourself So you can recreate that side of yourself at different moments in your life by tapping into different energies that you might not have been in touch with for many years.

Some of the archetypes are the innocent, the caregiver, the warrior, the seeker, the creator, the lover, the fool, and so on.

To illustrate, I will tell you about Susan. She is a resourceful nurse, and she is very decisive at her job while performing the caregiver archetype, but as soon as she steps into her home environment, she becomes the orphan archetype by being very submissive to her husband Martin, who plays the ruler archetype as the dictator at home. Susan is very sweet, but if you see her at her church, she transforms herself into the warrior archetype who can mobilise a crowd to march for womans' rights.

What I'm suggesting is that you can tap into another part of yourself for extra energy, power, and creativity by feeling like a warrior, creator, or magician whenever you work, read books, or make decisions.

So, if you think this idea makes sense, you could read more about Jung archetypes, decide to exercise your free will, and embody a particular archetype to give you more options to act in life. You could meditate and ask an imaginary advisor or your role model that embodies the trait you want to emulate, what kind of decisions you should take to progress in your endeavours.

I recommend a book called "*Awakening the Heroes Within*" by Carol S. Pearson. She describes 12 archetypes and applications for self-discovery. You will probably be fascinated by the hero's journey, and you may understand that to achieve success you will pass through struggle and awakening.

If you want to become an entrepreneur, you could start connecting with your warrior or magician archetype to overcome all the challenges with a spirit of power and triumph.

You can read a book by Richard Branson and feel like you are in his shoes, playing with uncertainties from his point of view to exercise the identification process with a role model.

Then whenever you have decisions to make, you can narrow down your questions about your target market, product applications, price or any other question related to your new venture. Ask the archetype or Richard Branson inside your head, and listen to the answer. Once you hear the answer, you know that the next step is to act on it.

I've wasted many years of my life waiting too long to make crucial decisions, and now I feel more confident with my advisors. I dare to ask Richard, and other personalities, some business questions like they were just in front of me. I value their answers and feel reassured to act faster and with more confidence.

Decision-making diary and feelings

I'm also guilty of having lots of ideas and not acting on them, only to stay in a loop of infinite possibilities and waste precious time.

What I've learnt is that you need to figure out just the next step, not the whole staircase. The following step will depend on the step you took, not the one you only dream about!

For example, you could think of two paths to take to create your new venture. You could find the right decision by focusing on each possible answer, and then connecting to the feeling you have if you were to follow each of the actions. If one answer feels better than the other, you can make a decision and move on to the next question, instead of repetitively thinking about the first question.

I found it very helpful to keep a little notepad in my pocket to track down my decisions, and wake up from the default mode of living life the same way. The act of thinking about a new action and writing it down gives the decision an official look, and creates a crystal clear instruction that I will then follow as if it is the only way forward.

The most important part of the entry is that I record the feeling associated with the decision, reinforcing that I made the right choice, and that it felt great to make a simple or important decision. This way I create more options to grow and take risks, because I'm conscious that I have a thousand possible new paths, I can choose from, every single second of my life.

To illustrate, you can read a couple of entries in my diary below.

15 Oct 2019 - 8:05 pm

Should I delete the Solitaire game on my phone?
Answer n.1: No, I can relax while playing it.
Answer n.2: Yes, I can waste a lot of time playing it.
I visualise and connect to the feeling of relaxing while playing it, and then connect with the feeling of not having the game and not wasting my time, perhaps saving an extra 20 minutes every day.

I feel like answer number 2. It gives me more satisfaction and I make my decision.

Conclusion: Yes, I will delete the game now. I feel great with a sense of liberation.

Action: I delete the game now.

17 Oct 2019 - 10:09 am

Should I organise my desk today?
Answer n. 1: Yes, I want a clean environment to work in, and will finally have it.
Answer n. 2: No, I have lots of emails to answer, and have no time for it.

I visualise and connect to the feeling of having a clear desk, and then a messy desk with emails answered.

I feel like answer n. 1 gives me more satisfaction, and I make a decision.

Conclusion: Yes, I know I've postponed it for a few weeks, and I have a good feeling that clearing my desk will give me a clearer mind too.

Action: I organise my desk right now.

Decide using a secret identity

I've learnt from Todd Herman, something that can be a game-changer, and it is as simple as changing your clothes.

Todd is a high-performance coach and advisor of Olympic athletes, billionaires, and entrepreneurs. He is the author of *The Alter Ego Effect: The power of secret identities to transform your life*, and he describes an enlightening study done at Kellogg School of Management in America.

They invited a group of students to participate in a study to solve a puzzle, and measured their performance while changing a variable that is constantly overlooked.

They divided the big group into three smaller groups that would have to solve a puzzle against time.

The first group was wearing plain clothes, and as expected, achieved average results.

The second group were given white coats to wear, and were told they were wearing painters' coats. Their results were similar to the first group.

The third group were wearing the same white coats, but were told they were scientists' lab coats, and to everyone's surprise, they performed the task in half the time, and made half the mistakes than the first two groups.

This phenomenon is called enclothed cognition, and you can take advantage of it by knowing that taking the time to dress up will have an effect on your behaviour, performance, personality, mood, thinking process, and confidence in your interactions.

Todd doesn't need glasses, but as he identifies himself with Superman, he wears glasses when he goes to meetings or engagements that require foresight, strength, and control, as he feels like Superman disguised as Clark Kent.

I know it's hard to believe that wearing glasses with clear lenses would have any meaningful impact on the wearer, but it does. Todd's book is full of stories describing how successful people found original ways to leverage this phenomenon to progress in their careers, and you can do it too.

While working from home, and even before knowing about enclothed cognition, I've changed into my suit many times before making an important business call so I would feel more professional, and I really felt the difference.

So, if you want to get in flow while writing an article about sports, you will probably do a better job if you dress up as an athlete. Working from home in your pyjamas might be comfortable, but if you are working on something challenging and want to get in flow, you can dress up for the occasion. Perhaps wear a piece of jewellery, or something that triggers a connection to someone you admire or emulate, to perform at a higher level.

You could find a connection to a professional that has the traits you want to acquire, or an actor of a movie you relate to, and you will feel empowered to perform differently.

Jung's archetypes can also be of interest to channel your energy into becoming more in touch with parts of your personality that would be helpful to certain circumstances. If you want to find a new way to grow your business, you could read about the magician archetype, and imagine yourself having special powers to find a creative solution to your challenges. Find the appropriate identity to suit your needs.

So now it's your turn to think about who would be the real or fictional character to help boost your powers and raise your standards.

As you are reading this book, stop for a moment, think of someone you admire, look them up on Google, read a little about them, look at their pictures, and think that your mind is connected to their mind while you keep reading the book. Focus on reading, and also on having new ideas that would be inspired by this connection.

You can put some clothes on that could be worn by them, or just use your imagination to tap into their way of being.

Judge this approach after you try it out, or if you want overwhelming arguments to support this experiment before deciding to give it a go, read Todd Herman's book.

161

It's much easier to get in flow if you decide to work while focusing on a specific trait to feel more empowered to achieve your goals.

Feedback

It is now evident to me that there is no such thing as a right or wrong decision. What is damaging to your development is lack of decisions and feedback.

If you had learnt about the way all successful companies achieved accelerated growth and prosperity, you'd already know that they had a string of bad decisions that led to good outcomes. The founders had a string of failures along the way, and had to pivot their original idea until it started to thrive.

Remember that taking risks and having good feedback is essential to bring flow into your life.

Metaphysical decision making

As you cannot predict how one decision will unfold, I like to base many of my decisions on the entanglement theory.

Every living being creates an electromagnetic frequency that can be in sync with a set of circumstances that involve a certain number of people. Some people follow their gut to make decisions as they allow invisible forces to communicate to them the most favourable path to take when they face a two-way decision process.

You emanate an energy field around you that can actually be photographed, using something called Kirlian photography. This field can be amplified by external factors, people, and even just thought.

What if you had a way to measure integrity or lack of it at an energetic level? What if you had a device to measure which choice would unfold more or less favourably than the other?

The good news is that there is a way to experiment between two distinct options. This can help you move forward with certainty and at a faster pace to achieve your dreams and experience more flow in the process.

Dowser

Dowsing is a controversial subject, and unless you've had first-hand experience with it, you may dismiss it as a bogus practice.

I was fortunate to have parents that were scientifically minded, and were also willing to experiment with dowsing amongst other mysterious subjects. Since childhood, I was exposed to pendulums, L-shaped metal dowsing rods, forked sticks used as dowsers, and telekinesis. We even had a large pyramid in our garden for a while; it could fit four adults.

Inventor Thomas Edison famously said: "I don't know what electricity is, but it's there, so let's use it".

I do not doubt that the subconscious mind can cause a pendulum to swing by amplifying slight movements of the hand. So I remain in a peaceful state, and let the invisible vibrations travel through my body to manifest a visible action that has a meaning attached to it.

When I was young, I was really impressed the first time I saw my uncle predict the sex of an unborn child. He took a long strand of hair from my cousin, and tied it to her wedding ring with a knot. He positioned the pendulum over my cousin's belly, and declared that if the pendulum started swinging clockwise it was because the baby was a boy, and anticlockwise meant it was a girl. It went clockwise, and we were in awe. I asked to try it too. He showed me how to hold the string with light pressure, and the dowser went clockwise again. And a boy was born a few months later. I just believed it was a given, and it worked time after time.

I use a pendulum that is rose quartz on a metal chain. You can use one with a bob made of metal, wood, or other natural material with varying effects depending on the person using it. Yes, if you experiment with a few of them, you will find what suits you best. Bear in mind that a small percentage of people will have absolutely no response from the dowser, and in that case, dowsing is not meant to help them make their decisions.

Its practical application in business and life decisions is very simple to understand.

Hold the end of the string between your thumb and index finger, and ask the pendulum to show you the

163

direction for "yes" and "no". It will swing one way and the other. Knowing the established convention, you can ask a question and have your answer. Be relaxed and connect with a specific issue, and let the pendulum give you the answer. You can test it out by asking if it's raining outside. Practise with simple things before going into more complex subjects.

Another example would be asking: "Will it be beneficial to my company to hire John?"

Alternatively, the question can compare two options. "Will I make better business connections by going to the golf club on Saturday, rather than going to Jack's birthday party?

What I like about this method is that you need to formulate the question very well to create a new possibility in your life. Once you find the answer, swiftly execute it without hesitation. You will stop thinking about the decision made, and think about what's next.

If I'm not decisive, I end up becoming very anxious to make the right decision, and waste a lot of time thinking about the pros and cons, postponing the decision and getting stressed.

As I bring you many new concepts in this book, you can use your dowser to help you decide if you should experiment with any of the ideas you are not sure about. If you get a positive answer, just do it, if you get a negative response, move on to the next topic knowing that you will find what is right for you.

If you like the dowsing experience, you can find much more about this ancient practice online.

The five-second rule and flow

Mel Robbins created a method to help you take action by recommending you start counting down slowly from five to one, like on the launch of a rocket into space, to empower your decision making muscles. Pulling the trigger, you start doing whatever you set your mind to do, right then. She says that if you have the instinct to act on a goal, you must physically move within five seconds, or your brain will kill it.

You can start experimenting with this method in the morning when your alarm clock goes off. Instead of reaching for the alarm clock to hit the snooze button, count down slowly from five to one in your head. If you dare, jump out of bed. Once you succeed in this simple task, you will start using the five-second rule to make other decisions too. Empower yourself to act whenever you have the hunch that you should do something important, and your power of decision making will grow stronger. Watch Mel Robbins' TED talk on YouTube, or read her book for a step by step action plan to build confidence in making decisions.

The skill of taking risks while making important decisions will help you open a better connection to your higher self, and open the opportunity to get into a state of flow.

The speed of decision

The question here is to analyse the exact time it takes to make the right decision.

You have some pre-conceived ideas about making decisions, so I want to question the idea of getting ready to make up your mind by bringing into context the fast paced world of video games.

Gamers understand the concept of APM which stands for Actions Per Minute and they can see the results of it on the score boards.

Starcraft players start with 10 to 20 APM as they take from three to six seconds to make a decision while playing the game. Experienced players can become confident to make a decision every second and raise their APM to 60. What is incredible on Starcraft - and other eSports games - is that professional players can reach 300-400 APM which makes them execute five to six actions per second.

Obviously, gamers will make mistakes and learn with their mistakes at a faster pace. This comparison is just an insight into how powerful your brain is to play in the real world. If someone, with similar education and work ethics as yours, can make twice as many decisions in a day as you can, they will build their decision making muscle stronger and will be more likely to get into a flow state by trusting their judgement and actioning on it.

Nearly perfect decision making

As you already know, getting in a flow state demands a high level of skill and challenge. What is surprising is that when you get into flow the activity seems to be effortless, despite its complexity. You stop doubting yourself, one action leads to the next, and you feel powerful and connected by executing the task like a highly skilled professional would. Your creativity is enhanced, and you end up with new solutions that can improve productivity.

As you develop yourself to enter into a state of flow faster, you can use some of the ways described to assist you on your decision-making process. This is a great access point to get into flow, and to develop your confidence to take more risks and thrive.

1.4.5 Predict new trends

The eagle is also considered the "king of the skies" and connects us to the heavens as it flies incredibly high. An eagle's power of vision is up to eight times stronger than ours. Combined with their ability to fly at high altitudes, they can see further than all other species, and can move swiftly. I will discuss the speed of change, and how to get in flow by using your excitement to see ahead and innovate. Staying connected with new trends, you will be capable of surfing the wave of innovation, spotting connections that most people with their feet on the ground will miss, anticipate what is yet to come, and find your fortune.

Peter Drucker wisely said: "The best way to predict the future is to create it."

Most of us cannot see that the world is radically changing. Every single day a new discovery or idea is on the market looking for finance or seeking partners to disrupt the marketplace.

If you research the new trends before they become mainstream, you will feel ahead of the pack, and your sense of urgency will be enhanced. You will be creating the future, and in this way, you will be more likely to get in flow because you are going to dive deep into your intellect to find innovative ways to succeed in this competitive world.

Remember to schedule in your diary a few hours to google "new trends, predictions and opportunities" in or out of your field of work.

It's proven that advertising and labels that contain the word "new" attract more attention. In the same way, your brain will engage in becoming more creative and expand to a state of flow if it is limited only by your imagination. If you have more questions than answers, discuss your predictions with friends, and you may discover breakthroughs that can lead to your fortune and more flow in your life.

Now is your turn to create something beyond your perceived capacities.

1.4.6 Create a Goal Map, prioritise and plan your diary hour by hour

When eagles want to procreate, they start the breeding process by building their nest, which can take one to three months. The pair will find an inaccessible spot on a cliff or at the top of a tall tree, and start creating a nest that will get bigger every year – it can end up weighing two or three tons.

They build the nest and return to the same spot year after year. With meticulous care, they intertwine the branches to have a safe structure, making it cosy by using grass and soft material inside, and surrounding the nest with thorns to protect their chicks. All of this requires prioritising, planning, and stress testing the strength of the nest to avoid a sudden collapse.

In the same way, you will be more likely to get in flow if you have a master plan to achieve a big goal, and break it down into tasks with deadlines. By planning your day with tasks to be completed in specific slots of time, you will focus better, and you will become more productive than if you have only a vague idea about what to do on any given day.

Prioritise, and give yourself a challenging time slot to accomplish your goals. One of the first slots should be used to create your bucket list, or your list of goals for one whole year. Then break it down into smaller parts, and

167

allocate the deadlines throughout the year ahead. Make these deadlines public, or share them with a trusted friend, or with your team. This way your reputation will be at stake, so you will be more likely to accomplish them, and flow will be your companion.

A great app to help you accomplish your goals is called StickK – www.stickk.com. You decide on a task, give yourself a deadline, and put your reputation at stake by sharing your progress on social media. Did you know that you will become up to three times more likely to achieve your goal if you put some money at stake? So place a bet on yourself, and increase the amount to hit the sweet spot that will really make you move towards your goals faster.

Create a Goal Map

As you are aware, your mind thinks in pictures. I want to share with you a great idea to stay connected to your dreams, and to take action to get there. You've probably seen, or perhaps you've created, a vision board to focus your attention on things that you want to create in the future. I had vision boards before, but they lacked structure. To combine the left and right side of the brain, I use the Goal Map format, which is the creation of Brian Mayne. It puts your conscious and unconscious mind to work for you. Below is a representation of it. You can use pictures instead of drawings.

The structure basically has a primary goal at the centre, and a few sub-goals on both sides of it. Then think about WHY you want those goals and draw on the top of the Map. You will have defined the "Emotional Drivers". The ladder creates the WHEN by establishing a timeline. The HOW are the actions you need to take, and they go on the right side of the ladder. Then you finish it by deciding WHO will help you achieve those goals, and write the names of people or organisations that will support you, on the left side of the ladder. That's it; you've spent time creating your future, and now you can have it as a screen saver or hang it somewhere to remind you of your big dreams, and the roadmap which will take you to them.

168

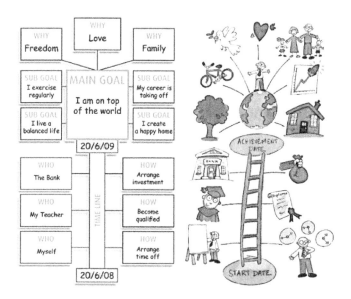

You can learn how to create your own Goal Map for free; use the easy to follow templates, or use the free online tool.

Go to the website below, and you will find both ways to create your Goal Map.

www.goalmappingonline.com

I hope you enjoy this as much as I do!

1.4.7 Having a buddy will help you give birth to your projects faster

Eagles lay one or two eggs per year, and then embrace a task that requires extreme focus and abnegation from both parents as they take turns to brood on the eggs for 35 days in the middle of winter. So, having a partner or a buddy to help you prepare the ground to accomplish your dreams, and also have the discipline to work on your projects consistently is essential. I will show you how to have many people to support you, and to hold you accountable to get into flow, to develop your plans, and to bring life to your ideas.

I know that life can be pretty lonely at times, so I advise you to find someone you like as an accountability partner to make your projects develop much faster.

As you now understand that organising your diary and allocating tasks by the hour is crucial to accelerating your success, I've got great news for you.

You can use a virtual co-working space to get into a state of flow more consistently. A significant part of this book was written while using Focusmate as it harnesses pillars of psychology that are proven to boost productivity by 200 to 300%. You can find the space at the following website:

www.focusmate.com

It is surprising that a virtual buddy can keep you accountable, and you need to try it to believe it. This website pairs you up with another person on a video call that is not intended to promote a conversation, but to help you focus while working on a project. To make it effective your sessions are a 50-minute stretch and you will talk to your mate for one or two minutes at the beginning of the meeting, stating what your project is and what you want to achieve by the end of the meeting. They will also share their objectives for the meeting, and you start your work. At the end of the 50-minute session, you will share your accomplishments and say goodbye.

As I write these lines, I'm connected to Gian in Italy. He is working on planning his studying schedule for the week. Just because I shared with him that I'm working on a new chapter of my book that explains how to hack into the flow state I get glued to the chair and 50 minutes pass by very quickly. I'm usually surprised when the session is over because the feeling is that only ten or 15 minutes went by. It's rewarding to see the results of my work after a session.

The human connection is a powerful catalyst of flow states. By entering this state, you will release essential brain chemicals into your system, including, dopamine, oxytocin, serotonin, and endorphins. These chemicals will induce productivity with less conscious exertion.

To better understand the power of Focusmate, I will highlight the five behavioural triggers in action while using it.

The factors in play to give you the edge are:

- Pre-commitment
- Implementation intentions
- Social pressure
- Accountability
- Specificity in the task definition

Once you commit to your project, you will identify the flow experience as:

- Intense and focused concentration on the present moment
- Merging of action and awareness
- A loss of reflective self-consciousness
- A sense of personal control or agency over the situation or activity
- A distortion of temporal experience – one's subjective experience of time is altered
- Experience of the activity as intrinsically rewarding and fulfilling. Even though you might be working, you will realise it will feel like play

If you create a slot in the diary for an activity, it doesn't mean that you will accomplish it. But if you book the slot with a real person on Focusmate, they will hold you accountable, and you will be immensely more likely to honour your appointment and get into a flow state.

I'm using it to help me get out of bed early by booking my first appointment at 7 am or even earlier. You will wake up early to join your buddy at 7 am because you need to keep your appointments or you will be penalised with a no-show on your profile.

You will stop snacking all the time. I have a buddy that told me that he lost 10 pounds since joining Focusmate because it gave him the discipline to stay working for more extended periods of time.

You can find clients for your business or make friends out of joining a Focusmate session with a stranger. If you like the person, I encourage you to invite them to have another meeting, or just have a chat offline and see how to leverage each other's strengths. Remember that you can check their profile and screen what kind of people you want to work with.

Remember to put your phone on airplane or sleep mode to avoid interruptions and really become productive. Don't check random messages or emails during the session. It's much better to schedule 30 minutes specifically to deal with all your emails during a session, so you create urgency, get things done faster, and find your way to get into a flow state as often as you want.

I can't live without Focusmate, and I hope to meet you there on an inspiring 50-minute session.

1.4.8 Experiments and research

If you want to raise your standards, you need to be willing to try new things, and do a few experiments to achieve altered states of mind. You can improve performance by measuring risk and reward.

As I help people read and think faster, I've been researching the nootropics market. Nootropics are well known as smart drugs or cognitive enhancers. Some of them may improve memory capacity, learning ability, focus, creativity, or motivation. Above all, I'm interested in substances that can help me get into the flow state more often.

A few drugs that are illegal in certain countries are now being used under medical supervision. I want to mention the work that's been done by MAPS (Multidisciplinary Association for Psychedelic Studies). MAPS is documenting the use of psychedelic drugs to cure PTSD (Posttraumatic stress disorder) and depression in record time when associating drugs and therapy. I mention that because by lifting these debilitating states of mind, people can increase their mental capacities. Some research is finding benefits to creating flow states while micro-dosing on psychedelics.

You can find thousands of business executives claiming that meditation helps them achieve a clear mind and better focus. I mentioned that I went on a 10-day silent meditation retreat, and I reached an incredible state of concentration and pure ecstasy. You could also explore the brain entrainment route or HeartMath technology to help you get into a coherent state and achieve better mental performance.

There are deep breathing exercises that can change one's mental state. I've done a few sessions of holotropic breathwork that made me transcend reality, and I even did some regression into traumatic events of my life with the intention of clearing blockages. The rebirthing was nothing short of incredible.

I've been following the Ice Man Wim Hof's method of deep breathing for more than two years. Following his recommendation I've had only cold showers for the last two years as part of a protocol that has been giving me more health, energy, and inspiration.

I've experienced altered states of consciousness while on a Shamanic ritual in Brazil. The ritual did not involve any drugs, but just a massive bonfire and intense drumming.

In Brazil, I also experienced the Ayahuasca ceremony which combines a plant juice containing the compound DMT with music and an elaborate ritual. The powerful experience made me realise how connected we all are.

Sensory deprivation or flotation tanks give you an incredible feeling of no gravity. As you are laying on a bath filled with very dense water at the right temperature, you stay laying on your back in complete darkness for an hour. This experience can give you similar feelings to deep meditation.

I've also experimented with fasting by going on a ten-day green juice fast followed by four days of water fast. My meditation was enhanced, and I had fantastic experiences during the process, which gave me useful insights. The practise of fasting is found in most cultures, and is a great detox process that can bring you many benefits, but it should be done under medical supervision.

If you are hooked on the popular habit of alcohol and cigarettes to get into a better frame of mind, you could at least try something new and have a different perspective of your life.

1.4.9 Focus on gratitude

Most of the time, we focus on what is missing in our lives and forget to be grateful for all we have.

173

The more you focus on abundance and feel grateful for the resources and things you have, the more likely you will increase your wealth. If you always complain about scarcity, you will attract lack by not recognising that you have a magnificent body, friends, and resources to change your situation.

Being grateful will rewire your brain. You will be more likely to get into flow if you appreciate what you have, and look into the future to find ways to grow your skills and abilities. Whatever you appreciate appreciates.

Start dedicating some time to be grateful either by writing three things you are grateful for every day, or by connecting emotionally with the source of your gratitude while meditating.

The most powerful insight I had about gratitude was at a shamanic ritual, while dancing around a bonfire under the power of heavy drumming. I connected with my Native American Indian heritage and felt the unorthodox gratitude of having hunted certain chosen animals for my tribe. But it was the day before going on a hunt.

Thanking God for what you're about to receive with enough conviction and specificity can bring your vision into reality faster as you create the accomplishment with certainty, and release it into the universe to take shape. Perhaps you can try this principle and see the power of gratitude in your life.

If you have a business, what about making a donation automatically every time someone buys something?

There's a charity called B1G1, which means that every time someone buys one thing from you, a donation is given to a project chosen by you. For example, if you had a coffee shop, every time someone buys a coffee, you would donate clean water for a day to a family in India which would cost just a few pence.

The big impact is that you would tell your customer that you made a specific donation in their name, and you can thank them for the support to your cause. There are countless options to join the charity, and you can find out more at:

www.b1g1.com

1.4.10 Synchronicity and flow

Synchronicity and serendipity are usually seen as random and mysterious subjects, but now I understand that they can be facilitated by flow, and also by pure intention.

To illustrate that, I will describe two experiences that coincided with two moments of completion as a writer.

Two years ago my friend Paul told me about an incredible adventure he had in London as a participant of the Synchronicity Walk, which is the creation of an eccentric American, called Todd Acamesis.

I asked Paul to invite me to the next walk, so he sent me the date and location of the next walk, a couple of months away.

I will describe below my two walks with Todd as if I am living the experiences in the present time.

Number nine and a reassuring message

I'm getting closer to finishing my speed reading book, and the day of the walk becomes my deadline.

It's 7:00 pm and I'm in celebration mode with Paul. A bunch of strangers gather together at the meeting point in Covent Garden in London. Todd introduces himself as a student of the mystical, and briefly explains that as his main line of work he teaches people how to have out of body experiences, lucid dreams and astral projection. He also created the Pandora Star which is a disc full of led lights controlled to blink at frequencies that can take us on a metaphysical experience, which I have deeply enjoyed at a later date.

He then explains that we will walk in central London without a fixed destination, and will use a pair of dice and a deck of cards he created to guide us.

The rules are quite simple. Firstly, we will toss the dice to find our lucky number. Nine was cast on the pavement therefore whenever one of us spot the number nine, we will interpret it as a sign, and will try to follow it at our own discretion. The walk starts in an ordinary crossroad, so we have four possible directions to choose from. Todd casts the dice again and we pre-determine that if we get one, two, or three, we will take the first direction. Four, five or six, will mean the second direction, and so on. We take the fourth direction as the number is 11. At the next junction, we cast the dice again, and follow the instructions until someone spots something unusual. A woman points out a black door with the number 10 on it; like the door where the Prime Minister lives in London. Then someone spots a small post-it on the door. We get closer, and the note has two words: "Please knock".

They are probably expecting a visitor, but Todd takes everything very personally, makes everyone get closer to the door and says: "They are asking us to knock. Shall we knock?"

With a naughty smile on his face, he knocks on the door, and a beautiful woman in her early 20s with long blond hair opens the door. Todd explains that we are on a synchronicity walk and asks if she wants to play with us.

As she agrees, Todd takes out a deck of cards that he produced himself, and asks her to pick one card to help us with the next set of directions.

She takes a card, and makes a face of authentic surprise. She shows us the white rabbit card, and tells us that she just received a pet rabbit as her birthday gift. And the colour of the rabbit was actually white.

We are taken by surprise, and then he asks what we should be looking for next. Firstly, she read out loud the text under the picture of the rabbit, "Follow the rabbit down the rabbit hole."

Then she said we should look for the sphere, and pointed us in a direction to go. We keep moving ahead while spotting the number nine here and there. Then someone points out at the number nine on a building, and as the group notices it, a very funky guy with a hat and a waistcoat steps out of the building. He quickly looks left and right, then glances at his watch, and starts a brisk walk down the road like he is late for something. Another person of the group says that he is our rabbit, and we should follow the instructions to follow the rabbit.

We agree that he could well be a modern version of the rabbit of "Alice in Wonderland," and we storm down the road on our frantic pursuit. At some point, my friend Paul tells us that the building we are facing is the central office of the emergency number, which is 999, or our lucky number nine repeated three times.

We decide to stop there, and ask the third person that passes by for help. The guy is sympathetic to our cause, and tells us to turn around and go back, and that we will find what we are looking for.

As we walk back, we spot an entrance of the Charing Cross tube station that is so inconspicuous that I had never seen it before, even though I've passed there countless times.

We remember that the instruction was to follow the rabbit down the rabbit hole, and decide to walk down the stairs to explore the access to the underground. We are shocked to see a window shop that didn't seem to be connected to any shop. Inside there was a real table with a top hat, and inside the hat was a cute white rabbit.

The sight of the rabbit was incredible, but as I walked along the shop window, I found the other part of the quest; the sphere that the girl told us to search for was in very good hands. "Alexander – The Man Who Knows" was holding a crystal ball, foreseeing the future.

Seeing the poster on the wall, Todd asked with certainty, "Who is Alexander?"

I stepped up, told everyone that I finished my book that day, and that I was a little insecure about the reception of it, but with such a colourful and inspiring image I was well reassured.

Then, just after that, another poster on the wall with "Open Dreams" written on it.

Todd declares that I am now the leader. I decide to go out of the rabbit hole, and to finalise the walk I stop two gorgeous girls on the street, briefly tell them about our walk, and announce that they won a group hug. They liked it, and we have a massive group hug to disperse into the dark night immediately after.

I printed the proof of the book, and went to an event that Tony Robbins was speaking at, in London. I was so confident that I had created the right book to propel my career to the next level. What I could see in my immediate future was to talk to Tony, and offer him a partnership in my business. So, I asked everyone at the event to help me meet Tony, and a miracle happened. I met Tony, and was invited by the CEO of the company organising the event, to speak all over the world.

While meeting with the marketing expert that would create the campaign to promote my workshops, I explained speed reading, but his excitement only appeared when I mentioned brain hacks and flow state.

He said that a workshop about brain hacks and flow state would be sold out very quickly, and the new book was born in my mind.

Two years later, I had repurposed my first book by adding a lot of new research and experiments with brain hacks on the field of flow.

Once again, I was about to finish this book, and decided to join a synchronicity walk. And I used the date of the walk as my deadline to finalise the book and celebrate.

Number seven and a world of possibilities

The meeting point was Todd's new venture called Pandora Spa – www.pandoraspa.com. I knock on the door, and Todd invites me into a spacious basement with very high ceilings. Inside there are eight lounge chairs positioned side by side, and fitted with individual light dials called Pandora Stars. At the central area of the Spa, there are massive gongs and huge crystals to induce altered states of consciousness.

I walk through the basement to join the others who were already sitting in a relaxing area with big sofas. I start talking to a young man called Piotr, and he tells me that

179

he moved from Poland to London that very same day, and he is all excited about his new life here.

Todd gives a 40-minute talk about astral projection, and shows us three special cameras that he is fine-tuning to capture the images of people projecting their body while sleeping. The conversation is intriguing, but it is time to hit the road and verify if we would have any luck finding synchronicity that night.

As the group steps on the sidewalk, Todd asks if someone wants to throw the dice to give us a direction to start our walk. My new friend Piotr asks to roll the dice, guessed it would be a seven, and it was.

The walk starts, and at every corner we must cast the dice to decide which direction to take, unless someone has a good reason to point us in another direction. I notice that the door of the Spa is number 34, which adds up to a seven. Great start.

A girl takes the dice and casts the number seven again, and we turn to the right. As we walk we start talking and my new friend points out that the day is the seventh of March. So I tell him that I'm here to celebrate the completion of my book after seven years writing it.

Someone else throws the dice, and the number seven appears again, so we take the direction that the dice dictates, and get to a courtyard where a company that empowers entrepreneurs to succeed is located. It is called London Real, and perhaps I should get in touch with them to promote my book, as it feels like a sign.

The dice needs to be thrown again, and the seven is the result, so we take the directions the dice tells us to take, and while walking someone spots the number seven on the entrance of a building.

The word Freeman above the number seven makes my Polish friend share his thoughts with us. He tells us that he is celebrating his new life in London, and he is feeling free to live his new life. Then he said that seven years ago he fell from the seventh floor of a building and survived the fall, but the anniversary of the date of the fall was actually seven days before. He tells me that the number seven is his lucky number, and said I should take a look at something. He bends over and pulls the trousers of his right leg up to show me a number seven tattooed on his calf.

Everything happens very quickly, and I don't want to break the flow by taking pictures. I'm just there, in the present moment living my adventure, but then I feel the need to register that moment and ask him to pose for me besides the Freeman sign.

The number seven is then cast for the fourth time in a row, so we keep walking guided by the dice, and enter a dark alleyway. One person from the group points out his car parked there and switches the alarm on, as he had forgotten to do that when going to the meeting point. So the confidence builds up at every step.

We get to another crossroad, and another girl throws the dice, and seven is cast for the fifth time on top of a manhole. Someone gets closer to it and says that the number seven is on the tag in the centre of the manhole.

The number seven is then cast for the fourth time in a row, so we keep walking guided by the dice, and enter a dark alleyway. One person from the group points out his car parked there and switches the alarm on, as he had forgotten to do that when going to the meeting point. So the confidence builds up at every step.

We get to another crossroad, and another girl throws the dice, and seven is cast for the fifth time on top of a manhole. Someone gets closer to it and says that the number seven is on the tag in the centre of the manhole.

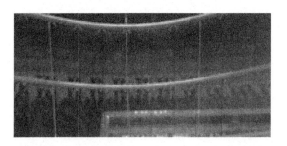

Todd decides that this is the perfect place to end our walk as we can see copies of ourselves reflecting all the possible parallel universes that might be available to us.

I then take another picture as I think of me being duplicated many times over by publishing my book.

That was definitely a happy ending. I tell Todd more about my flow state research, we decide to talk further in the near future, and we say goodbye.

As we walked around, I made friends with a ginger haired girl from Canada. She was with her boyfriend and a couple of friends. They wanted to grab a bite to eat, and I decided to join them.

I asked her what her job was, and she told me she worked in hospitality. I asked which hotel she worked at.

To my surprise, she said she worked at the Pullman Hotel. I was gobsmacked as I was there two days before having dinner with a friend, and I went there recently to coach two people on separate occasions. This is a hotel that I've been to just five times in 19 years, and three of those times were in the previous month. That couldn't be a coincidence. Then I ask the guy what he does, and he tells me he entertains at parties making soap bubbles.

That was intriguing because I worked with my friend Sam selling bubbles at festivals over the summer 18 years ago. The mystery was solved when he told me that he works with the same Sam making bubbles.

That was enough for me, and I left the coffee shop certain that there is some order in the universe, or perhaps I create the order around me while in flow. Who knows?

Be able to identify flow moments, start new ones, make them last longer and flow deeper.

Unlock your creativity

Ignite your creativity; apply what you've learnt from the first four visions to create a structure for achieving mental flow at the office.

The easiest way to get in flow is by reading long-form texts, especially books. So I will guide you on how to focus better to enjoy reading books. I will go into the detail of how to use your power to focus and read faster during the Second Quest.

The other way to develop your power to get in flow is by writing. To develop this skill, you need to create a bigger vision, and aim to be a leader in your field. I will expand on that during the Third Quest.

The most powerful access to flow is by taking a big challenge, creating a new project, or organizing an event to impact one community that you care about. In this way there is so much at stake, and you have so many ways to be creative. I recommend you find an accountability buddy or hire a business coach to bounce ideas off, so you can actually make your project take off.

There is another way to get in flow that seems to be difficult for most adults, but it can become a great source of pleasure. This is the art of drawing. I will show you a shortcut to develop this skill very quickly, and to open your mind to new possibilities.

After explaining how to get in Mental Quiet Flow while reading, writing and drawing, I will dive into Mental Loud Flow for a brief explanation about presenting your ideas, teaching, discussing projects, and brainstorming. This topic will also be expanded on in the Third Quest.

So let's start with the basics.

PREPARING TO FLOW

1.5.1 Have a control panel for feedback

Measurement is key if you want to improve in any area and immediate feedback is an important flow trigger. The best device to track you 24/7, and to guide you into flow is the Oura Ring – www.ouraring.com. It will measure sleep quality, sleep stages (REM, deep, light), recovery optimization, resting heart rate, heart rate variability (HRV), body temperature trends, respiratory rate, daily activity, steps, calories, activity balance, and meditation efficiency.

If you like the futuristic features of the Oura Ring you can purchase it with a discount at the following webpage.
www.humansinflow.global/hrv

If you don't want to buy the Oura Ring, you can choose from other devices that track some of your vitals, including the Apple Watch. A very important device to purchase is one that measures the heart rate variability (HRV).

If you decide to be coached by me to get in flow faster you will learn a great deal about the heart rate variability (HRV) and you will see something quite fantastic, which is to understand how well you are practicing your meditation or mindfulness.

Learn more about the HRV and look at recommended devices by visiting the webpage below.

www.humansinflow.global/hrv

I've been gaining invaluable insight about my mental performance while meditating. You will also understand what kind of practices yield the best results on your quest for flow.

1.5.2 Balance your day and night

With all this data, you can refine your strategy to get in flow, and measure the results achieved.

Having a great night's sleep is fundamental. I also recommend the Sleep Cycle app to help you wake up during a window of time where you are dreaming (REM). Being prompted to wake up during your dream stage will make you embrace the day with pleasure and energy, as opposed to waking up from deep sleep which will make you feel sluggish and tired.

1.5.3 Exercise

Although many people will look forward to getting in flow while practising sports, this book will guide you on your quest for intellectual flow.

An important part of being ready to flow is being healthy and fit. I recommend ten to 20 minutes of exercise in the morning. You will be able to adjust the time and intensity with the results you gather from the Oura ring.

Embodied cognition

Experiment using your body in new ways. Exercise, relax in a sauna or flotation tank, experiment with the force of gravity by going on a roller-coaster, try surfing, or basketball.

Express yourself by going to a dance class, play some percussion or another instrument, make art, or go to a church, mosque or synagogue to enjoy the feeling of connecting with God in a different atmosphere.

187

As you move your body, your brain learns to be flexible, and to think differently.

1.5.4 Meditate and understand heart rate variability

Eagles need to quickly learn how to be independent. In under two months, they will leave their parents, and move away from the nest to explore the world. As the young eagles start flying, they will find flow, which is a state of focused relaxation. I will describe the essential benefits of a relaxed state, which can be achieved in under five minutes, with the help of neurofeedback equipment. You will benefit by diminishing stress, and also by finding better clarity to make decisions.

The practical steps for the five-minute meditation are straightforward.

To improve your focus, you will do some breathing exercises that are based on the Heartmath techniques, which use biofeedback software to measure your state of mind.

I went to their lab nine years ago, and I was amazed to see all the changes that were happening in my mind and my heart, on a computer screen, while I was practising their short meditation training. Heartmath has an app called Inner Balance that trains you to shift and replace emotional stress with emotional balance and coherence. You will aim to increase your Heart Rate Variability (HRV), and this is the measurement to keep in mind while practising the meditation. The Inner Balance app requires that you buy the Inner Balance Sensor. It is a sensitive device that will be plugged into your phone or tablet, and will be attached to your ear lobe to measure a particular variance of your heart beats accurately.

I've already recommended the Oura Ring – it also measures the HRV and tracks various other vitals.

Take a look at their websites to understand how to stop feeling overwhelmed, anxious, and scattered.

Studies at Heartmath with over 11,500 people over 6 to 9 weeks have shown the following improvements: 24% felt more focused, 30% had better sleep quality, 38% felt calmer, 46% felt less anxious, 48% felt less fatigued, and 56% felt less depressed.

188

With a little practise, you will start feeling more inner calm, clarity in decision-making, and balanced composure, which can greatly reflect in your capacity of getting into flow state.

I think it is simple and can be of benefit to beginners or advanced meditation practitioners.

Firstly, make yourself comfortable by sitting on a cushion on the floor or on a chair, and keep still. Breathe deeply and evenly by counting slowly from one to five while breathing in, and by counting slowly from one to five while breathing out.

It is interesting to note that if you are tired or not motivated to do something, you will tend to exhale for longer than you inhale. You can relate to that if you imagine someone huffing and puffing, you can see them taking longer when breathing out.

By inhaling and exhaling for the same amount of time, you will become more balanced and relaxed. You will stop being tired or elated and become more harmonious.

It is easy to understand that a sportsman would be very happy after scoring for his team, and as a result he will start to breathe in for longer than he will breathe out. However, if he doesn't get back in balance, the likelihood of him playing well is diminished because he becomes overconfident. If he wants to keep scoring, he should be getting out of that elated state to focus and think straight. Heightened emotions can tip you over the edge and make you less focused, so the idea is to feel fulfilled, contained, and relaxed to achieve high performance in sports and at work, too.

You know that it is possible to measure brain activity with the Electroencephalogram (EEG), and also to measure heart activity with the Electrocardiogram (ECG). Your heartbeat synchronises with the rhythm of certain kinds of music you listen to, and in the same way, by focusing your attention (or your mind) on your heart, you start using biofeedback to connect and harmonise both frequencies. What scientists noticed is that you create stress when your head and heart are not in sync. However, you become calm and focused when they are in sync. The whole thing happens automatically when you focus your attention on your heart.

189

So keep breathing slowly and imagine that you are breathing from your heart, put your hand on your heart and feel it. This way your brain and heart start getting in sync.

Now it is time to imagine and connect with a beautiful moment of your life – a person that you love, or a special holiday place to bring you a feeling of relaxation, contentment, and gratitude. Hold this thought in your mind while breathing slowly.

That's it, you are doing the five-minute meditation. You can have your eyes open or closed while practising your meditation. However, if you close your eyes, your brainwaves will slow down dramatically, and your brain will start producing Alfa brainwaves, which will help you relax faster.

It is beneficial to do this meditation whenever you are sitting down to read, work or study. We often have troubles that infest our minds, which keep spinning around and inevitably become a distraction. To get rid of such thoughts, it is necessary to breathe slowly, and focus on ideas of a more pleasant nature. This way, you will break the repetitive cycle, and your mind will be ready to focus on new information, enabling you to have a clearer thought process. It is also great to do this meditation before an important meeting, or while sitting for your exams.

After five minutes meditating, keep breathing slowly from your heart, and start focusing on the text you want to read, or on the activity at hand.

It is essential to focus your attention, but don't become anxious to understand, just relax.

So stop reading now, and practise the five-minute meditation. I guarantee you will feel better and more receptive to learning while reading this book.

I recommend you practise meditation, even if just for five minutes, during your day. Ideally, you would be practising twice a day for a month to get the hang of it.

This is just the beginning, and if you like how you feel, then do it for longer. Sometimes I meditate for one whole hour or even longer, but the important thing is not the duration; it is the frequency.

Experiment with guided meditations, apps or various techniques like square breathing. Observe how they affect your HRV, and choose the one that brings you the best results.

As you learn how to control your HRV, I recommend a few minutes to be thankful for all you have, before focusing on wanting more of anything.

Gratitude is directly related to the level of happiness you can achieve, so start thanking people and circumstances in your life, opportunities that open for you, and also simple things like the smell of flowers or the smile of your child.

As you develop this practice, your electromagnetic field starts to emanate a different vibration, and you will be more likely to bring synchronicity and serendipity into your life.

Stimulate the Parasympathetic System

My research has indicated that many factors that stimulate the vagus nerve can promote overall coherence in the body and flow can blossom.

A few ways to prime your body that will strengthen your discipline are, measuring your heart rate (HR), your heart rate variability (HRV) and learn some rhythmic breathing with visualisation to bring coherence to your system.

Other routines that I recommend, and practice, are grounding (earthing) by walking/meditating barefoot in the park, or using a device with cables that brings the earth connection to you while at home.

It's been three years since I started only taking cold showers, so you can experiment taking a cold shower, or end your hot shower with a cold finish. It will give you a great feeling of being alive and gives a boost of energy to your vagus nerve.

Intermittent fasting gives more time to the body to recover and regenerate. A bit of exercise during the day will also move stagnant energy and bring a heightened meditation level.

1.5.5 Create time blocks

Block out 60 to 120 minutes of uninterrupted time, as you start to track your vitals and compare KPIs (key performance indicators).

You will be able to locate the optimal window to achieve ultimate performance as you notice how you behave over a period of time.

I'm usually much more productive at night, but it's wise to set one of these time blocks right at the beginning of the day.

Become pro-active and execute the tasks you set up for yourself the previous day.

To avoid being reactive, and to avoid interruptions, before starting the first time block, turn your phone onto airplane mode, tell everyone that you are having an important private meeting, and do not check your messages and emails.

1.5.6 Prioritise your actions

It's critical to prioritise your to-do list. I recommend that you learn how to create a Goal-Map, described in detail already, to create a big vision for your projects that speak directly to your left and right brain.

Being organised is fundamental to get in flow and I coach my clients to organise their life around the flow triggers, so flow can be accessible on a day to day basis.

Discipline and surrender

As being in flow is related to pleasure, accomplishments and purpose, many people think that by creating the conditions to promote flow they will be able to surrender and have a great time. This is a very biased truth because getting in flow requires as much discipline as it requires surrender.

So, to start strong you should have a life or business coach to structure your life and find the benefits only flow can give you.

Remember to prioritise:

● Top things to do – stay focused and accomplish more

- People to connect to – new people will add a new layer of depth to your projects
- Bold requests – raise your standards and bring more excitement to your life
- Dare yourself – take more risks to spice up your working day

1.5.7 Take risks

Risks immediately make you focus more, and this is why you will increase flow by practising radical sports in the ever-changing outdoors. Dopamine will really spike when you ski, or ride your off-road bike in the countryside.

Intellectually, you might think that more exposure to information can bring more flow, but your brain will filter more than 90% of the inputs to be able to make sense of anything it is focusing on.

So a great way to enrich your flow experience is to do the opposite; practice selective ignorance about subjects you don't want to waste time learning about.

For example, even though I'm Brazilian, I decided not to follow sports so I can't be active in a football discussion, but I can ask questions to stay engaged in the conversation.

Just like you don't miss the news while on holiday, you can stop reading the newspaper a couple of days a week, or avoid some sections by not even opening them. It feels risky not to be up to date, but swapping the newspaper for a business book can bring great insights. Go on a social media detox by not connecting on it every single day. Breaking the routine brings novelty to your life, so buy a magazine or a book about subjects you don't know much about.

People that take more risks feel more alive, so I invite you to think about a few unreasonable requests or bold actions that you could take today or in a few days. Schedule it in your diary and make things happen.

Going to a park to think unreasonably can be much more productive. Research done on creatives working in different environments showed that they are less creative in a room with a low ceiling. Their creativity can improve if they have a window with a view. They become even more creative in a room with a high ceiling, and are most daring and inspired when there is no roof at all over their heads. Steve Jobs was famous for having work meetings while going for long walks, and I think you can take advantage of this strategy too. Invite a friend to an inspired location for a business meeting, and enjoy the sun, or a beautiful rainy day.

1.5.8 Achieve any goal in an almost fool-proof way

If you need a helping hand to achieve more, check this out!

There is a free web-based service called www.stickk.com that can help you achieve your goals because of a *Commitment Contract*. You can also use the App *StickK* after registering on their website.

You will define your goal (read three books in three weeks, make a call to create a joint venture, write an article per month, quit smoking, or whatever you decide), pick a timeline to accomplish it, and put something at stake (whether it is money, or your reputation). You are up to three times more likely to achieve a goal if you put money on the line. *StickK* allows you to bet on yourself, and if you are unsuccessful in achieving your goal, they will donate your money to a charity, a friend, or even an organisation you oppose. For extra accountability, you can ask a friend to be your referee, and check in at least once a week. You can also invite your friends to be your supporters, and they will automatically receive weekly updates on your progress.

After defining your goal on *StickK,* you can set up daily reminders at a certain time of the day, so you will stay on track. For that, I use the App *Habit Builder* because it shows graphs of my progress with different metrics like the Apple Watch. It is great to be able to visually see my progress over a week or a month.

To engage in flow intellectually, I will explain how to get in flow while reading, writing, and drawing, as they are the easiest ways of starting and maintaining flow.

As you learn the principles, you will be able to expand and get in flow while thinking, solving problems, planning, working, and studying.

FLOW READING STATE™

1.5.9 Read books to flow

Getting in flow requires extreme focus, which kicks in after a period of time. So if you read a book you are interested in, you will be practising entering into flow, and will become more confident in achieving the flow state while practising other activities.

Reading books seems to be easy. But what most people fail to notice is that if they read at an average speed, they disengage easily, skip back to reread many times, and quickly decide to have a break or stop reading because the task becomes more of a burden than a pleasure producing action.

The solution is to learn how to focus your mind, and develop the ability to read 50 to 300% faster.

Your reading speed will vary according to the material you are reading, and your actual skill level. You will be guided on how to read as a skilled adult while reading the second quest.

Before you learn the techniques, I will explain some pre-requisites that will prepare you on your journey of learning to read books efficiently, and thereby awaken your passion for reading books, long-form texts, and articles.

1.5.10 Select authors that speak your kind of language

As soon as eagles are mature enough to reproduce, they have the urge to find a mate that will be their companion for life. Bald eagles' courtship involves an acrobatic manoeuvre known as the death spiral. To determine fitness compatibility the couple soars up to high altitude, hold each other's talons tight, and go for a dangerous dive while they cartwheel and tumble toward Earth, letting go only moments from reaching the ground, unless one of them leads their dance into a fatal crash. They perform this ritual every year to keep the flame of passion alive. I will now talk about creating flow by establishing compatibility with the author, their style, and the subject of the book. This will increase the possibility of you falling in love with the content, creating flow, and increasing pleasure while you read and learn.

I believe that Neuro-Linguistic Programming (NLP) is an incredibly powerful discipline, and reading some books about the subject could improve your reading speed and performance. It deals with human performance and excellence, and enables people to unblock the way they communicate.

NLP explores the relationships between how we think (neuro), how we communicate (linguistic), and our patterns of behaviour and emotion (programmes).

People can effectively transform their lives by understanding how to adopt new models of human excellence.

In effect, NLP is a powerful personal development tool which transforms the way you think and act to improve your performance both professionally and personally.

People use three main channels as their preferential way to communicate and understand the world. You might prefer to learn using the visual, auditory, or kinesthetic channels, and will prefer to interact and learn from people that have the same preferential channel. If you start to learn about NLP, you will recognise that if you don't like a particular book or article, it might be because the writer is using a channel that is not your favourite. For this reason you continuously disengage and get bored by the way the author shares information.

To illustrate this principle, I will tell you a personal story. I'm a visual person, and most people like me think by referring to images in their mind. I imagine things quickly and as a result, I end up speaking very fast. While growing up in Brazil, I would tell my father what I was learning while studying history, and then he would tell me many details of what I was learning, from his memory. He was a bank director and had a fantastic memory for history. His preferred channel was auditory, which deals with rational thinking, and for this reason he would speak much slower than me. The problem was that he would start sharing his knowledge at such a slow pace for me, that I would find it incredibly challenging. Now I

197

understand that it was not the content, but the form of delivery.

If you understand that each channel uses different words to describe the same situation, you will know if the author is talking to you on the same wavelength or not. If not, you can try to think as they think, or drop the book and choose another one that speaks directly to you. Maybe a friend of yours will love a book that didn't connect with you. So, comprehension will be affected if you read a book that you don't connect with, and you will indeed suffer trying to finish a book that has an underlying channel preference that you don't easily connect with.

So why don't you browse a few NLP books and choose one to read?

It will have a significant impact on your communication, not only because of the content, but mainly because of the way you get the message across. I recommend a few books and courses on the webpage below.

www.humansinflow.global/nlp

1.5.11 Finding your natural strength for mental flow

Eagles fly great distances to find good food for their eagle chicks, and they are confident that their family is protected at an inaccessible nest. But if for any reason another eagle, man, or other animal cross the line, and they feel threatened, they will not retreat until they win or die. Each animal has a strategy, which is different from other species, to find food, procreate, and care for their family. Lions will not be tempted to graze by the sight of a beautiful pasture, but you can be seduced into thinking you could make millions by investing in the stock market as your best friend does. If your profile is not suitable, you will have an average income, and will feel stressed and unfulfilled by investing in shares. Humans have diverse sets of talents, and knowing how to identify and use them can almost guarantee success and flow. In this topic, I will discuss the territory that is available for you to conquer. You have many abilities and talents that can be awakened and explored if you understand what your wealth profile is. This way, you will feel inspired, and will be able to leverage your strength, create synergy in your team, and feel on top of the world.

I understand that people have natural abilities in certain areas, but sometimes we push ourselves too hard to learn things that are almost out of reach for us in terms of flow and development.

The Wealth Dynamics profiling test can help you choose the right books for you. There are many profiling systems on the market, and I've tried several of them, including the Enneagram, Myers-Briggs, DISC and Spiral Dynamics. However, best of all is the Wealth Dynamics Profile, because it's not only about knowing more about yourself, but also about how to find your strength to work in flow. With this knowledge, you can find the right people that can leverage your value in a mutually beneficial way.

The reason for mentioning Wealth Dynamics, is that once I took the test, I could clearly see why some successful people share the same profile as I do, and by reading their biographies and books, I became much more in tune with myself. I was also inspired to read more.

There is nothing better than reading about the kind of people we like the most. Ourselves!

Even if I choose to read a book that is not about my profile, I can appreciate it, and I will know what to focus on, without having to worry about parts that don't resonate with me.

I'm confident that you will find it fascinating. You will learn how to get in flow, and will create wealth in your life.

It totally changed the way I see work and money, so go on, take a quick look at it.

You can find more information about the test on the following webpage.

www.humansinflow.global/wealth-dynamics

1.5.12 Book summaries can boost your confidence

To make you more confident while taking the challenge of reading a book in two or three hours, I suggest you take advantage of reading a book summary before reading the whole book. This way, you will know what areas of the book you should concentrate on, and will look for examples and stories in your reality to illustrate the theory presented.

By reading the summary, you will know the core ideas of the book upfront. Therefore, you can increase your reading speed, and not feel insecure that you might lose something important while reading. As you relax, you are more likely to get in flow.

Follow the link below to find the best sources of book summaries in the market.

www.humansinflow.global/summaries

1.5.13 Find a great place to trigger flow

You can choose a spot in your house that you always use to read or to work. The dedicated space will ensure your mood changes, your mind clears, and your brainwaves adjust rapidly to help you get in flow. You will have created an anchor for a good state of mind to focus, work, read, and learn.

Alternatively, you can read books using the Book app on iPhone, or download the Kindle app on your phone, and read while on the move, instead of checking your messages or getting lost on Facebook. Create some priorities, and remember to read a page or two while waiting at the post office queue, or whenever you are moving around on a bus or on the tube.

1.5.14 Ergonomics and flow

I remember my Judo master, called Sensei Kenjiro, talking about posture, "That's how you can recognise someone's power". I believe you can tell a lot about someone by the way they hold themselves.

Years ago I went to a Japanese restaurant in Brazil called Kamikaze. It was quite famous for having amazing food, and also because the owner, Mr Kazuma, was usually moody. He could be rude, and would often insult some of the customers. People would go to the restaurant to have a bit of fun with the moody Japanese owner. I love the culture, and that time was an opportunity for me to learn something.

I went there with a group of friends and a new girlfriend. I ordered some fantastic sushi, and decided to eat with chopsticks instead of a fork. I was managing it quite well. Suddenly, I dropped a roll of sushi back on the plate because I wasn't holding it well enough, and then I felt the presence of the owner by my side. He smiled. I thought that was unusual, and he said, "Trying to eat with chopsticks and not doing a good job!"

I was just happy because I hadn't dropped any food on my lap, however, he was not encouraging. So I said, "I'm still learning."

He then said something very wise and rude at the same time, "Yes, you better learn it! Be aware that animals bend over to eat. Humans raise the plate! You are a silly boy." He laughed, which was followed by the laughter of my friends. I joined in with the fun.

He was calling me an animal, and I am one.

In fact, it looked like I was eating from the table just like a horse. I immediately raised my plate, and it all seemed much more natural and civilised.

I never forgot that lesson at the restaurant, and therefore I want to tell you that it is much more comfortable and civilised to raise the book, iPad or Kindle while reading, than bending over to read the book flat on the table.

The reason is this: our head weighs about ten pounds or five kilograms. If you are reading a book flat on the table, your head will be hanging over the book, and you will have to use the muscles in your neck and back to keep that position.

So, if you start reading a book, you will feel fresh and bright after five minutes. Most of your energy will be directed to comprehension even though you are spending a reasonable amount of energy keeping your head in that position. You are not body aware, but from time to time, you will be fidgeting a little, and may cross one leg, or scratch your arm. Nothing wrong with that, we fidget and still understand what we read.

The problem starts if you stay reading in that position for about 10 or 20 minutes. Then your head will start to become heavier and heavier. You don't notice it, but your energy will begin to shift from your brain to your neck and then down your back. You start burning extra oxygen because your body needs more of it to keep your head hanging. At this point, your concentration will begin to get

201

redirected to your body, and you will start to lose track of the content of the book.

You get distracted because you are spending too much energy just to keep your head hanging. Time passes, and things get worse. Eventually, you get fed up with the book, assuming that it is boring, or far too complicated to understand, even if that is not the case.

Reading performance over time:

Comprehension

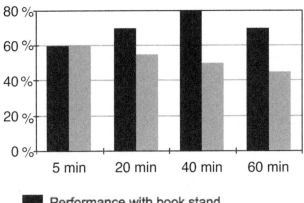

I created the graph to illustrate the dramatic increase in performance if you don't bend your neck while reading. To avoid wasting energy and to be more focused with better comprehension, you could use your hands to hold the book, document, Kindle or iPad in a better position or use a book stand like these:

A simple stand is holding a book and a Kindle.

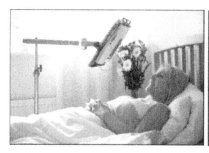

A versatile stand is holding a book.

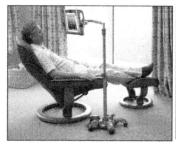

A versatile stand is holding an iPad.

You can buy a great book stand by searching on Google for "book stand."

It will make a massive difference to your attention span. Your computer screen should also be raised; while maintaining good posture, your chin should be level with the bottom of the screen, so lift it up. If you have a laptop, you can find a laptop stand to raise the screen, and you use another keyboard and mouse to make the experience more ergonomic and comfortable.

By keeping your back and neck straight, you feel more focused and have better comprehension.

So simple and so overlooked! Next, have a quick break to stretch. This is important. If your body feels tired, it demands so much energy to keep functioning that it is challenging to focus on reading.

So please stand up, take a deep breath, raise your arms, put your hands behind your head, tilt your head backwards and sideways, and then go for a little stroll. This will make a significant difference when you sit down again to read. Your mind will be fresher, and you will perform much better.

Your phone is changing your posture

Many people complain of chronic back and neck pain, and the mobile phone is certainly contributing to the problem. While standing up, your head should be aligned with your body, but many people project their head forward as a result of constantly looking down to check their phone, tablet or laptop, and they are changing their posture forever.

As I said, your head weighs ten pounds (five kilograms) which is about the weight of a bowling ball. If you were holding a bowling ball with your two hands in front of your chest you know that the further out you hold it, the heavier it feels, and you need to use more energy to keep it up. So bending your neck 45 degrees will increase the pressure on your neck's vertebrae by five or even six times. Translating pressure into weight would mean that if you bend your neck 45 degrees it would be like holding a 50-pound head (25 kilograms).

The more you keep hunching while working on your laptop or checking your phone, the more likely you will develop neck and shoulder pain. By constantly stressing the neck vertebrae, there is the possibility of a cervical nerve becoming pinched, causing headaches or making the pain radiate down the arm and hand.

This is such a severe condition that it has a few names including Tech Neck Syndrome, Text Neck Syndrome, or Gameboy Disease.

Young children are more vulnerable as their spine can grow stiff with their head projecting forward, increasing back problems, which can lead to disability later in life. Other complications from bad posture are linked to obesity, depression, spinal disc herniation, and high blood pressure.

If you keep your head projected forward, you could develop the "fatty neck hump" which are fat deposits on the back of the neck formed to protect this injury.

Fatty Neck Hump

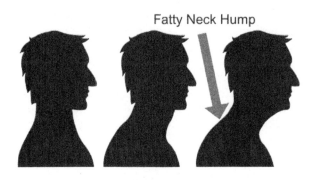

So the challenge is to improve your posture to prevent painful years ahead.

EyeForcer

A clever solution to help children and adults keep good posture is called EyeForcer. It consists of a glass frame that has sensors to measure the angle from which you are looking at your mobile devices. Whenever your posture needs to be adjusted, it will flash tiny lights to warn you, it will display a message on your device, and it will shut down the mobile device or video game if a child keeps that bad posture for longer than a specified amount of time. You can find out more about these frames at the following website:

www.medicalwearablesolutions.com

Ergonomics and performance

The experience that I had at the Japanese restaurant was the beginning of my obsession with ergonomics. I became fascinated with chairs and the body. I've learnt that chairs usually have a 90-degree angle between seat and backrest, but our bodies tend to be more comfortable when it is at 100 or 110 degrees. Think of the front seat of a car, it's not 90 degrees, is it? So, based on some

206

pictures of ergonomic chairs from Norway that have the seat tilted down, and also a knee rest, I started to produce my own line of ergonomic chairs in 1996 which sold very well at trade fairs in Brazil. It was an innovative design, and really made you comfortable by allowing you to sit with good posture, even without a backrest. If you have the opportunity to try one of these, then please do, to understand what I am saying.

I love design, and now I understand that good posture can affect your performance by helping your body to become more relaxed and receptive, and also by allowing you to breathe deeper.

Photograph of one ergonomic chair I have produced

Ergonomic chair and laptop stand
gives you great posture

Another trend is the "standing desk" which is a desk that you can raise so you will be able to work while sitting down or standing up. An alternative is the "treadmill desk" allowing you to exercise while working. This might be strange for some people, but this is a very good way to relax the tension in your spine and stay focused for longer.

If you complain of tension and stress in the neck or back area, you should look for a solution to your problem. By improving your posture, you will better your chances of finding flow while working.

Google "standing table," "ergonomic chair," or "ergonomic equipment" for your home, office, and especially for your children. Visit a shop to try their options and buy what suits you best. I'm sure this is an investment that will pay off.

1.5.15 Micro-movements and flow

This topic might seem obvious, but it's not. If you move your head sideways while reading, you are probably not aware that you are doing it, so pay attention and stop moving your head sideways to save energy that can be used to improve your comprehension levels and lead you to flow.

1.5.16 Break the spine of your book

I recommend you break the spine of your book, so you can flick the pages quickly. If you keep the book half-closed, your reading speed will suffer, and you want to have the least resistance to get in flow.

FLOW WRITING STATE™

1.5.17 Write blogs, articles and books to flow

The second easiest way to get in flow is by writing, and you will be more likely to explore this gateway to flow if you have a big reason to share your ideas.

I have dedicated the whole third quest to show you how to hack your way to becoming a leading expert fast.

Reading more books will help you have more ideas, and by deciding to position yourself in your industry as an expert, you will need to target a niche, write a book and share your ideas loud enough to feel confident that the message can stand out amongst all the noise in the marketplace.

FLOW DRAWING STATE™

1.5.18 I believe you can draw

The training to achieve the flow state includes drawing, and most adults reading this lines will be tempted to skip this topic because they don't see themselves capable of drawing, but I have great news for you.

As a child you were certainly very happy to entertain yourself for hours with a pen and a piece of paper, but after going to school you started to develop your left brain to become school smart, and this brain cannot draw well.

So you started to be critical about your drawing skills and stopped developing this invaluable talent.

I will show you how to start drawing well. It is easier than you think.

1.5.19 The impact of the right side of the brain on finding flow

Young eagles cannot catch fish due to refraction error of the eye, but as they keep trying, the refraction error resets, and they become great at catching fish. Eagles fly great distances, they can spot a white rabbit in the snow, and also locate their prey even if they're camouflaged, because they can see ultraviolet light which allows them to track the urine trail of prey escaping. In order to develop these skills, the eagle will need to start using new parts of its brain, and I will show you how to harness the right side of your brain to get in flow, to remember names and faces and to achieve feats that will surprise you, like a quick lesson on how to draw well.

If you want to watch something unusual just go to TED Talks www.ted.com and search for Dr Jill Bolte Taylor. She has a talk about the brain that is worth watching.

She is a brain scientist, and she talks about her experience of having a stroke and seeing the world being controlled from the right side of her brain, which lives in the present and is not controlled by time.

The left side is linear, methodical and keeps thinking about the past and future. It categorises and details everything with language, and communicates internal and external worlds.

I have had a similar experience described by Dr Taylor during meditation.

While meditating, I had moments when I was really connected with the right side of the brain, and I felt like a genie liberated from a bottle. This experience was like an awakening for me, it was a feeling of total integration and super awareness that I want to experience again, and many people have been researching and experimenting new ways to get to this higher dimension faster.

You know how the internet connects people, well, I felt like I had been plugged to the internet. It was like knowing everything and nothing at the same time. I was feeling much bigger in size and was also so light and free.

From this experience, I got some clarity, and I understood that by explaining the difference between the left and right side of the brain, you would be better able to develop your reading speed and memory. Keep reading, and you will be ready to fly.

Left and right side of the brain

Left Brain	Right Brain
Can comprehend	Can "get it" (i.e. meaning)
Detail oriented	Big picture
Language and reading	Symbols and images
Time oriented	Not time based
Past and future	Present
Person's name	Person's face
Fact rules	Imagination rules
Safe	Risk taking

Now I will explain the differences in more detail.

The right side of the brain can read faster and get in flow.

When you read in the traditional way, it's by looking at the letters sequentially from left to right so you understand them. Talking is also performed by the left side brain, so when you read and say the words back to yourself, it's the left side brain that's active. The right side brain works differently and sees the bigger picture.

So, the left side brain is concerned with logic and is sequential and linear. The right side brain finds the meaning by creating the big picture.

By the way, it is interesting to note that both eyes are connected to both sides of the brain; however, each side of the brain is connected to each side of your eyes.

Hooked on details or more holistic

The left side pays attention to the details, and the right side is more holistic; it absorbs everything at once.

While the left side works with words and language, the right side works with symbols and images.

You use the right side to see an image, and in less than a second, you notice all the details. However, the left side describes what you saw in words, and you may use a thousand words to do so. Can you see the difference? Instead of a second to see and take in the information, you will use a few minutes to describe what you saw with words.

If you look at a TV screen with magnifying lenses, you will see a lot of dots, red, green and blue. If you can see the colours individually you are too close to the screen. This is the way of thinking of the left side brain, too many lights but you can't see any images. If you move away from the TV, you will start seeing the eyes and nose, a little bit further you can see the whole face and, eventually, the entire screen with all the details of the scene.

Your left side brain is the default mode to the activity of reading.

Whole words can be seen as icons with the right side brain, and then you will be able to silence the inner voice inside your head.

If you have a red tulip before you, you will recognise the flower, but you will not say inside your head the words "red tulip."

To speed read you will just look at words as icons that represent ideas and will acknowledge the message without pretending to say the words in your mind, or pretending to hear their sound to understand the meaning of words.

So, this is a big secret. Look at words like they were images.

For example, if you see a Coca-Cola sign painted on a wall, you don't need to read Coca-Cola, you just know it is Coca-Cola. With words, it works the same; once you build your vocabulary, you can recognise expressions and read by recognising words as unique images.

On your computer's desktop, you have an icon of a printer, and you click it to "print one copy of the document." This is the "right side of the brain." It is straightforward.

If you don't click on the icon of the printer, then you will have to go the long way, which is the words route or the "left side brain." You click on "File" on the top bar, then click on "Print" and then you wait for the dialogue box to pop up. It takes a couple of seconds, and then it appears clearly on your screen. You realise that you don't have any settings to change and click OK. That's it, and the page will be printed.

You will find the same principle all over the computer. Icons for "right side brain," and its equivalent wording route if you prefer to use the "left side brain."

If you know about Neuro-Linguistic Programming (NLP), you will quickly understand that we have three favourite channels to communicate with the world. The visual, auditory and kinesthetic. The icons are the visual representation or channel. The words invite you to read and listen to them in your mind, and they are auditory. And you can also reach out to "Control+P" or "cmd+P" to have the same printing done by using the learning and memory accumulated in your muscles, which is a kinesthetic experience.

If you see a word and it looks wonky, it is because you know that it is misspelt. You will see that your spelling will improve after looking at words as if they were images, which are recognised by the visual channel. If you are more auditory, you might make a mistake while spelling a word because this channel is more concerned with the sound, and you create the graphic representation of the sound, which might incur you into making a spelling mistake.

Meditation can develop the right side of the brain

I've done a lot of martial arts in my life, and I am attending Kung Fu classes at the moment. The interesting thing about the lessons is that, on top of practising to train our bodies, we have some meditation sessions where we sit on the floor and imagine our body being strong. So Kung Fu is not only an exercise for my body, but also for my mind. I spoke to the master, and he assured me that meditation is essential to harness your focus and with focus comes power. This way, I learnt that meditation would be a good practice to follow if I was ever to have a great focus.

Knowing that meditation would be of good help for my fidgety mind, I decided to Google for a good place to go and learn.

I wanted results, and surprisingly, I found an intensive retreat called Vipassana. To my surprise, the retreat was free of charge, and I found amazing reviews about them.

They have centres all over the world and I chose one in Hereford, which is three hours away from London, and booked my place. A few weeks later I took the train to their fantastic venue in the countryside.

This is my self-portrait meditating

I lived like a monk for ten days, sitting on the floor with my eyes closed for ten hours each day.

There were a few rules though. The first one was that I was not allowed to talk to anyone for ten days. I was going to spend ten days in silence, complete silence.

I would hear the master teaching the techniques, but I could not talk about it.

The only time I was allowed to talk was in case of emergency. We could ask the master a question at the end of each day, but I had to ask a direct question about problems with the technique and not a philosophical, existential or intriguing question.

I remember going once to this special meeting where people were allowed to ask a question for a few seconds. It was an exciting event because I'd been silent for five days and just had my first insight into the ethereal world.

I was all excited about telling the teacher that I had been to a fantastic place where time stood still, and I was entirely in bliss seeing that the whole universe exists inside me.

His answer was the most bizarre. He said: "This is very dangerous. To go to the other side is very dangerous. The problem is that you will want to go there again because it is such good fun; however, every time you want to get there, it can become harder to find the way.

The best thing to do is to stop wanting something to happen and just do your work of sitting down to meditate. Things will happen because you allow them to happen and not because you want them to happen."

This talk took my smile away and made me think a lot about the way I expect things to happen. To make things happen, we actually need to focus on the present, and this was a revelation to me.

So, I've started to focus more on the practice without forgetting the final result. My mind began engaging with my higher thoughts, and I've started to clear the clutter.

I feel much lighter now.

I can observe the big amusement park that exists in our minds. We mostly look for pleasure on the outside, but there is a lot of fun inside ourselves.

The exciting thing is that the more you focus on the present, the more you start to slow time down and more things start to happen.

Not talking was just the beginning of the restrictions. I could not read anything at all. No new ideas were allowed. This was quite challenging, but at the same time, I felt relieved not having to search for information outside my own self.

Then came the worst part of the deal. I could not write! I was looking forward to having plenty of time to think and register my thoughts, but I could not record that on paper.

But unknowingly, I was going to be able to flip the switch and deprive my left brain of information that mostly came in words, and the left brain had a rest from having to function.

Meditate, stop feeding the left brain with words and it quiets down, giving space for the right brain to expand so you enjoy more freedom of choice, and feel the connection with your most powerful self.

Thinking back, I wasn't aware that a big challenge like that would bring such tremendous results. I had insights with lots of ideas, and not being able to register them made my mind stretch and find ways to remember long conversations I had with myself. This made me trust my ability to remember. Just by thinking again about something makes you remember it more because it is cumulative. If you focus on something for around five seconds, you have a good chance of retaining it.

I believe that reality is created by extreme focus, and it demands effort and determination. What I do has never been done before, and I have to imagine things before they become real. So, to remember the ideas, I started to develop my imagination and create vivid stories in my mind. I could hold essential thoughts by creating a visual representation of the information. The more details I created, the better the recall.

Most people don't even grasp the fact that our world is powered by imagination. They forget to imagine, and nothing extraordinary happens as a result.

Once you find something that is in line with your highest values and your heart's desire, focus on one project, and you will start to attract coincidences to your life. Concentrated effort can bring you surprising results.

This was a radical way of learning how to focus my mind, and I was ploughing my way through it. It ended up being an incredible time in my life!

In a nutshell, this was the challenge:

- Ten consecutive days
- Ten hours sitting down to meditate every day
- No talking
- No reading
- No writing
- No eye contact

Just focus, focus, focus.

These are some of the exciting discoveries that I made during the ten-day meditation retreat:

While meditating, I started recognising some differences between the left and right side brains.

To sit down each day and meditate for ten hours was very intense and tiring. Time would drag every time I sat down for a one or two-hour session. This is because in the left side brain the minutes are always ticking away, and I would get very anxious to get to the end of the session. One hour would feel like a three or five-hour session. It's bizarre to have all that time just not to think.

I also had a pleasant time walking in the fields or on a path cutting through some woods. It was a beautiful place. It was terrific to have the time to look up at the sky and appreciate how tiny our planet is; we are the observation point, where everything begins. Nothing is real unless it reaches you. The experience is real if someone is there to observe it; otherwise, it is just potential. So you bring things to life by being the observer.

It was fascinating to sit down for hours waiting for a man to ring the bell. That was the sound I would anxiously expect when I was meditating. I would also dread waiting for this sound if I had to start my meditation again, as I was already tired.

Einstein said something very curious about the relativity of time:

"Put your hand inside a hot oven for a minute, and it seems like an hour. Sit with a pretty girl for an hour, and it seems like a minute. That's relativity."

Now I understand that we can distort the fabric of time according to the side of the brain we are more connected to. The left side of the brain creates anxiety, while the right side of the brain creates relaxation.

All that frustration that grew out of the anxiety of wanting time to run faster, only prepared me to pay attention to the present moment.

Then I was sitting down for another one-hour session, and suddenly I saw time stop. I felt like I was there, where time stands still. My whole life had frozen in time.

The pain in my back and legs had been intensifying steadily, but suddenly there was no pain in my body, and I felt so calm and confident. I was really focused and felt like I had never been more alive in my whole life. I was, and I stayed in the same position without moving a millimetre for more than four hours. Time did fly this time.

The man came with his bell after one hour, but I didn't care about it and preferred to miss my lunch and stay there enjoying myself. The energy inside me was tremendous, and at this point, I had an insight into why I felt the need to teach people to read faster. It is all down to exploring my potential, so I don't have a TV set, and I spend my time experimenting and observing how the mind works.

218

If you are operating on the left side brain, you will be distracted by driving your attention to the past and future. Regretting things you have said and done, getting anxious about all those things you want to do, those things that have a small probability of happening in the future. You are just worrying for no reason.

So, if you learn how to connect with the right side of your brain, you will be living more in the present, which will help you to focus, to find flow and remember more of what you read.

1.5.20 Drawing and the right side of your brain

You can draw well, and I will show you how.

Safety and risk-taking

The left side of the brain is based on learning what is right and wrong, and by reconsidering all the time, we end up trying to minimise risks to be safe.

The right side brain does not restrict our options by choosing the safe route; it wants to go along paths never travelled before to expand and learn in search for fulfilment.

Now I will teach you how to tap into the power of the right side of your brain to learn how to draw. It's easier than you think.

To get started, I will ask you to do a simple exercise. I'm sure that you will be surprised by the results.

This is based on the teachings of Betty Edwards from her book *Drawing on the Right Side of the Brain* and, after 10 minutes of drawing practice, you will be amazed by the results, especially if you think that you are not good at drawing. I will show you an easy way to draw quite well, and hopefully, you will enjoy it!

Please copy the drawing below on a blank piece of paper.

You might not like drawing, or you may believe that you are not very good at it, in that case you will skip this exercise. I would, however, recommend, that you do attempt the exercise, which is designed to help you learn how to draw effectively. You will learn how to switch from the left to the right side of the brain in an instant. Speed reading is similarly all about left and right together.

You will have good fun teaching some children or friends how to draw in a matter of minutes.

Get ready and start copying it now. You will be spending about one or two minutes on it.

Start it now!

Well done!

Your left side brain is usually in charge of your everyday life, organising the sequence of the steps you take to function in the world.

Now let's say that you take up drawing classes, but all you can draw is a stick man. The simple drawing of a man is a creation of your left side brain which is not artistic and, being time-oriented, you try to draw a man using the fastest way to represent the idea. It doesn't waste time. Even if you attempt to draw a man by copying from another drawing, the left side brain will pay little attention to the details, and you will draw using symbols that represent the preconceived idea of the image that you have in your mind. You draw like a child using the quick way to understand symbols for mouth, eyes, and face that are a shortcut to represent the idea of a head.

Drawing well is about being able to see. If you could see like the artist sees, you would be able to draw. It is not a matter of dexterity, but it concerns slow observation and attention to visual detail, which are not traits of the left side of the mind.

The trick is to turn the image upside down to do the next drawing.

I know it is strange to do it this way, but there is a good reason for that:

If you don't rationalise, and give names to all the parts of a man's body and clothes, you will start copying just the lines and will pay attention to the length, angle, and shape of each line, as if you were copying a map with rivers, roads, and fences, where every little detail needs to be observed carefully.

Now you will take your time and start to copy the next image, while avoiding saying the parts of the eye inside your mind. There is no rush, so slow your mind down, observe every detail and enjoy. It would be great if you could put on some music to create a pleasant atmosphere.

Start copying the upside-down image slowly and enjoy the process. You will take longer to do it, and it doesn't matter! Just copy the image and don't worry about the time. Remember that the right side of the brain will now become activated, and it is not time-based. Just do it nicely, and you might find yourself in flow.

So, now you can draw the image using a fresh piece of paper. Spend as much time as you want to finish it, or draw it as many times as you want.

As you probably slapped random lines to draw the eyelashes on your first trial, but now you will have to pay attention to every single detail to draw each eyelash exactly as it appears in the image. To help you get started I'm displaying a detail of the image, so you can see all the details and copy every single line as you see them.

Now, carry on and draw the whole image.

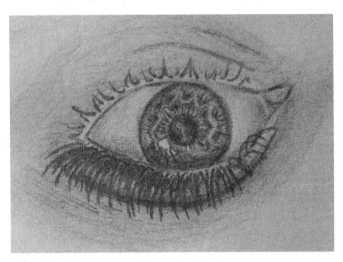

Good try!

Now turn the drawing the right way up and see how different it looks from the first one. It's not good or bad, it's just different. I believe that you could see more of the details and got a different perspective from the drawing.

Some people who do this exercise get very excited, because they understand that they can actually draw something well for the first time. It is a great feeling of accomplishment because you've learnt something new.

Now I suggest you go one step further and draw the image below, slowly.

Well done!

You can practice more, choose another simple image to draw or follow a few drawing lessons on YouTube. I suggest you search for "RapidFireArt" on Youtube for easy to follow lessons. You will find the lesson to draw the eye with all the details by following one of their lessons.

Just slow down, relax with a nice music and practice drawing something else and you will be easily entering the state of flow and developing your artistic talents that were probably hidden for a long time.

The switch

Give the left side brain something in which it's not interested, and the right side will take over and open the doors to another dimension of flow. A place where time runs slower, your perception is heightened, and the task will be carried out in a better way, giving you a holistic and more focused understanding.

In fact, to flow read, you will actually slow time down. You will see everything, and ideas will make even more sense than before.

Slowing down can be very rewarding if you want to learn how to play an instrument, cook or even to create romance in your life. It's all about perception, so set a timer for one, two or as many hours you want to focus one just one thing, and don't look at the watch until it rings, you will be tempted to look at your computer's clock so cover it. This way you will immerse into the time inside the time.

Relax and slow down to flow, feel the feeling that you are enjoying your time.

MENTAL
LOUD

FLOW

This interactive way of flowing demands dynamic engagement, and flow will be likely to appear if you are focused on overcoming a challenge, while presenting to a big audience, teaching, coaching, learning, discussing projects and brainstorming.

So be aware that your aim is to focus on the engagement fully by being present, and not trying to get in flow. Strangely, if you acknowledge that you are in flow and share that with people around you, you are very likely to get out of flow automatically. So don't think about flow while flowing, just focus on the interaction as if you would be happy to stay there forever.

FLOW SPEAKING STATE™

1.5.21 Learn with the intention of sharing

Can you imagine how much attention I put on the world to be able to find meaningful information that can help you use your mind better?

I'm really keen to learning and even more eager to share, therefore I have spent years of my life writing this book, to give you the cutting edge information, to upgrade your brain. I also coach individuals and give talks to huge audiences to help them perform better, and I think you should do the same.

Listen to audiobooks and podcasts, read books and summaries and watch videos to keep learning, and change the channel to stay stimulated. Read, listen or watch videos actively, instead of passively, to activate RAS.

You will be more engaged in any activity, and you will develop your memory if you have the underlying intention of sharing what you are learning. Be brave, post a Tweet, write a blog, write an article or a whole book. Go to Toastmasters and practise your public speaking skills, give talks, record a Facebook live or post a video on YouTube about everything you learn, and you will be surprised how you will engage even more to get into flow, become more creative and you will be more keen to continue reading and learning.

1.5.22 Present and teach

As you know, getting in flow demands preparation and risk-taking, so exposing yourself by sharing your ideas in public will add that extra layer of depth to your focus, and you will benefit from experiencing excitement and fear of being judged or criticised.

By knowing that you will be under the spotlight, you will start paying attention to the way other people deliver their speeches, create suspense, pause or bring the crowd to laughter.

I'm certain that we teach what we want to learn, so take it seriously by preparing your slides, rehearse and gather a few friends to have a live rehearsal before the actual delivery date.

1.5.23 Discuss projects and brainstorm

A low key way of practising to expose your ideas can be to present while discussing a project, and being vocal to make suggestions, even if you don't have all the data to back you up.

Be daring as your ideas might trigger other ideas that can result in the success of your projects.

You can always suggest a brainstorming session with your colleagues to find more freedom to be silly or over the top, as a brainstorming session will allow you to say whatever comes to your mind, without the fear of not being totally rational. Research about brainstorming and set one up at the company you work, or gather a few friends and run a brainstorming session to see if any new ideas pop up. Perhaps you will start a new company, or make a bold move in your career as a result of taking the time to listen to your subconscious mind, and acting on the good ideas.

1.5.24 Pay attention and invent

Being able to impact one of the communities you belong to can bring great satisfaction, and also inspire you to explore new possibilities in your life.

By enrolling other members of your community in your project you will hold each other accountable, and will maintain high integrity to achieve more than planned as the community gets tighter.

You can also develop trust to create a team that can create group flow, and perform at an excellent level.

Another approach is to focus on creating something new. It is very likely that your new idea comes from a problem or frustration you have in your life. Being critical and aiming to solve problems that can benefit you, your friends or the world at large are great motivators of flow and will develop your creativity further.

Think of impacting a large number of people, and suddenly you have a big responsibility on your shoulders.

You might need to create a business plan, a PowerPoint presentation, or a prototype to enrol people that will become investors or partners in your new venture. These are incredible motivators to achieve the flow state.

Entrepreneurs can face the most challenging conditions to develop a successful company, and will work countless hours in pursuit of turning an idea into a reality. They will develop a concept, fail, waste time and money, recoup the investment, pivot the idea and work through the night to deliver a project on time to make it successful.

This might sound like hard work, and it is, but not many people can see the satisfaction created by this massive challenge in creating meaning in someone's life, and deep satisfaction of achieving a fleeting success with tons of flow.

So what could be a project or idea that you can create?

1.5.25 Gamification of a project

Most of us grew up receiving gold stars and special treats for some minor but important achievement on a game.

Adults still acknowledge someone receiving a medal at the Olympics, the Nobel Prize or a trophy at your neighbourhood's snooker tournament. Winning first place on anything is something intrinsically attractive and valued.

You may not collect football cards any more, and instead collect watches, high hills, or support a team by buying shares, betting on them and having an executive box to watch the game live with your friends.

Simple games became sports with the introduction of rules and official judges.

Video games are bringing crowds together in large events and are now widely called esports.

Esports have tournaments that gamers pay to watch, buy merchandise, learn and join the party in Cosplay. Esports are spreading quickly and gaming is being introduced as an effective learning method.

Google's famous 20 per cent time to work on your own project is the inspiration here. As an employee you can work one day a week on a project you come up with, and you can have as many engineers on your private project team, as long as they volunteer to work with you. No one will be assigned to your project if you cannot enrol and register them yourself. It is like inviting friends to create a new game, so they have discussions, laugh a lot and push the boundaries to create incredible products and services.

It's your turn to join forces with friends or colleagues to create a project that can have a deadline no longer than six months. Have measurable goals and make it happen.

Flow requires creativity, so it's time to think of projects linked to your profession, a cause or a hobby. Break it down by having mile stones and a buddy to check in with you.

I have parameters to help my clients dream big and create new ways to expand and grow during a nine-week programme where game features are carefully designed to engage you on accomplishing your vision.

Brainstorm some ideas and take one up to apply the learnings from this book, and get in the zone like never before.

1.5.26 Gaming industry

The video games industry generated $138 billion per year, while the films and music industry combined generated $61 billion a year. Games for mobile alone are around $65 billion, and I bet you didn't see this coming (Global Games Market Report by Newzoo - 2018).

Electronic sports or esports are propelling video game international tournaments to a new level of interest, where professional gamers are finding stardom and wealth in this ever-growing market. The International Esports Federation is organising to include esports in the Paris 2024 Olympic games as a demonstration sport.

Esports generated £400m in revenue in 2016, with a global audience of about 320 million and the numbers are growing quickly.

1.5.27 Gamification to achieve serious results

The influence of games is spreading into our lives in imperceptible ways, and I'm discovering new strategies to combine game psychology to help you achieve flow in engaging and exciting quests.

According to gamification expert Yu-Kai Chou the average age of gamers is 35 years old, 68% of them are over 18 years of age, and 47% are female. More adult women are playing games than under 18 males.

Great results have been achieved by market leaders, and I will give you a few examples to illustrate that gamification is serious business.

You can have a LinkedIn profile and display a great variety of information that will help you do more business or get a job. As people upload whatever they think is important on their profile, they forget to look into what could be added to boost their searchability and impact. With that in mind, a few years ago LinkedIn engineers introduced a game-like progress bar at the top of each person's profile. This bar shows you the completion rate of your profile. Whether you are an employee in search for work, a sales representative, or a respected professional, the constant reminder that your profile is 78 per cent complete will motivate you to spend a few extra minutes to fill the gaps on your profile. It is upsetting for you to see that you are not displaying 100 per cent of your potential profile, and as higher engagement brings better results, this strategy is simply a no-brainer.

1.5.28 Focus on a project, not on the money

Whenever a professional wants to work with me, they have a discovery session to find out if their expectations can be met, and I offer them a challenge to measure the degree of success to achieve flow.

Their challenge is to create a project that has a few metrics, and money is one of them. But if their main goal is just to make a lot more money, there will be no chance of developing their flow muscle with me.

Investment bankers and stock market traders have an expression for being in the zone by saying they are "in the pipe", when they are super focused to make the best buying and selling decisions and profit from being in flow, but the learning process starts by finding a project to focus on.

If we find common ground we can create bespoke principles of engagement that can be conducive to creating flow, and they can incorporate gamification triggers and systems to get there faster.

They must develop a project that is self-contained and personal, or focus on a part of their career ambition to stretch their skills in a creative way.

Money cannot be the primary motivator, but money will certainly start flowing in abundance into their lives, if they learn how to harness the principles of ultimate performance.

Once they learn the principles to become engaged and motivated on their project, they can also use the principles to improve the way they study, market their products and services and also learn how to have more fun during their free time.

1.5.29 Game-like thinking to flow at work

My clients enrol on a nine-week training programme to learn how to develop gamification applied to work and lifestyle, to have more fun in life and accomplish much more.

Different types of people are motivated differently, so they will explore the application of the eight core drives of gamification developed by Yu-Kai Chou.

The core drives motivate everything that you do, and they are:

- Core Drive 1: Epic Meaning & Calling
  You are motivated because you are part of something bigger than yourself. Working with charities brings it to life.
- Core Drive 2: Development & Accomplishment
  You are motivated when you feel like you are improving and achieving mastery. Nike+ breaks down data to measure development which brings motivation.
- Core Drive 3: Empowerment of Creativity & Feedback

You are motivated when you can dare using your creativity to solve problems. The AIDS virus protein structure was an unsolved problem for 15 years. When the problem was transformed into a game, the solution was found in 10 days.

- Core Drive 4: Ownership & Possession
  Ownership will make you want to improve whatever you do. This principle is used successfully to teach algebra.
- Core Drive 5: Social Influence & Relatedness
  Being part of a community will change your attitudes and habits without you noticing. This principle can help people lower their utility bills.
- Core Drive 6: Scarcity & Impatience
  You are motivated towards something that has limited supply. The Kickstarter crowdfunding platform uses it with success.
- Core Drive 7: Unpredictability & Curiosity
  You are motivated by wanting to explore the unknown and by chance. It can help people obey the speed limit and drive more carefully.
- Core Drive 8: Loss & Avoidance
  You become more motivated to avoid losing something you have, than by gaining something you don't own. The alarm clock that donates to an organisation you would hate to support, if you touch the snooze button, is a good example here.

After familiarising yourself with the core drives you will understand how to select the ones that can support your flow quest, and will start applying them to achieve the outcome of your project.

1.5.30 Player types and context

Another factor to create flow is the understanding of your style for motivation, and Richard Bartle's Four Player Types can be insightful as he separates people into four types.

- Achievers
- Socialisers
- Explorers

- Killers

The context of gamification will become broader when you start exploring other applications in non-game contexts as you will understand the division below.

- Workplace Gamification
- Lifestyle Gamification
- Product Gamification
- Marketing Gamification
- Career Gamification
- Health Gamification
- Productivity Gamification
- Education Gamification

1.5.31 Flowing down the rabbit hole

My efforts are focused on inspiring and motivating people towards their work beyond the paycheck incentive (Core Drive 4: Ownership & Possession) or the threat of losing their job by not working hard enough (Core Drive 8: Loss & Avoidance). Understanding the nuances of your workforce will help you understand how to make a difference with engaged, disengaged and also actively disengaged employees. According to Gallup's 142-country study, 13 per cent of employees are engaged at work. The big difference is to understand that the 24 per cent of the workforce that are actively disengaged at work are engaged in other activities and pursuits. Analyse the motivators and you can transform any organisation and drastically increase their bottom line.

Performance can be evaluated in the workplace, but a new level of sophistication can be achieved by new tracking systems and devices.

The cultural revolution of tracking personal data is giving birth to the "quantified self" revolution. If you add the "Internet of things" and "big data" you will have more elements to use in gamification to achieve your life goals.

According to Yu-Kai Chou special attention should be directed to finding your game, analysing your initial stats, formulating your skills trees, connecting your allies, finding the right quests and beating the game.

So, if you want to enter the rabbit hole to find your flow, get in touch. It will be a pleasure to challenge and support you to create an exciting life and career.

Hack a smooth and simple way to read faster.

The *Horses Read Quest* has four insights to help you focus and read faster.

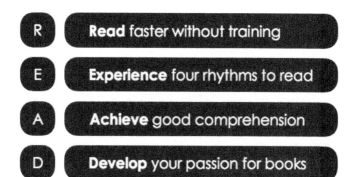

R — **Read** faster without training

E — **Experience** four rhythms to read

A — **Achieve** good comprehension

D — **Develop** your passion for books

Time to read the Second Quest

Reading Speed in Words Per Minute	TIME
At 100 WPM	5.2 hours
At 200 WPM	2.6 hours
At 300 WPM	1.7 hours
At 400 WPM	1.3 hours
At 500 WPM	1.1 hours

Reading Speed in Words Per Minute	TIME
At 600 WPM	52 minutes
At 800 WPM	39 minutes
At 1000 WPM	31 minutes
At 1200 WPM	26 minutes
At 1400 WPM	22 minutes

To illustrate the process, I will compare the act of reading faster to learning how to ride a horse. Once you understand the process, you will be ready for the experience.

The challenge

Horses are the oldest allies of men which have increased productivity, and they were first domesticated 6,000 years ago, on the grasslands of Kazakhstan, Ukraine and Russia. They replaced manpower, and even now our sophisticated machines still use horsepower to measure their power output.

I'm using horses as an analogy to flow reading because they are the basic units of the industrial revolution and thanks to men's ability to read and write, the industrialised world has developed in incredible ways over the years.

Humans are obsessed with measuring everything and have even found out that light travels at 186 miles per second (300 Kilometres per second). A surprising fact is that the vast majority is unable to tell with confidence if they are slow, average or fast readers.

The most understated, transformative, disruptive and creative technology ever conceived was the invention of the written word. Words allow us to store and transmit information so ideas can endure time but apparently, no one is concerned about our reading speed. Teachers have been teaching people to read, but as soon as learners become proficient readers, teachers cease to train the students to become fast readers. You can pursue excellence in any field, and reading performance can be doubled in a matter of a few hours, so let's sort the basic units of mental power by teaching every single human being that reading fast and well can be mastered quickly even in late stages of life.

Humans can learn to mount a horse and make it walk, trot, canter and gallop and, similarly, I am determined to help people double their reading and learning abilities. I can assure you that if you can ride a horse, you can learn to read much faster than you do now.

238

HORSES READ QUEST

Vision One

READ FASTER
WITHOUT TRAINING

"In times of change, learners inherit the earth, while the learned find themselves beautifully equipped to deal with a world that no longer exists."

Eric Hoffer

By reading this vision you can expect to improve your reading speed on a computer screen from 10–100%+. No kidding!

Can you imagine riding a beautiful horse in a 3D virtual environment? That's what you are going to do to get started.

You watch the horse approaching through your 3D glasses, then you jump into the saddle, and the mechanical horse starts moving. You feel the fresh breeze on your face as you gather speed, racing over vast green fields. As you direct the horse towards the woods, you jump over a log and feel exhilarated as you think you are riding a real horse. There will be more surprises on your journey!

I will show you how to read using simulation software, and you will start reading faster as if by magic. The words will rush towards you, and you will understand the text at an astonishingly fast pace. In this way, you will get ready to start speed reading books too.

2.1.1 How fast do you read?

You may think that you read slowly, or perhaps you think you are an average reader, but how do you know? Who would you compare yourself with? There are no set standards. There might be occasions when you get bored and distracted, read a few paragraphs, and then skip back to reread a paragraph that you can't quite remember reading or didn't understand. Does that sound familiar?

The benefits of reading faster

Once you have learnt to speed read, you will be more focused, and your comprehension will be enhanced.

Your expectations and real life

I have provided a space below so that you can write down your expectations of improvement after reading the book and practising the basic exercises. What do you think you will achieve in terms of improvement?

Will you improve 10%, 30%, 50%, 100% or more than 112%?

Because we spend so much time reading throughout each day, I believe that even a 30% improvement would save valuable time. You could be saving in excess of three or four years of your life if you spend much of your time reading.

There is no right or wrong, just have a guess. How much do you think you will improve?

Write it down here or make a note in your diary.

I expect to improve: _____ %

You can get back to it at the end of the book and you will be surprised by the results.

You should aim to improve by 112%. If you set this as your target you will be more open to achieving a big change in your reading performance. Most people improve 100-200% or more. If you aim to improve by only 30%, you may be expecting me to prove to you that you can speed read; however, the only person that can really make it happen is you, so be ready to get more confident and increase your brain power.

Read a book like you are watching a movie

Can you imagine choosing a book to read, yet reading it as if you were watching a movie? I will show you how to read a book of approximately 200 pages in two to four hours in a motivating way.

If you are choosing a DVD to watch, you peruse the back cover to see what the movie is about, the actors, the plot and, perhaps, the running time.

Let's say that the length of the movie you've chosen to watch is one hour and 55 minutes. Although we don't always think about this, it can be reassuring to know how long it will take to watch the entire movie. On the other hand, if you were to pick up a book, it is likely that you will have no concept of how long it will take to read it. In the back of your mind you may know that you read four books the previous year, so that it takes on average three months to read a book – which is demotivating, especially if the book is "thick".

I will show you that using simple maths, you will know beforehand how long it will take to read a book of any size.

Learn brain hacks, and you will be surprised that reading a book in three hours is really possible.

Getting your reading speed above average

Reading in the traditional way is considered to be slow reading. We live in a fast-paced society and if you read slowly, you will easily get bored and distracted. And you're likely to lack motivation to read, whether it's for study, work or pleasure.

People talk on average at speeds that range from 150–250 words per minute (WPM). You can see from the following graph that this is the same speed at which most people read.

Based on my own experiences, I estimate that, on average, children tend to read at 150 WPM, teens at 250 WPM, rising to 300 WPM for students at university; however, after finishing their degree, most adults probably slow down to about 200 WPM. Many of the high-level executives I've worked with had an initial reading speed of around 400 WPM, while in the general population you would find one in 100 adults that read at more than 700 WPM.

What's important to understand is that everyone can boost their reading speed. It doesn't matter which category you're in or if you are a native or non-native English speaker.

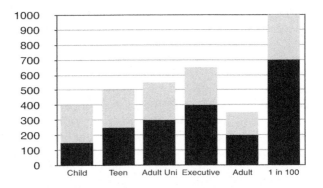

Expected improvement after reading the book
Reading speed before learning with the book

Based on more than thirteen years' experience teaching people how to read faster, I believe that the younger you learn, the more significant the improvement.

Many of us can learn to read at 400-700 WPM. At this pace you might think that the voice inside your head will be going at the rate of a horse racing commentator. In fact, what happens is that you start to go faster and the voice inside your head starts to disappear, until you become a truly silent reader.

2.1.2 Test yourself – measure your reading speed

First of all I want to show you how to measure your reading speed so you can see the improvement every time you measure it by yourself.

This simple test will really open your mind. This is the beginning of your training. Let's set your standards.

You will achieve better results if you measure your reading speed twice, on two different books (you can use a paper book, Kindle, iPad or tablet). Your reading speed can vary when you read different subjects, so I want you to see if there is any difference between books. You will also rate your comprehension of what you've just read.

First of all you need to choose the right kind of books to make the most of the training.

Your books should be:

- Non-fiction books that you want to learn something from
- Easy read book, nothing complex to start with
- Books with 10-12 words per line
- Books with continuous text. Avoid books with many bullet points

Non-fiction books are best to learn how to speed read. After you get the hang of it, you will be able to speed read your fiction books, articles, emails and tweets too.

I will guide you through the process while you watch a short video. I will give you exactly one minute to read your book and you will find out your reading speed in words per minute (WPM). You can also use the timer on your phone to measure your reading speed.

When your minute expires, you can stop and mark the line you read. Think about what you've just read to rate your comprehension level from 1 to 10.

To help you do this through the training programme, ask yourself: Did I follow the author's train of thought? Do I remember any details from the text? According to the answers that you give, rate your level

243

of comprehension and then keep track of the results on your control sheet.

Next, count the number of all the lines you read. Remember that you are working with averages so count full lines and short lines. Then multiply the number of lines by the number of words in one line, and you will have your reading speed in words per minute.

To find the average number of words per line, count the number of words in three full lines and then divide the result by three. You can then round the result down.

For example, let's say that you counted 32 words in three lines. Dividing 32 by three is 10.7 words per line. Rounding 10.7 down you have 10 words per line. If you read 22 lines and each line has on average 10 words per line. Multiply 22 by 10, and you will find that you are reading at 220 WPM.

Next, go to the control sheet and write down the results.

Go now to the website below, and I will guide you through the process.

www.humansinflow.global/test

Test yourself twice and keep track of the results on the control sheet to be able to see your improvement.

Keeping track of your progress

Great! Now that you know your reading speed please jot it down on the appropriate boxes for "Test 1" and "Test 2" or in your diary.

CONTROL SHEET

			Reading speed increase in %
Test 1 Baseline	Reading speed WPM		
	Comprehension 1-10		
Test 1 Baseline	Reading speed WPM		
	Comprehension 1-10		▼
Fastest Zap	Reading speed WPM		%
	Comprehension 1-10		
Fastest Metro	Reading speed WPM		%
	Comprehension 1-10		
Test 3	Reading speed WPM		%
	Comprehension 1-10		
Test 4	Reading speed WPM		%
	Comprehension 1-10		
Test 5	Reading speed WPM		%
	Comprehension 1-10		
Test 6	Reading speed WPM		%
	Comprehension 1-10		

* WPM (words per minute)

This is what the results mean

Most people read at the same speed they talk; so if you talk fast, you probably read faster than those who talk slowly.

On average, adults read from 150–250 WPM. Below is a guide to show you where you are now. If your reading speed is:

- Below 200 WPM, you are a slow reader
- Between 200-300 WPM, you are an average reader
- Between 300-600 WPM, you are a speed reader
- Reading between 600-1000 WPM or above, you are a super speed reader

2.1.3 Read faster without training

Your inner voice slows you down

Having learned to read out loud at a very early age – and having gained a good proficiency – the teacher then tells you to read silently. The outcome of this guidance is that your voice gets trapped inside your own head. Inevitably, this inner speech ends up limiting your reading speed, albeit, you fail to realise this. You believe that everyone experiences the same thing; however, you also understand that some people have the ability to read faster, which you determine must be a blessing from God. In fact, God supplied us all with the ability to silence this voice and read quicker.

That is what we will be doing here; improving your reading power.

Silence your inner voice

First let's see how the brain works.

If I start speaking slowly – but very slowly – you get bored.

If... I... start... to... speak... even... slower... it... becomes... so... boring... that... you... will... disengage.

But now if I speak rather quickly... you get more interested and things make more sense. Don't you agree?

That is exactly what happens when you read slowly. Soon enough you will get bored. If you learn to go faster you start using your mind's eye to create the images described in the book. By imagining them you become motivated and you are more likely to remember what you read because you remember ideas that you create in your mind. You don't, and I repeat, you don't necessarily remember the words in the book, but the ideas that you create in your mind. We think in pictures all the time but we don't realise that.

Going faster you stay engaged, and become more focused.

The video game analogy

Just as with video games, you start a new game slowly. However, as you become accustomed to the game, you become faster and more efficient. This progress becomes more fun and you know that your brain will continue to learn and improve even quicker. I am certain that you will enjoy the exercises for speed reading and will adapt very quickly because they work just like video games.

Pay attention to the voice in your head; do you stop to take a breath like you are reading out loud? That is not necessary! Are you giving more emphasis to certain parts of the narrative?

You can read faster and it is not difficult. I will show you how.

To start, you will be learning to speak less mentally with fewer words in your mind. Just start to make a conscious effort to say only the bigger words inside your mind and don't waste your time saying the linking words like "and", "or", "but" or "the". They will not disappear from the paper and you will understand the whole text. You will probably save yourself 20–30% of your time by avoiding the words that are not charged with meaning. Just repeat mentally the bigger words and you will start speed reading; your focus will improve and you will be reading faster and faster the more you do it.

Go on, start saying the bigger words inside your head and avoid saying the linking words. See how much you can learn this way. I bet you will get the meaning of it without any extra effort.

I will put a black mask over the linking words throughout the next few paragraphs. Almost 33% of words are hidden and I believe you will get the ideas quite easily. You can start now! This is the first attempt of reading 33% faster.

Go ahead, read 33% faster by saving time looking only at the important words I've selected for you.

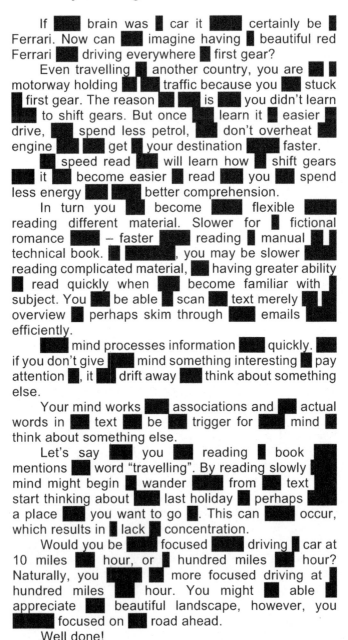

How you shift gears

If ▮ brain was ▮ car it ▮ certainly be ▮ Ferrari. Now can ▮ imagine having ▮ beautiful red Ferrari ▮ driving everywhere ▮ first gear?

Even travelling ▮ another country, you are ▮ ▮ motorway holding ▮ traffic because you ▮ stuck ▮ first gear. The reason ▮ ▮ is ▮ you didn't learn ▮ to shift gears. But once ▮ learn it ▮ easier ▮ drive, ▮ spend less petrol, ▮ don't overheat ▮ engine ▮ ▮ get ▮ your destination ▮ faster.

▮ speed read ▮ will learn how ▮ shift gears ▮ it ▮ become easier ▮ read ▮ you ▮ spend less energy ▮ ▮ better comprehension.

In turn you ▮ become ▮ flexible ▮ reading different material. Slower for ▮ fictional romance ▮ – faster ▮ reading ▮ manual technical book. ▮ ▮, you may be slower reading complicated material, ▮ having greater ability ▮ read quickly when ▮ become familiar with ▮ subject. You ▮ be able ▮ scan ▮ text merely ▮ overview ▮ perhaps skim through ▮ emails efficiently.

▮ mind processes information ▮ quickly. ▮ if you don't give ▮ mind something interesting ▮ pay attention ▮, it ▮ drift away ▮ think about something else.

Your mind works ▮ associations and ▮ actual words in ▮ text ▮ be ▮ trigger for ▮ mind ▮ think about something else.

Let's say ▮ you ▮ reading ▮ book mentions ▮ word "travelling". By reading slowly ▮ mind might begin ▮ wander ▮ from ▮ text start thinking about ▮ last holiday ▮ perhaps a place ▮ you want to go ▮. This can ▮ occur, which results in ▮ lack ▮ concentration.

Would you be ▮ focused ▮ driving ▮ car at 10 miles ▮ hour, or ▮ hundred miles ▮ hour? Naturally, you ▮ ▮ more focused driving at ▮ hundred miles ▮ hour. You might ▮ able ▮ appreciate ▮ beautiful landscape, however, you ▮ focused on ▮ road ahead.

Well done!

Early speed reading experiments

It dates from before the Second World War. The Royal Air Force had to train pilots to distinguish friendly planes from enemy forces in a very short space of time.

While in a situation of combat, it was necessary to acknowledge if the plane approaching from the rear was an enemy or an ally. Naturally, such behaviour and instincts were vital for survival.

One method to expand peripheral vision was to have pilots look at a cinema screen and flash images of different planes at a distance. The idea was to train them to recognise and remember a still image fast and precisely.

They flashed small pictures of planes for one second and the pilots could recognise them.

In one of the pictures they could see an image like this:

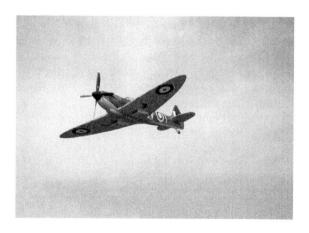

This is a Spitfire, a British war plane.

The groups of pilots were shown a new set of pictures for just one fifth of a second and they were surprised that most could recognise them so well.

A third set of pictures were shown for one tenth of a second and many could identify the planes, too.

The most amazing thing was that, after training, some pilots could identify the planes in less than one thirtieth of a second. According to RAF files, some of the top pilots would recognise a plane in one hundredth of a second, which is quite remarkable.

The trainers were so impressed with the results that they decided to expand the experiment and had a great idea:

What about flashing text, word by word, very quickly?

Would the pilots be able to read it?

They started flashing the words 50% faster, and the pilots understood everything. Then 100% faster than the average reading speed and the pilots were able to understand the messages. After further training, some of them were able to read even faster.

The pilots couldn't read faster on paper like they did on the screen

But there was a problem. The pilots would read very fast from the screen because their eyes were stationary and the words were coming towards them. However, when they were given a book to read, they had to move their eyes across the lines and reverted to reading slowly again on paper.

The secret was in harnessing the power of the right side of the brain instead of reading slowly with the left side of the brain.

Try it yourself and read faster! No effort required.

Watch the demonstration if you want to see how clever your brain is. You will speed read on the spot.

Now you will be able to see what the pilots saw. I will flash images of planes in rapid succession and one of the images won't be a plane but an animal. This will prove that you can assimilate information very quickly.

After that you will be able to speed read as if by magic.

For example, if your reading speed is 200 WPM (words per minute) you should watch the video that will flash words at 210 WPM and 315 WPM. You will experience reading 50% faster, and I believe you will find 315 WPM easier than 210 WPM.

I believe that you will understand the whole thing at this fast pace. It's really incredible...

If you've taken the test already, you know how fast you are reading and will be surprised with the results. Sometimes numbers talk louder than words.

If you didn't take the test, go to the webpage below to test yourself; if you've done it already, just skip the following line.

www.thespeedreadingcoach.com/test

Watch the planes and read faster on the spot.

Go to this webpage and select the appropriate video to watch based on your reading speed. Push play, and relax... Try a faster speed to test yourself.

www.humansinflow.global/flash

Well done, you are a speed reader already! Just do the maths to see how much faster you can read. Keep track of your improvement on your Control Sheet on page 235 under "Fastest Zap" or write it down on your diary.

Congratulations!!!

Did you watch the summarised version of The 7 Habits of Highly Effective People by Stephen Covey?

I have prepared it to be flashed 500 WPM. If you watch, it will only take you less than seven minutes to understand and learn the essential ideas from the book. This is really a no-brainer if you want to become highly effective.

It is like a video game; the more you play, the easier it gets. It will also help you to expand your peripheral vision, which will help you read any text faster.

I'm creating a library of summaries of great books so you can read them super-fast.

After watching the videos, you can also start using the software to read faster from your screen. It is FREE and very effective in helping your mind start accepting information at a faster pace. It will help you read normal text too.

I recommend you give it a try.

Just go to the following website, copy and paste the material you want to read inside the box, select the speed you want to read it at and then it flashes the words in a very effective way. You don't even realise that you're reading at a faster speed!

Check my website for the Free software that will help you perform better than ever.

Go to this page to try it out.

www.humansinflow.global/freesoftware

Now I will start to explain to you how to speed read a normal text without the software.

I'm sure that you are going to love it!

2.1.4 Preview and review

To preview a book it is important to understand that you should have a pretty good idea why you are going to read that book. This should set your purpose to read it. I flick through it, read the back cover, table of contents and a little from a couple of chapters. Finally, I look at the book and I have a feeling if I should read that book or not. And then I follow my instincts.

Reading a great book means that you read that book and the timing was right.

By reading a book for a specific purpose or with some intention you will find many good things in any book, because you are looking for them. I aim to find just one good idea from reading one whole book, and I end up finding quite a few ideas because I'm looking for them. If I find one great idea while reading it, I might consider it a great book.

Then comes the review, which means taking notes, creating Mind Maps or a summary.

You remember more of what you read if you write a summary using your own words, which is an active and a much better way than copying the words of the author.

2.1.5 Secrets to guide your eyes

Keep reading and saying only the key words inside your mind; did you forget to do it?

Knowing that you can absorb information faster, I would like to guide you through the first step of trying something straightforward, yet very powerful.

The idea is to use a pointer to help you move faster while reading. By using a pointer, you will start to focus better.

Your eyes naturally follow motion, so moving your pointer under the line you are reading will help you go faster because you will stop lingering for too long on each line and will also avoid regression.

You will make your eyes glide smoothly along the lines of text.

By giving your eyes something to focus on, you can create a rhythm to your reading and increase your reading speed.

Just understanding this alone will help you improve your reading speed by 10–30%.

Children begin pointing out words as they learn to read. However, as they develop their skills, they are discouraged from pointing out each word as no one expects them to read faster than their talking speed.

To get started you should use a pointer every time you read anything because it will help you increase your reading speed from now on.

Pick a book that you are interested in and want to use for your practice. It is best if it is non-fiction because you want to extract useful information from it. As you improve your focus, you will be surprised how many times the information is restated in a factual book. It is best if the book is not too technical, without too many bullet points, graphs and charts, as it really needs to be a continual text. Biographies can be factual but they are not a great choice to start with. It's preferable to choose a book that contains 10-12 words on each line. This will enable you to read with greater ease. If you are using a digital format, then make the pages big enough to have an average of 10 words per line.

It is OK to use a book you have already read. This is to learn the techniques and be confident while applying them. Once you get used to reading this way, you will naturally apply what you've learnt to any material you read.

If English is not your first language, you may also like to use books in your mother tongue; some people find it easier to learn this way and then apply it to written English.

The best option would be to keep reading this book and applying the techniques you learn while you read. I recommend that you read each chapter twice, if you feel the need to do so, in order not to worry about missing anything because you know you will be reading that chapter again. Give it a go and check the results later. I'm sure you will be surprised at how quickly you progress.

Now you need to choose a pointer. A long pointer like a bamboo skewer, a drinking straw or a chopstick is best. A long pointer is practical but you can also use a pen or even your fingertip. Moving your finger around, you will notice that your arm will grow tired quickly, but it will work the same.

2.1.6 Become a maestro to read in style

To make your horse run faster you will need a good stick to motivate it to accelerate and change the virtual gears into a faster pace. Some people think that whipping the horse is cruel but I think it is more like an embedded gesture that communicates that the rider is giving the horse the freedom to transform its energy into speed and you will see them enjoying the ride together.

A strong horse likes to be handled by a powerful rider and will try to throw over a weak or timid one.

As you are preparing yourself to develop your reading power, I will show you how to use a stick to signal to your brain that you want to increase your speed.

Reading can be compared to music as a way to entertain your senses, so I will create an analogy between the way the maestro conducts an orchestra by their baton with using a pointer, to create a new harmony to read.

To be a maestro also means to be a distinguished figure in any sphere, so I want to help you develop your reading skills to raise your standards.

The process is simple, and I've created the acronym BEBOP to guide you, as Bebop represents a musical revolution.

Bebop was developed in the 1940s, and it is the first type of modern jazz. It created great controversy because it was not melodic like traditional jazz but had lots of improvisation and extended solos of each member in the band. Some Bebop musicians I appreciate are Dizzy Gillespie, Charlie "Bird" Parker and Thelonious Monk.

So my BEBOP will revolutionise the way people perceive and interact with the written word by creating new flexibility to speed up and slow down while reading.

BEBOP stands for:

- B aton
- E ncourage to Advance
- B e Biased
- O ne Great Idea
- P itch Range

1. Baton

As you will be interacting with your book, your challenge is to make your eyes move around in new patterns. Being a maestro, your instrument will be a baton or a pointer, that will guide your eyes into new dynamics so you can explore your reading potential.

Whenever the maestro points at a member of the orchestra, he expects a complex harmony or a big chunk of the music to unfold. You will use your baton to guide your eyes along the lines, and you will be taking chunks of 2, 3 or 4 words at the time.

As you will understand later on about the power of the right side of your brain to help you take bigger chunks of words, you will start using your left hand to hold the baton, especially if you are right-handed. The reason is that the right brain is connected to the left hand so you will start to make this connection awaken some powers you were not aware you had.

2. Encourage to Advance

The maestro is in front of the orchestra to make all musicians move forward, even if someone makes a mistake the show must go on.

As you use your pointer to guide your eyes, your intention is also to keep going forward. Resist the temptation of skipping back to reread while in the middle of the page, finish reading the page to let the information settle in your mind and only go back to rereading it if after having finished reading the page you still have the urge to double-check some information.

By moving forward with enthusiasm, you will naturally begin to stop saying all the linking words mentally but will still understand the ideas in the text. Remember that the linking words form 33 per cent of any text, and if you put some pressure to speed up your pace, the first words that you will stop saying mentally are the linking words. Because they are there just to fulfil their grammatical role, you will see them but will not waste time on saying them inside your head and you will naturally start to read faster. With practice, you will begin by saying less and less words inside your mind and achieve speeds of over 500 words per minute. If you are not limited to reading at the speed that you talk you can achieve reading 1,000 or more words per minute. To be effective, you should never move your lips or your tongue while reading and your eyes should be relaxed.

3.   Be Biased

If you've ever played an instrument, you already know that whenever you listen or watch a band or an orchestra playing you will be hearing the instrument that you play better than all other instruments because you are biased by your interest and experience.

If you don't play a musical instrument you will miss out on the complexity of the song; if you don't sing you will probably misunderstand a few words because you couldn't be bothered to read the lyrics and understand the whole message and if you don't dance you will not appreciate the level of difficulty of a performer choreographing intricate movements in sync with the song.

Similarly, you will not be able to notice and absorb all the information and nuances from a book. You cannot grasp the entire information in detail in a book because you are always biased and blind to many other aspects that grab your attention. So keep reading and expect to understand what relates to you, and this could represent a comprehension level or 60, 70 or 80 per cent of the content. Be happy and read on because if an idea is important, I guarantee it will be repeated, similarly, there is usually a chorus that repeats the same lyrics or music.

4. One Great Idea

One song essentially has one central message, one article has one important topic, and a book has one main idea that will unfold.

You will be reading non-fiction books to learn something, and the author is there to help you understand their lifetime body of work. Unlike a Sherlock Holmes detective story, you will still follow the train of thought even if you miss a few details here and there.

Remember that there are plenty of unnecessary details throughout the lines you read so stay focused on the main idea you are getting from the text, and you will see the number of times the authors restate an information using a different context or examples.

We can only appreciate the music because there is silence intertwined in it. I highlight the importance of having a few seconds of silence whenever you read a great passage or reach the end of a chapter. Look up and use this moment to think about the main points of the text. Whenever you stop and remember the main ideas, you crystallise your memory, and you will remember the ideas you created in your mind more efficiently than the words you read. This is an exercise to help you understand actively, and it will also stimulate your creativity and imagination.

5. Pitch Range

As the music unfolds, you can measure the distance between the lowest and highest tones, or sound waves, that a voice/instrument can produce and establish the pitch range of a particular piece or song.

It's easy to understand that a slow song can make you feel relaxed, and an upbeat one can make you feel like dancing.

The analogy to the pitch while reading is profound because our brain produces specific brainwaves while you are chatting with a friend and other kinds of brainwaves whenever you focus on reading a book or studying. Your brain will produce mainly low beta waves while you talk to a friend and this is a great match, but if after the conversation, you decide to read a book, your brainwaves will be low beta to start with, and this frequency will make you distracted; therefore you will read without proper focus. By using the pointer, you will help yourself focus by guiding your eyes to read at a slightly faster pace, and this way the beta waves will intensify their activity, actively engaging your mind and you will be surprised to find yourself more focused on reading just because your brain will start producing medium and high beta waves. As you keep resisting the temptation to skip back to rereading, your brainwaves will keep increasing. Other kinds of brainwaves will be generated, and you might even enter a flow state and forget about time while you really enjoy the book.

I will explain how to get into flow state later, but to begin with, use a pointer to help you start changing your brainwaves, and you will feel the difference it makes to help you develop a better understanding of what you are reading.

It's interesting to note that we talk about cycles in nature and cycles can be represented by waves. You might want to stay entirely focused for one hour and achieve the flow state, but our waves of focus are usually much shorter. For example, you start reading a book and begin to focus your attention, but you break your concentration every time you feel the need to fidget. Then after ten minutes, you feel the urge to have a cup of tea and break the focus. Your attention will keep increasing, but suddenly it will decrease just to pick up again a while later.

The more you get into the habit of setting a more extended period of uninterrupted time to read, study or work, the more likely you are to get into flow and have two, three or even five times more done in the same amount of time. I recommend that you stay focused for at least 30 minutes at the time and to make this happen, you should turn your mobile phone into airplane/sleep mode or cancel all notifications, just like I do, so you too can boost your productivity to incredible levels.

If you feel a little anxious or tired while increasing your reading speed remember to take a deep breath and relax your body and eyes. This simple act will help you stay focused longer.

2.1.7 Start reading with a pointer, and just let yourself flow

Now it is time to put the theory into practice.

You know it makes sense to read only the words which carry essential meaning, but you've probably noticed that making this distinction while reading is a complicated task.

The good news is that by using a pointer, you will do this mental gymnastics of silencing the inner voice automatically. The pointer will make you move your eyes faster, and you will not linger on any word for too long, making you see them all and read faster.

Linking words are just like wallpaper, they don't hold the house together, they only make it look good.

Now, take a pointer or a pen and keep reading this book using it. Just push yourself a little bit to help you go faster.

You can start now!

Are you already using a pointer? That's great!

Give it a try; this is the beginning of your training. It is easy, and it will help you perform better from now on.

I believe that you will feel like creating a pace for yourself, and the information will start flowing in, at a different speed. It will feel like you understand more with less effort.

This is the magic of using a pointer.

2.1.8 Skipping back to reread is a waste of time

You will avoid skipping back if you understand this simple idea. Based on experience, I estimate that we skip back to rereading about 30% of the time. If you become more focused and start skipping back only

259

10% of the time, you will be reading 20% faster without even applying any technique.

One Page Forward Method

From this point on, I advise you to stop going back whenever you don't understand something you read. Read the entire page before going back to reading it again. The information you've missed is very likely to reappear before the end of the page, or you will come across the same information but restated in a much clearer way. So don't panic and keep moving forward.

Most of the time, you go back without being aware of it. Involuntary eye movements make you skip back to double-check the information without you noticing what is going on. What is essential is to be aware of what you are doing and stay in charge. Don't let your eyes dart back on default mode. If you decide to go back, be aware of what you are doing.

If you know that you can always go back, you don't focus, you get distracted, and your brainwaves don't start changing to give you better comprehension.

The habit of going back undermines your confidence, and you end up getting bored and you stop reading the book or text because you don't become engaged enough.

Of course, you are free to skip back but try not to do so and keep your mind switched on to engage again and follow the train of thought.

So, skip back only if it is imperative to do so. Tension creates engagement, and by the end of the page, your mind will get back on track, and you will get most of the content anyway.

If we make a comparison between reading a book and watching a film, I will point out some important correlations:

I'm from Brazil and I've been living in London for more than 19 years. Whenever I'm watching a film, I really need to pay attention because there are so many accents that come with new regional words and expressions that make it impossible to understand everything I listen to. It is also very difficult to grasp certain lyrics in music and quite often I miss bits of information in face-to-face communication when the person uses words that I'm unfamiliar with.

The *Oxford English Dictionary* lists more than 750,000 words; and according to the Google/Harvard Study, there are more than 1,020,000 words in the English language, and each word can have multiple meanings. The English *Wikipedia* has 5.9 million articles (2019) and it averages 800 new articles per day. So, now I know that even if I wanted to understand everything that I see on television or a film, it would be impossible for me or any other native speaker, too. There will always be some accents that we find difficult to understand. We are soaking in cultures that change words and create expressions. If I am watching a movie and I don't understand what someone is saying, I carry on watching it without pausing and I catch up on the plot later. Sometimes I try to understand that weird accent from Scotland and I understand what I can. I know, my accent is weird, too. I'm Brazilian. So there will always be noise in the communication because more and more people are learning how to speak English.

Depending on your profession and social class, you will develop a particular vocabulary that will help you expand yourself in new areas of knowledge. A clever doctor might read a simple brochure for financial services and it will appear to him to be a completely different world, which is why we hire advisors so they can translate the language to us and we can make a wise decision. It's all down to vocabulary.

Sometimes you are watching a film on TV and you go to the kitchen during the commercial break to get something to snack on and you get back more than three minutes later. Do you get desperate for missing part of the film? Not that much. Do you switch the television off because you've missed three minutes? No, you carry on and try to catch up with the film.

Whenever you start reading a non-fiction book, you should apply the same principle of keeping going. If you miss something that doesn't seem to be very important, you could just carry on and try to catch up with the development of the book and be aware that if you miss three minutes of a film, it would equal to

261

around three pages that you've skipped. The author will be very likely to repeat the same idea in different words because they want to explain something very well to a big audience and this takes repetition. Normally, books do not have a *Sherlock Holmes* plot that if you miss one tiny detail you will be missing an important clue to the mystery. The authors are on your side and will help you understand a concept using examples and analogies so keep your cool and read forward as much as you can.

So, just remember that we can't understand it all because there are more than one million words in the English language and, according to the Global Language Monitor, a new word is created every 98 minutes. We use around 3,000 words for ordinary conversation. For more advanced conversation you will use 5,000 but you will need more than just the words! You need context and expressions, too.

According to David Crystal, a world-renowned expert on the English language, a person starting school knows 500-6,000 words; before starting a degree they would know 50,000 words, and by taking a degree they would know 50-75,000. Most of these words are passive vocabulary, which means that they might understand the words but will never use them.

According to Professor Alexander Arguelles, a language learning expert fluent in eleven languages, the number of words we know grows with education and I quote his findings below:

"250 words constitute the essential core of a language, those without which you cannot construct any sentence.

750 words constitute those that are used every single day by every person who speaks the language.

2,500 words constitute those that should enable you to express everything you could possibly want to say, albeit, often by awkward circumlocutions.

5,000 words constitute the active vocabulary of native speakers without higher education.

10,000 words constitute the active vocabulary of native speakers with higher education.

20,000 words constitute what you need to recognize passively in order to read, understand, and enjoy a work of literature such as a novel by a notable author.

The maddening thing about these numbers and statistics is that they are impossible to pin down precisely and thus they vary from source to source."

The following graph is a simplistic representation of vocabulary and the number of words in the English language.

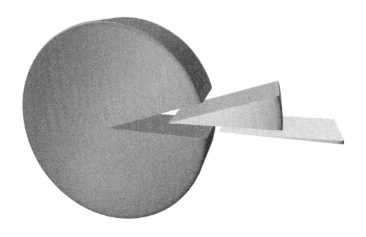

0.5% - Native basic vocabulary is 5,000 words

5% - Native vocabulary after Degree is 50,000 words

95% - Natives with Degree will not learn 1,000,000 words

Stay engaged

Relax and read with a purpose. If you read a whole book and find just one great idea that you can implement in your life or work, then the book was really useful. So read and keep searching for that one good idea. It might happen that you will find more than one, but the intention is to read actively instead of reading passively. If you have a question in your mind you will be able to take your own conclusions and will get the big picture anyway. New words will come and go; just pay attention to the message and look up a word that starts appearing quite often. There is a way to learn and remember new words that I will explain when I talk about the right side of the brain.

Keep reading with your pointer because it will help you to start going faster and you will get more focused while reading.

HORSES READ QUEST

Vision Two

EXPERIENCE FOUR RHYTHMS TO READ

"Change the way you look at things and the things you look at will change…"
Wayne Dyer

By reading this vision you can expect to improve your reading speed from 20–90% or more!

If you are familiar with horses like me, you already know that all horses have four basic gaits.

They can walk at 4 mph (6 km/h), trot at 10 mph (16 km/h), canter at 14 mph (23 km/h) and gallop at 30 mph (48 km/h). As they go faster, their legs move in specific ways.

When they trot they lift each diagonal pair of legs alternately. When they gallop all their hooves are off the ground at the same time during each stride.

In the same way, you will increase your reading speed if you understand the natural reading speed paces that suit your reading needs.

2.2.1 Easy practice with pointer and rhythm

Just by using a pointer, I believe that even at this stage you will be faster already. It might be hard to register 5% or 10% improvement, but if you are 20% or 30% faster, you have probably noticed that you are not skipping back so much to re-read and are moving along the lines more smoothly.

Keep using the pointer while reading the next set of instructions. Your eyes will get used to the new system in no time at all. It's important to synchronise your eyes and your hand. The results will speak for themselves.

Keep reading with your pointer

If you are right-handed, start moving your pointer with your left hand. This way you will be using the right side of the brain and the results will be even better. I will explain about the right side of the brain in more detail later. If you are left-handed, keep using your left hand.

If you didn't like switching hands at all you can keep using your right hand.

Your brain is amazing, and if I would compare it with a real machine, I would say it is a Red Ferrari.

Most people have a Ferrari for a brain but they go everywhere in first gear. This is a waste of time and petrol and you will strain the engine...

Now you will start to shift gears and will start to go faster with less effort and more comprehension will follow.

Remember that you always start in first gear and then you shift gears up as you go along. Go faster when you can but if you find difficult terrain, you slow down to third, second or first gear again. Be flexible and remember that your gear stick is the pointer that you have in your hands.

Now you will start shifting gears...

The metronome is your gear box

You will be using a metronome, which is a little machine, software or App used by musicians to help them play music at exactly the right pace by following a rhythm. If you play the piano, drums, guitar or any other instrument, you are probably familiar with it. If you have never heard of it before, it is easy to understand. You can learn how to play a song, but if

266

you play it too fast or too slow, it won't sound good. So, the metronome will help you play at a constant rhythm and once you get used to the clicking sound, your fingers will start moving with the rhythm automatically. At this point you can switch the metronome off and you will be playing the song at the right pace.

I'm borrowing the metronome from music to help you increase your reading pace. To get started you will find the rhythm that matches your reading speed right now. You play the metronome and keep reading with a background sound. Once you are comfortable with it I will increase the pace, and you will use the pointer to make your eyes start moving faster in sync with the sound. The increase in understanding from the text will follow shortly after.

2.2.2 On your mark

Before I show you how to use the metronome to instantly improve your reading speed, I want to share an interesting way to boost your mental power.

We all feel a little insecure before trying something for the first time, so I want to share a scientific way that can help you become more assertive.

Boost your confidence to succeed in two minutes flat

Amy Cuddy is a social psychologist, and she noticed that men and women that occupy a position of power usually have higher testosterone levels which are associated with confidence and risk-taking. They also have lower levels of cortisol, which reflects a lower level of stress.

She observed that powerful people have body language that displays their dominance. They find ways to take more space by expanding the space their bodies take up. Examples of these power poses are:

- Sit down on a chair, put your feet on the table and put your hand behind your head

267

- Someone celebrating their victory in an athletic competition would open their arms while reaching for the skies and tilting their heads up
- Stand tall, shoulders back, chest out, spread your legs and put your hands on your hips like the Wonder Woman or Superman

Just by sitting down on your chair and spreading your arms out, or over the back of your chair, will show your dominance.

This discovery is the result of a series of studies. In one study a group of men and women were interviewed for a job. Half of the participants held a power pose for two minutes, just before the interview, and a saliva sample was taken before and after.

The other half were instructed to sit down with their legs together and make themselves smaller. Some would slouch with their shoulders rolled inwards, which is the typical posture of someone using their mobile phone. The second group stayed in this position for two minutes, and a saliva sample was taken before and after.

The surprising result of this study is that the people that held a power pose before the interview were more relaxed, assertive and confident. The interviewers wanted to hire the ones that were power posing and also evaluated them more positively than those candidates that were making themselves smaller before the interview. The results also showed that those that were power posing immediately raised their testosterone level by 20% and lowered their stress by dropping their cortisol level by 25%. The group that was scrunched up had opposite results by lowering their testosterone by 10% and showed a raise in their anxiety by a 15% increase in their cortisol.

So, now that you are about to try something new, you will perform much better if you have a higher level of confidence and a lower level of anxiety. I am now inviting you to choose a power pose and hold it for two minutes before you start the speed reading exercise. It will rapidly change your hormone levels and also make you perform better at reading.

You will boost your confidence, enthusiasm and your willingness to take risks instantly. You will feel like you are doing the right thing, will adapt to the new reading speeds with ease and will have a better comprehension of the text.

So, pause for a couple of minutes before doing the exercise with the metronome and the pointer. This is a decisive moment! You will build your confidence to read faster and the results can last a lifetime. Choose a power pose and feel the power growing inside yourself. If you decide to go to the kitchen to make a coffee, before you hold the power pose, walk like a champion would walk. You will definitely feel the difference.

Remember that this is a strategy that you can use anytime you want to be more assertive and confident.

If you want to watch Amy Cuddy explaining the *Power Posing* experiment in a TED Talk, go to the website below and search for her name. She also wrote a fantastic book called *Presence*.

www.ted.com

Now you are ready to speed read!

2.2.3 Get set

How to read faster using the metronome

You will have to go to the webpage below for this exercise.

www.humansinflow.global/audio

Once you are there, you will play the video that is suitable for you, based on the results of your reading speed tests.

For example, if your average reading speed was 200 words per minute, and your book has ten words per line, you will play the video with 20, 25 and 30 beats per minute (BPM). This video plays all three rhythms in sequence. The first rhythm is intended to be close to your actual reading speed.

Please choose the appropriate video to suit you.

You need to follow the rhythm and read one line per beat. Considering that every line has ten words on average, you will be reading at a speed of 200 WPM. Just multiply the rhythm by the average number of words per line in your book to know at which speed you are reading.

You can practise the exercise by continuing to read this book or choose a book that has on average ten words per line to make things easier.

The rhythms will start at 20 beats per minute, which means that you will hear 20 little "clicks" in one minute, like a clock ticking very slowly.

You should be using your pointer to help you keep up with the pace and will read one full line at every single beat. Move the pointer, under the words, from the beginning to the end of the line slowly and in sync with the rhythm. Every time you hear the "click" you should start a new line, so you will cover one line for each "click". If you don't like using the pointer you can try with your fingertip instead.

You will start reading at 200 WPM. You need to keep up with the rhythm for two minutes to get the hang of it. I will increase the speed from 20 to 25 and to 30 BPM. Your left side of the brain will find it difficult to follow, so your right side of the brain will kick in and start giving you the comprehension that you want. This will happen more so because you will start to expand you peripheral vision and will be able to see and understand more words at every fixation.

After reading at 200 WPM for two minutes, I will then increase the pace to 25 beats per minute or 250 WPM, after which time, you shall try to read for two minutes at 300 WPM, which is 50% faster than 200 WPM.

If you have a shorter line at the end of a paragraph, spread all the time you have in that line and linger there so that you keep in sync with the rhythm.

It is best if you move your fingers and wrist instead of moving your whole arm to make your pointer go sideways. Less energy spent moving your body will result in greater comprehension.

At the beginning of every new rhythm you will have to get used to it, and in a little while your comprehension will start to improve.

If you don't have good comprehension don't worry, just keep up with the exercise to get comfortable at one reading speed. You will understand the mechanics of reading faster in the next few chapters and your performance will keep improving as you learn more about your reading skill.

2.2.4 The secret sauce

Now I am going to share with you one of the greatest secrets of this book. As you start to read faster, your comprehension will decrease. Comprehension will only arise as a result of you being stable in one of the rhythms. You might be surprised to notice that a faster pace might give you better understanding than a slower one, so try them all. Some people need just a few minutes to adjust to a new pace, while others might take a few hours.

Choose to focus and understand. I tell you that you can!

2.2.5 BEBOP System

Become a maestro to read in style. Read the summary of how to move your pointer for better results below. I made the full explanation about it at 2.1.6 – page 244.

Baton – A pointer helps you take chunks of 2-5 words at a time by switching the right side of your brain on while reading so you will begin to stop saying all the words in your mind.

Encourage to Advance – Avoid the habit of skipping back to reread by forcing yourself to get to the end of the page. If you really want to reread you are free to do so if you are aware of what you are doing. Don't let the autopilot take over and you will become more confident to take the information in.

Be Biased – Each one of us sees the world according to our values system, so we naturally see all those things that relate to us and are blind to what we don't think is interesting. Read with the intention of finding connections with useful information and by trying to use them you will develop your memory with confidence.

One Great Idea – Fortunately there is a lot of repetition on non-fiction books so keep looking for the main idea and don't worry if you miss a few details here and there. Stop and think for a moment whenever you find valuable information. This way you crystallise your memory by creating it.

Pitch Range – By using your pointer, you will start to focus your attention to reading faster, and as you keep moving forward your brainwaves will begin to change to medium, and high beta waves, which are the best brainwaves to give you better focus and understanding. As you progress, you are more likely to get into the flow state and really become more productive.

2.2.6 Go!

Keep using your pointer and play the video that suits you on the webpage below to start reading with the metronome. Start it now!

www.humansinflow.global/audio

I recommend you choose another book of your choice for the practice, but you can carry on reading this book.

These six minutes have changed many people's lives as you will have the first experience of reading at three different speeds. Everything is very new and you are just stretching your power to digest information at a different pace. You will start changing gears in your mind.

This is just the beginning!

After having your first experience with the metronome, I want you to think about it. Which pace worked best for you?

Each person will achieve different results. Those who begin the course starting at 200 WPM might feel confident to increase their reading capability while improving on their overall comprehension to 300 WPM. It can take some time to gain full understanding; however, as long as you stay in one particular rhythm long enough, your brain will find a way to give you the comprehension you deserve.

It is fascinating to me when someone goes from 200 WPM, to 500 or even 600 WPM, with great comprehension. To do this requires having the ability to relax and as the peripheral vision expands, the results can be outstanding. This is the moment when the left side of the brain gives up full control and starts to support the reading process, while the right side takes over. The act of reading becomes a whole-brain activity.

This is the first time you have experienced this accelerated way of reading, and you will develop more and more with continuous practice.

Once you finish listening to your video, you can then decide which speed you liked the most.

Go to the webpage below to listen to a free metronome online, and select the new rhythm to keep reading your book.

http://a.bestmetronome.com

The best metronome you can get is a free App called **Pro Metronome**, which is available for iOS and Android.

Download the App and once you open it you can change the T.S. from 1/4 to 1/1 by touching on it and adjusting with the minus (−) sign. Then select the rhythm that will help you get consistent in one single reading speed.

The App is great because you can speed up the beats one notch at a time and get the perfect rhythm to read any text. Make sure it plays just one sound throughout and not two different notes.

This is how the **Pro Metronome** App looks like:

If you want to programme a sequence of beats to suit your needs you can upgrade to the *Practice Mode* £0.79 (this is one of seven possible upgrades). Open it by clicking a little clock at the bottom of the screen. You will be able to create a sequence of rhythms like the examples below by choosing the **Automator** and **By Time,** once you are inside the **Practice Mode.**

- 15, 20, 25, 30 beats per minute, that will play in sequence. Six minutes each
- 45, 55, 65, 75 beats per minute, that will play in sequence. Five minutes each.

I have many sequences to choose from on my website, but by upgrading the App you can change the sequences as much as you like. This way you will have more control on finding the best possible rhythm to improve your speed and achieve good comprehension.

Don't forget to use your pointer and you will keep improving as you read this book.

2.2.7 Raising your comprehension

Your brain is prepared to understand whole expressions at once, so stop holding on to individual words and start to recognise expressions. Soon enough you will start to foresee the future and will reach the conclusion before the author reveals their own point of view.

Using the metronome, you will notice that you can follow the new pace; however, your comprehension suffers a lot, and therefore, you can't link everything together in your mind because it will seem too quick at first.

The brain is so clever that if you can't perform a task well, it will find a way to get the best results. And the results come fast.

The metronome goes from 30–100+ beats per minute, so don't be nervous as it is possible to read at 1000 WPM and beyond. This can be achieved when you are reading something that you feel comfortable with, which is the result of practising with the metronome. The more you practise, the better the comprehension. Imagine being inside a dark room. For a moment, you can't see a thing. However, after two or three minutes, you begin to get used to the dark and start to see. Reading faster works in much the same way. The more you practise, the more consistent you become, and the greater your comprehension will be.

The following graph illustrates that whenever you go faster your comprehension drops. But keep your speed stable and your comprehension will get better and better until you can understand everything that is relevant to you.

Comprehension level drops when you start to read faster and increases if you keep reading at a certain speed for some time.

Comprehension in %

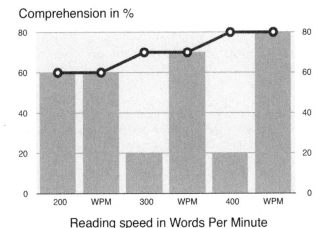

Reading speed in Words Per Minute

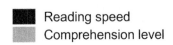
Reading speed
Comprehension level

We filter information all the time so you will remember things that are relevant to you. You will never remember everything written in a book, as that is not possible.

A lot of text is just padding and doesn't come with much content; it is just light commentary about what the author is about to present you with, so learn how to skim through parts that you might think are not relevant. Don't feel guilty about jumping around if you are reading a non-fiction book. You should have a purpose and look for things that are important to you.

You can choose the rhythm that you are most comfortable with whilst you are reading. Read for around half an hour or more. You can always change the track if you wish.

Knowing that your comprehension levels will drop if you go faster will help you to relax with the knowledge that such levels will increase if you spend enough time reading at that very same speed. Don't be anxious; read for some time with your metronome.

Continue to practise with the metronome.

2.2.8 Many subjects will not interest you, but

If you are talking to a group of friends, you will feel connected with the information that is meaningful to you. Sometimes, however, you will disconnect because someone is talking about a subject that you are not interested in at all and your mind switches off. Let's say that someone is talking about their kids and you are not really interested in them because you don't have any children and can't relate to their drama. You disconnect and don't pay attention to what they are saying because your mind is filtering reality according to your own way of seeing the world. If you *are* interested in children there will be many subjects that won't attract you like politics, football, fashion or the Middle East conflict. You keep learning certain subjects and others you simply ignore.

We filter information all the time with the RAS

There is a part of our brain called the Reticular Activating System (RAS) that gives us the ability to consciously focus our attention on something. In addition, the RAS acts as a filter; dampening down the effect of repeated stimuli such as loud noises or visual pollution, helping to prevent the senses from being overloaded. In fact, the RAS helps us to function in life by constantly deleting, distorting and generalising information to be able to cope with two million bits of

277

information that reach our five senses and our conscious and unconscious mind every second.

Can you remember a time when you were planning to buy a new car? Maybe a Mercedes Benz for example; suddenly you see so many Mercedes around that it can be quite overwhelming. The same might be said for women who are pregnant – they notice lots of other women who are pregnant everywhere they go.

Have you had the experience of learning a new word and suddenly you open a book and there it is again. Moreover, you might switch on the radio and you hear that same word repeated yet again. That is the RAS that stopped filtering that strange word by giving it meaning and now it appears in your virtual landscape.

So, by filtering information you are constantly selecting to pay attention to certain things and deleting other items from your conscious awareness.

In the same way, you will not understand many things in a book or text because your RAS automatically erases information that you don't relate to.

Based on that observation, I want to reinforce that you should avoid skipping back to reread as much as you can because your RAS will also find relevant information for you. I believe that it makes more sense now.

You can get frustrated because you don't have enough vocabulary. But remember, if you are learning a subject you should expect to find new words in the same way you know that the author will explain the new concepts in different ways, and then you will be able to grasp the information. It is therefore useful to know, that to learn any subject, you will have to learn new words and will need to improve your vocabulary. The English language has more words than any other language. Just to put it into perspective we have at least four times more words than Shakespeare had available in the 17th Century (according to Karl Fisch and Scott McLeod. YouTube: Did you know? Shift happens). Remember that it is not only the number of words that make a language but the number of new expressions too.

A solicitor has a different vocabulary from a doctor or a stock-broker. They just happen to know more words as a perk of their trade. Some words they've learnt without much explanation and others they had to ask someone or they have looked up in a dictionary.

We are all limited by our ignorance and you will expand your experience in this world if you add new words to your vocabulary.

100% Comprehension doesn't exist

Pareto was a mathematician who created the well-known *Pareto Principle*, which is also known as the 80–20 rule. It states that in general, 80% of the effects come from 20% of the causes. This principle can be applied to many fields and just to give you an example, I could say that 80% of your profits come from 20% of your customers. This is true for a big proportion of businesses. Now applying the same principle to books I could say that 80% of the important information will come from 20% of the content of a book.

Generally speaking, non-fiction books are not a detective story. You may think that if you miss a little detail you will jeopardise the whole book but you won't.

Relax, I believe that 20–50% of what you read is just padding! Hold on, it's not what you think!

I wrote this book with a few key messages and I repeat myself 20-50% to reinforce the main ideas with theory, history, examples, stories and practice.

I like the analogy of thinking that each chapter of a book is a beautiful room in a house. The author will guide you through many long corridors to show you each room. The corridors might have paintings on the wall, carpets, flowers and light features and you glance at them but don't pay full attention to these details because you are really interested in the room you are about to enter. Whenever you enter the room you might be enchanted by it and all the details that make it so special. The room will make a big impression on you. So focus on the room and don't worry too much if you don't remember the details of the corridor.

Even if you score 100% on a comprehension test you cannot say that you know 100% of that subject because our mind filters reality. So, as a result we see a reality that is moulded with our preconceptions and is focused on our interests.

It is incredible that we can only see what we are programmed to see. All those advertisements for broadband didn't really exist until I decided to look for a new provider. They are not there because I can't see them. Do you understand how it works?

My advice is that you shouldn't be so hard on yourself while reading because 100% comprehension doesn't exist. You will always stumble on a new word or expression, but you shouldn't be any less motivated to go ahead.

If you find a golden concept in a chapter of a book, it will be a concept that you will find the meaning of even if you miss a little bit here and there. I'm not advocating being superficial. I'm just aware of our limitations and extreme standards that we think we can achieve. I just want you to relax. Keep reading in search for new ideas or concepts. I hope you can enjoy reading more because an average book will become a great book if the timing for reading it is right. So read more and progress in life faster.

2.2.9 See your blind spot here. It exists

Sometimes we have a psychological blind spot and we can't see our glasses while they are just in front of us. What you might not know is that there is a real blind spot on each of our eyes. In the back of our eyes there is a specific place where there are no light detection sensors because that area is occupied by the nerves that link the eyes to the brain.

To see what I mean, observe the following picture. Just cover your left eye with your hand and stare at the letter X at all times. Your right eye should be straight in front of the letter X. Slowly move closer to the X, until the moment that the rabbit disappears completely from your field of vision – as if by magic. This is because your eyes can't see from that angle and the blind spot hides the rabbit.

X

If you can't find your keys in the morning, you have a mental blind spot. Then a relative comes and picks up the keys from under your nose and you are astonished, realising that the keys were in front of you all that time and you couldn't see them. This is called "scotoma".

In the same way, you have a mental blind spot if you can't see certain matters in life because you don't pay them attention. Your blind spot can be football, the stock market, gossip magazines or any other area you know very little about and there are areas of knowledge you are not even aware that exist.

There is a lot to learn in this world and books are a perfect source of education. You can create a window of interest in your life by deciding on the areas that you wish to learn more about.

Each one of us see the world in a different way

The Reticular Activating System is responsible for opening these windows of perception so you can see the world in a very particular way. The RAS gives you focus and if you have a question in your mind, it will start looking for an answer inside your memory banks and will be searching for the answer at all times and places. This is important because if your purpose is to read and focus your attention on *"What is in it for you"*,

you will find something that you can apply and take advantage of.

But if you don't start reading actively, you will end up reading the whole text and remember very little of it. So, the tip is to "Think" of a reason or outcome when you get a book to read. The purpose doesn't have to be directly connected to the subject you are reading. You will find what you are after.

For example, if you are frustrated with your meetings at work, you can focus your attention on finding better ways to run them. You might find the answer reading a magazine at the dentist or reading a book about entrepreneurship.

This is the RAS in action. Having a purpose, directs your judgment in a way that will give you more and more arguments to protect or develop your point of view. If you support a football team or a political party, you already know that you see reality very differently from your opponents. We think things are good while they think things are bad, and vice-versa.

As a general rule, you will learn much more from a conversation or a book if you know what kind of information you are after, because you start using your inquisitive mind instead of reading passively.

I've heard some successful people say that:

"The quality of your life will be directly connected to the quality of your questions."

I believe that you will be more successful if you ask better questions. I think this is a great way of thinking.

Because we watch too much television, we end up getting used to receiving information in a very passive way.

Studies have shown that watching TV stimulates the production of low alpha waves in the brain, which are usually associated with meditative states. While meditation can promote insights and relaxation, watching a lot of television promotes unfocused daydreaming and it can weaken your power to focus (no wonder people are more suggestible while watching TV).

I haven't had a TV for many years; however; there was a time when I was hooked on it. If you keep watching television for too long every day, you are probably addicted to it. If you are a parent, please consider controlling the amount of TV your children watch or perhaps challenge the whole family to have one full week without the TV. You know you can live without a TV set if you are on holidays in a foreign country so hide your TV in the garage and see how it can change the way you and your family use your time.

Remember that reading stimulates your creativity, imagination and memory.

2.2.10 Developing your focus

Persistence is fundamental to focusing your mind

When I read *Outliers* by Malcolm Gladwell, I learned that most people who succeed are those from families or cultures that teach people to persist at what they are doing for longer. For example, solving a maths problem before giving up on the task.

It makes a big difference if you only spend 20 seconds before giving up than if you spend two minutes before asking for help. Those that go a little bit further – go all the way and persist – will achieve great results. If you look for the answer you will find it.

If you persist and read a book with a purpose, you will use the book to help you find a solution for any problem or challenge you might have. Have an objective to read and you will be reading actively instead of reading passively and getting distracted.

Meditation can help you read faster

Another way to harness your mind power, develop your focus and improve your reading performance is to practice meditation.

After many years dabbling with meditation, I decided to study it properly by jumping into the deep end and enrolling myself on a ten-day silent meditation retreat. To sit down on the floor for ten hours a day, for ten consecutive days was a gruelling experience, but to my surprise, I learnt how to really focus my mind. As a result, I had the privilege of understanding the world from a new level of consciousness and experienced a state of ecstasy I didn't know existed.

Fortunately, I found new ways to achieve deep levels of meditation that are easily accessible to someone without any previous training. I will explain meditation further in the book, but you can look at the following webpage to start familiarising yourself with meditation.

www.humansinflow.global/meditation

HORSES READ QUEST

Vision Three

ACHIEVE GOOD COMPREHENSION

"It is not the strongest that survives, nor the most intelligent. It's the one that is most adaptable to change."

Charles Darwin

By reading this vision you can expect to improve your reading speed by a further 10–50%, so why not try.

When riding a horse, whenever you increase your pace, you will be unstable in the saddle until you learn how to move your body in synchronisation with the horse.

When reading, your comprehension could also be wobbly when you introduce a new pace. As you get used to reading at a faster pace, you relax and start to feel confident. Once you start reading at a consistent and stable pace, your comprehension level will rise.

2.3.1 Watch the eye tracker in action

Your eyes move in strange patterns to read, so in a moment I will show you the eye tracker in action, and you will see a person's strategy to read in real-time. It is an incredible sight! But before I do, I will show you the mechanics of reading so you will understand how it is possible to read faster.

First you need to know how your eyes work.

Your eyes can see things clearly when you hold them still. If an object is still, the eyes must be also still to be able to see it, and if the object is moving, the eyes must move with the object to be able to see it clearly.

If you pay attention to a person reading the paper or looking at a computer screen, you will notice that their eyes keep jumping throughout the lines.

Your eyes keep shifting and focusing on to every single thing they want to see clearly. In fact, they change focus or move around once per second.

The following text shows the eye movement while reading.

The dots are the places where your eyes stop while reading. Notice that they actually stop five or six times on each line of text.

If you prefer to watch a video with real time eye movement, then please go to the link below and see how your eyes behave while you read. I think it is incredible.

The eye tracker combines software and cameras that focus on the eyes of a person so it can show precisely where the person is looking at. The demonstration is very important to watch because you will see how you read in real time and how you can get distracted because of involuntary eye movements. Go to the webpage below to watch it.

www.humansinflow.global/eyetracker

Your eyes stop far too many times per line to be efficient

I bet you are surprised to have seen the eyes moving while reading. When you read, it is important to synchronise the speed by following each word with the movement of your eyes. Your eyes keep moving their central focus and stop every second.

Because you are reading at the same speed that you talk, you have no reason to move your eyes faster.

Typically, they would stop six times on each line; like in the following paragraph, if you were reading at around 250 WPM:

    .   .   .   .   .   .

Read faster to get more focused while reading.

You will see all the words in sequence and will stop six times over the line. You don't read each line in a smooth fashion; in fact, your eyes will be jerking from one group of words to the next.

Stop less times and you will see more

Now, to speed read I will help you go faster, your eyes will be stopping fewer times on each line and you can still see and understand all the words.

If you were to stop six times on each line, the next step that I will show you is how to stop just three times, and as a result, you will be reading 100% faster. Simple isn't it? If you end up stopping only twice on each line you will be reading 200% faster. You will get used to expanding your peripheral vision and instead of seeing two or three words every time you stop, you will start seeing three, four or even five words at a time. Because they are in perfect sequence, you will understand the meaning without much effort. It is just a matter of practising a little bit and your brain will get used to it.

It is also interesting to notice that you will overlap your field of vision every time that you move from one fixation point to the next, so you see the words you are reading at least two times while reading a typical line. What a waste of time.

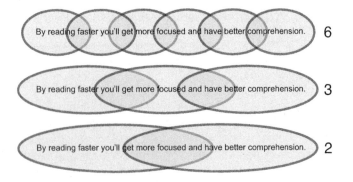

6

3

2

Now stop for less time each time you glance

The second way to enhance your reading speed is by jumping ahead as soon as you get a glimpse of the words. Just move faster and your brain will catch up and start enabling your comprehension. Just like it is difficult to play a video game in the first few minutes, it then gets much easier and you keep chasing the performance and speed. You can get tired eventually but it is stimulating to go faster.

When you read a line, the eyes keep jumping and stopping. The jumps take almost no time, but the fixations can take anything from one and a half seconds to one quarter of a second.

This way the eye takes short gulps of information; in between it is not actually seeing anything, it is moving from one point to another. We don't notice these jumps because the information is held over in the brain and integrated from one fixation to the next, so that we can perceive a smooth flow. The eye is rarely still for more than a couple of seconds. Even if you feel the eye is completely still by looking at a question mark, it will in fact be making some small movements around the point. If the eyes were not constantly moving in this way and making new fixations, the image would rapidly get fuzzy.

A slow reader, who pauses at every word and skips back reading the same word two or three times, will not be able to understand much of what they have read. By the end of a paragraph the concept is usually lost, because it has been so long since the paragraph had begun. By constantly re-reading, their ability to remember fades and they start doubting their ability to remember at all.

Their ability to read diminishes and the person re-reads more, then loses more trust in their memory and finally assumes that they don't understand what they are reading.

Let's say that on average you stop your eyes for one second. If you start stopping for half a second you will start reading 100% faster again. If you stop for one quarter of a second you will be reading 300% faster again. Do you remember that you could see the image of the planes in the video at one tenth of a second and the chick was flashed at one thirtieth of a second? So seeing a word at one quarter of a second is really possible.

2.3.2 More practice and the quantum leap

To help you understand the quantum leap you just made, I want to tell you a short story that illustrates what you've been through while practising to read with the metronome. You will be surprised to learn what happens inside your mind.

If you drive a car in your city or town, then you are driving most of the time at 30 mph (50 km/h); however, if you drive on the motorway, you gather speed until you are driving comfortably at 70 mph (110 km/h). Suddenly, you see a sign that indicates a small town ahead and you should slow down to 30 mph (50 km/h). You hit the brakes and slow down to a speed that seems to be slow enough to avoid getting flashed by the speed camera, which will ultimately result in a fine. Then you look down to check the speedometer and you realise that you are actually travelling much faster than 30 miles per hour (50 km/h).

It is very interesting how your brain gets used to the higher speed and then it doesn't want to slow down to levels that were acceptable before. You actually reset your mind at a faster speed.

It is important to know that:

When your mind is stretched to a new dimension it never goes back to its original shape.

Once you begin to speed up with your pointer and rhythm, you will start to feel comfortable at higher speeds. Naturally, you will begin to read faster. The mind starts to take in information using the right side of the brain; it is working so quickly that you don't have time to say the words in your mind.

Another secret of speed reading is that if you start reading at an even pace – let's say 500 WPM with the help of the metronome and the pointer – your comprehension will catch up.

This is the same principle of video games. You start playing and it feels very fast. Keep playing and your brain will get used to that speed because it is steady. Your response will enhance in a matter of minutes; an improvement which can be measured by your scores.

In the same way, your brain will give you the comprehension if you keep a steady pace for some time on one rhythm. The amount of time will depend on each individual person and also be variable according to the complexity of the material you are reading.

After continuous practice, you will read faster. The secret is to keep reading at a speed that is not too demanding, until your brain gives you that comprehension.

The insight

The magic happens because your brain works with feedback; whenever your eyes stop at the right place for the right amount of time you will have some comprehension. Your brain keeps track of the right strategy that yields the best results and will tend to repeat it. When this happens you will start understanding the text you are reading at 300, 500 or even 700 WPM. You should keep focused on the text but the actual process of developing is unconscious and relies on the coordination between brain, eyes and your pointer.

Be aware that different books will require an adequate reading speed, so try a few speeds to find the best one for a specific text.

Now decide which speed you liked the most and select the rhythm that will help you get consistent at one reading speed.

Keep playing the metronome to read this chapter.

Don't forget to use your pointer and you will keep improving as you read this book. Use the pointer with each of your hands and notice which one gives you the best understanding.

2.3.3 Important words can distract you

Did you know that words are not so important in face-to-face communication?

Research done by an expert in communication, Dr Albert Mehrabian, shows that only 7% of face-to-face communication is down to words. This is incredible because 55% of the message is expressed by facial expression, body language, eye contact and eventual touch. However, 38% of the content is delivered through the pace that we talk, volume, tone of voice, accent, pitch and much more.

Now you can understand why it is so difficult to focus your attention on reading material.

You read at the same speed that you talk and while you receive 100% of the message, the information given through words amounts to only 7% of the content. So only 7% of your effort is directed to the words and you can understand the whole conversation.

So, if you start reading a book at the speed that you talk, you would need only 7% of your energy to be able to understand the text. This way 93% of your attention needs to be redirected, otherwise your mind will start drifting away from the text and you will lose comprehension.

Your mind can process information very fast, but if you don't give it something interesting to focus on, it will disengage and get distracted. The problem is that you have too much mental power that is idle. Most people think it is difficult to speed up their reading because it will demand too much energy and focus, but in fact, they need to redirect their energy and comprehension will arise. It might sound like a paradox but it is not.

The important words hook you out of the text

Your mind will look at words that will trigger memories or random thoughts.

For example, let's say that you come across the word "trouble". If you read slowly, your mind can stop concentrating on the text and you start thinking about "trouble". Maybe your Tax Return or perhaps you will imagine how your client might react to a late delivery. You keep imagining things outside the book and it goes on and on.

The mind works with associations and will visually connect new ideas with others that lie in the unconscious mind.

Your brain loves speed

Our mind loves speed because fast is fun. As you learn to go faster you will start using your mind's eye to create the images described in the text. Your imagination will be activated, you will become more motivated and it is then that memory is created. It's not the words in the text but the ideas that you create in your mind that you will remember.

Another example of the brain working at speed would be playing a video game. The game has many levels and the higher the level you reach, the faster your brain has to think and the more exciting it gets.

With a bit of training you will develop quickly and will have more fun, either on computer games or while reading because your brain loves speed.

2.3.4 Getting ready to read really fast

Now that you've read with the metronome and have been reading faster by using the pointer, you are ready to stretch yourself a little more and start developing your comprehension levels even further.

The first time you used the metronome sequence I was helping you to stretch your mind. Now we will be doing the same exercise with a twist.

This time I will play three rhythms in sequence, i.e. playing 30, 40 and 50 beats per minute. I will also stop playing the beats after playing each rhythm for about a minute. You should keep reading at the same pace you were reading while in silence by moving your pointer at about the same rhythm.

Once you reach 50 beats per minute (BPM), I will start going backwards and play 40, and then 30 BPM. I am sure that it will start to get easier because, after stretching your mind and reading at 500 WPM, your mind will become more active and you will read faster with less effort. Even if you didn't understand much at 40 or 50 BPM, your mind was working hard to gain some comprehension from the text and you will find it much easier to read at 30 or 40 BPM after reaching 50. I will play the beats to get you started on each rhythm and you keep the momentum going once I stop the beats.

Do you remember I said it feels very slow driving at 30 miles per hour shortly after driving at 70 miles per hour? The same principle will work when you read at 30 BPM just after reading at 50 BPM. Your brain will get stretched again and comprehension levels tend to increase. You can practise on any book of your choice.

2.3.5 BEBOP System

Become a maestro to read in style. Read the summary of how to move your pointer for better results below. I made the full explanation about it at 2.1.6 – page 244.

Baton – A pointer helps you take chunks of 2-5 words at a time by switching the right side of your brain on while reading so you will begin to stop saying all the words in your mind.

Encourage to Advance – Avoid the habit of skipping back to reread by forcing yourself to get to the end of the page. If you really want to reread you are free to do so if you are aware of what you are doing. Don't let the autopilot take over and you will become more confident to take the information in.

Be Biased – Each one of us sees the world according to our values system, so we naturally see all those things that relate to us and are blind to what we don't think is interesting. Read with the intention of finding connections with useful information and by trying to use them you will develop your memory with confidence.

One Great Idea – Fortunately there is a lot of repetition on non-fiction books so keep looking for the main idea and don't worry if you miss a few details here and there. Stop and think for a moment whenever you find valuable information. This way you crystallise your memory by creating it.

Pitch Range – By using your pointer, you will start to focus your attention to reading faster, and as you keep moving forward your brainwaves will begin to change to medium, and high beta waves, which are the best brainwaves to give you better focus and understanding. As you progress, you are more likely to get into the flow state and really become more productive.

Start playing a video from the second set of videos now!

Go to the webpage below or open the Pro Metronome App and select the individual rhythms or create a bespoke sequence to play.

www.humansinflow.global/audio

Select the right video for you and get ready with your pointer!

2.3.6 Karate Kid and you

Do you remember *The Karate Kid* film? If you've never seen it, I'll tell you the story in a few words.

Mr Miyagi, an old karate master, comes out of retirement when he is befriended by a teenager called Daniel, who is constantly being beaten by bullies at school. Daniel pleads with him to teach him karate in the hope that he can learn to defend himself.

294

Mr Miyagi agrees to teach him the art of self-defence but on condition that Daniel will commit to any request that he asks of him – without question. The training begins with Daniel having to sand the floor at Mr Miyagi's home, paint his fence and then wax his car.

Daniel, feeling frustrated of having to work and not having any karate lessons, complains to the master, who tells him that his training had already begun. To prove it, he threw a punch at Daniel and said with his commanding voice: "Wax on!"

The boy – obeying without thinking – blocked the punch with precision.

Daniel was learning karate while waxing the car because he was coordinating mind and body. In the same way, you will train your mind to see differently by using your pointer. Once your eyes learn how to move and stop over the lines, you will have good reading speed and comprehension. After some time practising, you will not need the pointer anymore. Your eyes should go where you want them to go and the pointer is a fundamental part of the training.

2.3.7 Choose a rhythm to practise and get good at it

The secret lies in going at a higher speed of, let's say, 400 WPM by following the rhythm of a metronome. If your normal reading speed is 200 WPM, you will be reading 100% faster with some help from your pointer.

In the first few minutes you try to coordinate the pointer though the rhythm and the comprehension will not be very good. Perhaps ten minutes later you will get the hang of it and then you can see the words rushing in sequence at a faster pace.

Your brain loves a challenge and it performs very well when you try to play a video game for the first time. The improvement can be seen second after second. You learn the tricks, your mind gets sharper and your coordination becomes first class.

That is exactly what we will be doing. Make your eyes go fast and then your visual perception will start to kick in and you will then see more and understand it better because you are more focused. These are the results of switching the right side of the brain on. It will come alive when the task at hand is not suitable to the academic left side of the brain. The shift is made automatically.

Choose 400 WPM and keep the pace for some time. If you don't understand it, it is because your left side of the brain likes safety and will try to retreat to the traditional reading pace. But if you stay there, the left side will come out of its comfort zone and will be ready to give up. The right side is very holistic and understands the big picture and will take over the situation. This is the moment that the text starts to make sense. This is the big shift. You will start using your whole brain to read, instead of reading only with the left side of your brain.

You should read with purpose in mind or perhaps a question.

One that I like is this: How can I use this information?

Being in this frame of mind, you will be reading actively and not passively. Ask any question and you will activate the Reticular Activating System (RAS). If it were not for the RAS, you would become paralysed being faced by so many interesting things everywhere you go. The RAS make things easier. It helps you focus your attention.

So, choose one of the rhythms of the metronome and practise reading with it for half an hour. You can always switch it on and off while keeping the same pace. The comprehension will increase and you will become more confident to read faster and absorb the message from the text you are reading. Pick up another book to practise. After playing one of the video sequences to warm up, choose a rhythm to read for half an hour, and get good at it.

Don't move your mouth while reading

If you mumble or whisper the words while reading, you should stop doing that because it holds you back in terms of speed and your reading will be limited.

By wiggling your tongue inside your mouth, you will hold yourself back in terms of performance, too.

Measure your improvement

You can test yourself again; let's see how fast you are going just by using the pointer and the metronome?

You can ask a friend to time you or use the timer on your phone.

Time yourself for exactly one minute while you read your book and keep track of your progress.

Chances are that you have improved a further 10–40% just by using a pointer and the metronome to help you get more focused and stop skipping back.

If you didn't improve much, don't worry because I will show you other exercises that might be more beneficial to you. Much more to come! So keep reading.

2.3.8 Expanding your peripheral vision

The pointer will help you control your eyes

If you hold a pointer and make a spiral in the air in front of a person, their eyes will follow your pointer in a round swoop.

But now ask them to move their eyes in a spiral motion like before, but without the pointer as a guide, and their eyes will move in a jagged way, and not in a round spiral at all.

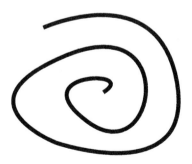

Using the pointer your eyes make a perfect spiral.

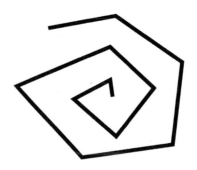

Without the pointer your eyes move around
in a jagged way.

Try this exercise with a friend and you will see that without a pointer the eyes go places that they were not supposed to go.

If you read with a pointer and train your eyes to read faster, after some practice, your eyes will know where to go and you won't need the pointer any more.

Expand your focal vision

I think that the way we are taught to read might have a massive impact on the speed with which you feel confident to read, perhaps for the rest of your life.

I believe that children should learn to read with the Analytic Phonics, also known as the Whole Word, approach instead of Synthetic Phonics, which teaches each letter and its sound before going into creating words.

Instead of absorbing two or three letters at a time, we can absorb four or five words at once and have good comprehension. Just expand your pericentral vision and read faster.

Having a scientific mind and based on a book called *Dyslexia Breakthrough* by Collin Corkum PhD and Jerri Girard-Corkum PhD, I found evidence that the way we are taught to read can activate only the very centre of the central focal area in the retina, which is called foveola. Some people will read slowly for the rest of their lives if they don't start to expand their focal vision. The earlier you learn how to expand your vision, the better.

As you can see in the image below, the foveola measures 0.35 millimetres in diameter, which is wide enough to focus clearly on four or five letters. If you read only with the foveola, which most of us do, your eyes will have to move far too many times to read. Some people might develop dyslexia as a result of this self-imposed limitation on the field of vision.

If you learn to read using the fovea, which includes the foveola and measures 1.5 millimeters, you will be able to read four or five words at once or five times more information than with the foveola alone. This way you can achieve a very good reading speed and read from 400–800 WPM.

The Parts and Functions of the Retina

◯ **Central focal area (foveola)**
– 0.35 millimetres in diameter
– Readability: 4–5 letters
– Average reading rate: 200 WPM

⬤ **Pericentral focal area (fovea)**
– 1.5 millimetres in diameter
– Readability: 4–5 words
– Average reading rate: 500 WPM

⬤ **Peripheral vision area**
– Gives general information outside the focal areas

The exercises in this book will help you increase your focal vision, so you will become confident in reading fast and efficiently.

Please note that you should remember to start using your pointer half an inch (1 cm) after the beginning of the line and stop your pointer half an inch (1 cm) before the end of each line. Your peripheral vision will see the words at ruthe extremities of the pages without having to go all the way. If you move your eyes from the beginning to the end of the page you will be using your active vision in the margins and this is a big waste!

The intention is to save fractions of seconds everywhere, so the result will be a great improvement.

Stop moving your head sideways

Some people move their heads sideways while reading one line of text. This is not necessary; your eyes can do the work and by not moving your head you save energy which can be used on comprehension. Can you imagine reading 100 pages of a book? You would be moving your head sideways 3,000 times. This really is a waste of energy.

Your head should be relaxed. Don't move it, just move your eyes.

This is ideal:

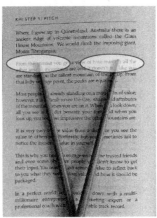

Start half an inch in and finish half an inch before the end.

This way you will expand your active vision.

You should avoid this:

If you move your pointer through the whole line you will waste your active vision in the margins and miss the opportunity to expand your pericentral focal vision.

Practise eyerobics to develop your pericentral focal vision

Now that you've learned the basics you should keep reading the book using your pointer. Use it all the time and don't worry if people look at you using a pointer to read. They will actually be surprised to see you moving your pointer or pen down the page very quickly. If they ask what you are doing, you can just say that you are speed reading.

At this stage of the training you will be activating your brain to start expanding your focal vision to be able to see three, four, five or even six words every time you stop your eyes on a line of text. The easiest way to activate the brain is to move your eyes faster. With practice, your focal vision will naturally expand

and you will start moving your eyes less while you learn more because your focal vision will have developed enough.

Watch films with subtitles

I recommend you watch movies with subtitles and you can practise speed reading just by glancing at the text and developing your pericentral focal area. Read the subtitles of a film in English; you will notice that, although you may not understand many of the words the actors are saying, you are still able to follow the story. As a result, your comprehension will increase, and your mind will work better to read the subtitles and also have the time to watch the scenes of the film. Watching a movie in a foreign language is even better because you will rely on your speed reading ability to follow the plot. This is a great exercise.

2.3.9 Computers can read and you can foresee the future

Bag of words on computer vision

There is a model in computer vision that is called "Bag of Words model". For example, "a good book" and "book good a" are the same under this model because it ignores the word order. This model can give you a lot of information about a text if you consider the Natural Language Processing. This means that computers can now read a text email and answer it without anyone looking at it.

Knowing that our brain is a sophisticated computer, I would like to introduce you to the "Bag of Letters model", which will give you great understanding of a text even if the letters of a word are jumbled up.

Read the text below with your pointer and don't linger on the words; your mental computer will give you the meaning of the text anyway. Some people have already noticed that they can read faster when the words are all jumbled up than when the words are written in the normal way. This is because it is very difficult to say a word in your mind if you can't say it

302

out loud. This way, they end up avoiding the mental chatter and understand the text anyway. Strange but true.

Now it is your turn to try it for real. Get your pointer to help you move forward faster and read the text below.

This is relaly amzaing. Even thuogh msot of the wodrs beolw are jublmed up you can stlil undesrtand the txet. You can crack the cdoe if the fsirt and lsat lerttes are corrcet and will strat raeding fsater tahn you wuold raed the txet if it was wirtten in the tratidional way. It's diffiuclt to suond the wodrs isnide yuor haed as you raed the wodrs wrttien in a diffrenet way so you will strat reaidng fatser withuot noiticng.

This is graet becuase to be frnak I'm raelly bad at seplling.

The relevant message from this text is that you will have better comprehension by not focusing on individual words. The brain can process text more effectively if you can recognise a few words at a time.

Take a look at the word below. What does it mean?

Etinesin

You are probably puzzled because you've never seen this word before.

But if you read the word inside a sentence it becomes much easier.

Ablert Etinesin is accliemad as one of the gretaest and smertast siecntsits of all time.

If you have the bigger picture, all the words make more sense.

Grouping words together will help you read more effectively and you will increase your reading speed, too.

Now you can also understand that we read using mental templates that give you meaning inside a context. We think that the words are important but expressions are even more so.

If you can raed somehting and can geuss waht is coimng nxet you will be albe to undsertand the txet and strat foresieeng the futrue.

You can predict what the author will say

Sometimes you read new information; other times, the information is completely expected and you can then skip it without loss of comprehension or just use your pointer to speed up one or two lines.

The idea behind speed reading is to become flexible and go faster when you can and slower when you need to. So, you will probably be going a little faster now and a little slower when there is a need for it. If you start reading for longer, you might gain a second wind, which will give you a lot of comprehension whenever you get into a flow. You will probably forget you are reading and will have a smooth experience.

I was born in Brazil so my mother tongue is Portuguese, which is a language based on Latin like French, Spanish and Italian.

If you've ever learnt one of these languages, you might agree with me that Latin languages are more casual and you can say the same thing in many different ways. People in Britain are usually polite and you can almost predict the next few words they are going to say when talking to someone. The English language is full of expressions that will be repeated endlessly.

You can be reading in any language and you will always find those expressions that are full of meaning but can be read almost like one single word. Whenever you notice that a well-known expression is coming just jump a little ahead.

Pay attention to the fact that most authors keep using the same jargon of words and expressions, and this is called a literary style.

Finish the sentences and you will understand what I mean by predicting the future.

He didn't mind all the shouting. He was cool as a _____

Stop that! Don't cry over spilled _____

Their shop is always busy and they are selling like hot _____

If you learn another area of knowledge you will then be faced with new words and expressions. Once you become familiarised with them, you can also speed read them. If you stumble upon a word two or three times, it is a sign that that word is quite important to learn; however, if it doesn't appear again just move ahead without regret.

You know more than you think so trust that you are following the train of thought and move ahead faster and with confidence.

Measure your improvement

You can test yourself again; let's see how fast you are going?

You can measure yourself by reading the next chapter for one minute.

You know what to do so keep track of your development.

Chances are, that by just avoiding the margins of the book, you will improve both your peripheral vision and your speed reading by a further 10–20%.

2.3.10 More practice using your awareness

You cannot expect to read faster if you don't train your eyes to go faster. This eye exercise will make the muscles of your eyes get fit very quickly, but you need to stretch the muscles to keep relaxed and strong.

Now I will show you how to relax your eyes and you can do it in two different ways:

If you close your eyes and squeeze them together for a few seconds, you will release the tension from them. So, now blink your eyes a couple of times, squeezing them together or open them very wide, look up, down and sideways. Do it a few times and feel your eyes relaxing.

The other way is to rub your hands together and when you feel the heat on your palms, cover your eyes with your hands to energise them. It feels good.

This is how to move your eyes down the page

Once your brain starts to process information faster, the eyes will start to move less and will see more, due to the increase in focal vision.

In the example below I've underlined the area that you would be covering with your eyes when you start reading new text or start a new chapter or article.

The idea is to create a smooth transition from the traditional way of reading into speed reading.

You can observe that the eyes would cover the first few lines in the traditional way so you can get the first impressions of the passage very clearly.

As you become familiar with the text, you will start speeding up.

Read the text below, concentrating on reading only what is underlined and see if you can understand the text.

If you go from the beginning of the line until the end you would waste your peripheral vision on the margins.

If you pay attention to the text you can figure out if there is something interesting to come or something that you can foresee. A lot of the time the author is waffling – even repeating – therefore if you got the message you will even be able to skip a few lines because you can see what is coming next.

You will learn that you will gather speed as you keep reading and get into flow. As you move forward you will feel more confident in not reading all the lines and also will start expanding your peripheral vision even more.

Practice with your pointer will give you more control and you will build your confidence by getting the message.

Great! You are doing very well and just by learning these principles you will be reading faster automatically.

Parallel Reality

Now the big surprise. Whenever you keep reading and start to go above 500 WPM, your eyes will stop moving sideways as much. Instead of both eyes converging to the same words, they will start to move along the line in a parallel gaze, which means that each eye will see different words and your brain will integrate the message in an instant.

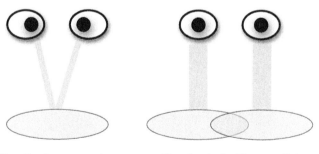

Reading by converging
150-500 WPM

Reading by looking parallel
500-1,000+ WPM

The following lines show the eye movement of someone reading at 500 or 700 WPM. Notice that the underlined words on the left will be covered by the left eye and the words underlined on the right will be covered by the right eye. This is just a schematic representation of the eye movement. You will start to go down the page quite quickly once you start to read faster and your focal vision will expand even more.

At the beginning of the practice you were making both eyes move along the lines very fast and the intention was to activate your brain to receive information faster. Once it gets used to this new stream of information it will be natural that they start gazing at the lines in a parallel motion. You won't need to move your eyes sideways so much and will naturally develop speed by seeing more while moving your eyes less. This is really incredible and this is the reason I call this stage "Parallel Reality".

To get you really confident, to read faster you should practise reading newspaper and magazine

They are great because the narrow columns are much easier to read than long ones. Articles have a catchy headline and you can get the information you need quite quickly if you feel secure to plough along. If by the end of the article you feel that you didn't get the main points, then just read the article again at a good speed. It is also very reassuring to read an article again because only then do you realise that you understood most of the text. It's harder to retrieve information than recognise it by reading for the second time.

If you concentrate on the centre of the line, you will find the words easier to define. Don't get scared if you start seeing two or three lines at a time and understand the message in narrow columns.

You start by reading the first few lines from beginning to end at a slower pace. Then you stop covering the margins and start to go faster. Whenever you follow the train of thought, keep connected to the main message. Be flexible to skip, scan and skim the text aiming to get the core message. As you get the message you feel more confident to go faster in the next article.

Sometimes you will be moving your eyes in a slight zigzag motion down the page. If you know a little bit about the subject you are reading you will find the new information amongst the padding. As you get more confident you might start to see two lines at a time and even skip a few lines that have information that is not relevant. I'm trying to show that each eye will stop in a slightly different place.

Practising free flow

Now let's practise again. This time things will start to get easier.

You will choose the rhythm that you think you are more comfortable reading and you will read with it for 30 minutes.

If you feel like changing tracks halfway, that's fine.

It is also good practice to play one rhythm for some time and stop the beats but keep reading on. After a while the beats will be inside your head. It is good to make the transition between having the beats on and off and keep the reading in a new flow.

This is like the stabilisers on your bike when you were a child or the person holding the bike from behind while you were trying to balance. It is a happy surprise to notice that you are riding without any help but at the same time you felt supported.

Please remember to go forward and avoid going back to re-read a line all the time. Try to go until the end of the page before deciding to go back. If you miss something it is OK, try to pay more attention and you might find out that the important information will appear again somewhere else before the end of the page.

Get ready and practise on another book for about 30 minutes before reading the next chapter.

2.3.11 Bounce around and be in charge

The Bouncing Style

If you don't use the metronome support you can use the "Bouncing Style".

Knowing that your eyes follow movement you can move your pointer across the lines and stop two or three times over each line and develop your reading ability. This way your peripheral vision expands and you give yourself a pace to read that will push you to improve over and over again.

It is enough to stop fewer times and get the big picture, see the important words and move on. Your mind will give you enough detail so you can understand the content.

Try it now; keep reading this book until the next chapter and practise by using a pointer or a pen. Stop two or three times on each line and remember not to linger on each stop too long. Your eyes can see an image in less than one hundredth of a second so trust yourself and the comprehension will follow. Dare to go faster... and miracles will happen.

START BOUNCING NOW!

2.3.12 Reading with a pointer on your computer

As you may have noticed, reading with a pointer can be very practical if you are reading paper material or if you're reading on your iPad or Kindle; however, if it's on your computer screen, it can feel a little awkward. My advice is to hold your pointer halfway between the screen and your eyes. This way, you can introduce a new rhythm and get used to it while bridging the transition from using a pointer and reading without it.

You can also use your mouse cursor to guide your eyes through the lines, although I prefer using a pointer. Try out both options and do what suits you best.

It is also interesting to notice that some people hold their books or reading material too close to their eyes. Once you start speed reading, you will be expanding your peripheral vision and will be able to hold your book a little further away. This can help you adjust the best distance for yourself by moving the book back and forth.

2.3.13 Music Sync

To support your reading with a rhythm, and also give you the flexibility to change reading speeds seamlessly, I've created the Music Sync.

You can experiment with music tracks I've selected for you or use a song that you like.

I prefer to use electronic music and "House Music" style is my favourite. You can listen to them by going to the webpage below.

If you choose a fast paced track with 116 beats per minute you will not cover one line per beat like you were doing with the metronome, but you will synchronise the beats with the "Bouncing Style" and bounce once per beat.

For example, if your book has ten words per line and you bounce four times on each line, you should touch the line four times and also listen to four beats on each line. At this pace, you will be reading at 290 words per minute. If you feel that you understand the text well you can switch to bouncing three times per line while listening to just three beats on each line. Your reading speed will increase by 34%, and you will be reading 390 words per minute. Once your understanding improves you can start bouncing only twice on each line, your reading speed will increase by 49%, and you will be reading 580 words per minute. Then if the content starts to become a bit more challenging, you can begin bouncing three times again, and your reading speed will decrease from 580 to 390 words per minute in a smooth way.

The music is much softer and fluid than the metronome, and at this fast pace, you can feel free to speed up or slow down without changing the rhythm. If you enjoy the precision of the metronome, you can also set the metronome to a faster pace and use the same principle of the Music Sync to bounce.

Keep changing to increase your level of flexibility and adapt to the difficulty level of the material you are reading. Refer to the table on the following webpage to find out your reading speed, accordingly to the number of words per line of your book or text as you play the tracks.

www.humansinflow.global/musicsync

2.3.14 Set yourself a realistic routine and great goals

Success in a new ability comes when learned properly, practised daily and used in your everyday life.

If you commit yourself to practise the techniques you've learnt and read at least 15 pages per day, you will change your life for the better.

Remember, it's not enough to "learn" how to speed read; you need to practise all the steps to master it! You can improve from 20% to more than 100% by practice alone!!!

With your best intention you plan to read regularly and set yourself a target of 15 pages a day, but the chances are that you will start strong but will give up after a month or even less. New Year's resolutions work the same way.

What I want to teach you is a system that will keep you motivated because you will always reach your target, every single day, and with almost no effort!

Choose a book that you really want to read to start using this system.

Using the *Minaxi Target*

I love the system that combines a mini and a max target, that I've named *Minaxi Target,* which will help you reach your goals and establish a new routine avoiding failure from the start.

I recommend you to set a target to read 15 pages of a book every single day!

This may seem reasonable but there will be some days that you will not have the time to read the 15 pages. A couple of days like this and you break your routine, and before you know it, you've stopped your daily reading habit all together. This happens because you break the chain of events that would stay strong if your life was boring and uneventful; but it is not. You need to deal with unexpected events that will take you off track. For example, you are invited to a party and so you don't have the time to read your 15 pages. You decide that to keep on track you will read 30 pages the

313

following day to compensate but then it feels overwhelming and you don't read anything again. This is the beginning of the end! Don't get trapped in a commitment that is too difficult to keep up. Give yourself a little flexibility and it will be much easier to stay on track!

I would like you to think that you have a mini target that would be very easy to achieve, which is just one page a day. It's going to be very easy for you to keep your commitment now! You can read one page in bed, commuting to work, during your lunch break, or you can even keep a book in the bathroom for a quick read.

The good thing is that some days you will start with the one-page challenge and before you know it, you will have read 15 pages, which is your real target. Other days you will be really engrossed with the book and read 30 pages; this is the max target!

What's important is that your target is easily achievable and it will lead you naturally to the next target, and with little effort on your part.

So, decide today to pick up a book and start the *Minaxi Target* to help you create the habit of reading books.

You can track your progress by using your diary. Mark on each day how many pages you've read and you will become more motivated to read more and more every day of your life.

The example above is my personal *Minaxi Target*. You can do the same as me or choose the target that feels right for you.

Stop using the pointer

At this stage you can stop using the pointer, while maintaining the bouncing technique, using only your eyes. You will get the hang of it and your eyes will have an internal rhythm to follow. Your peripheral vision will expand and you will get to a new comfort zone in no time at all.

The bouncing technique works very well for books, but it is especially good for reading small chunks of text like emails or small articles. Practise for yourself and measure the results!

A new strategy to bounce

After spending some time practising, you will see that you don't need to point two or three times but just once on each line and go down in a slight zigzag.

The easy way to experience this is by reading an article in the newspaper. The headlines are usually very catchy phrases that leave a question in the air. This is the reason you read the article, to find the missing link or a specific piece of information. So, now get the paper or a magazine and try to read by tapping your pointer just once on each line. The columns are narrow and in no time, you will be able to see two or three lines at once, perhaps more than that. You can also use this technique on books.

Now start reading with or without your pointer. Apply the techniques described above and go on a zigzag. I believe that you will be surprised to understand the text because now your RAS will make all the relevant information stand out.

The text below is simulating a column of a newspaper or magazine to make you understand how easy this technique is.

Start the zigzag now!

2.3.15 There is a lot of repetition in books as you can see by now

I believe that we talk a lot to say very little, and when you are reading a non-fiction book you will realise that 20–50% of the

315

information is just padding and repetition. Don't worry too much if you miss a sentence because it is very likely that it will come back again in the conversation.

I found this quote from Mark Twain that is very insightful:

"I am sorry to write such a long letter. I didn't have time to write a short one."

I've been very interested in producing book summaries and I found out that the English language is redundant for up to 70% of the time, according to Dr John Davies, who leads the Semantic Technology research group at BT and developed a software to summarise text called *Prosum*. This significant figure means that we repeat ourselves all the time. Exactly like I've just done now. I said redundant and I guess you know what redundant means, however I've explained it and written: "This means that we repeat ourselves all the time." Do you realise how much repetition there is out there and we don't notice it is just repetition?

Now I'll repeat myself for the third time and I'll give you an example:

"The little boy went to school in the morning."

It seems a simple sentence but notice that when I say boy it almost implies that a boy must be little, little boys go to school and, apparently, in England if they don't, their parents can go to jail. And I don't even need to mention that the school is in the morning. Got it?

So, as you can see, I kept repeating myself in different ways and we do it all the time; so keep reading forward and notice how much the same ideas are repeated.

My intention here was to repeat a few concepts I find interesting and useful. Repeating so you will remember how much people repeat themselves while talking and writing.

Read faster to get the big picture by seeing what matters and being able to skip, scan or skim what is just padding.

2.3.16 Squeezing or revealing text

As you experiment reading without the pointer, you can use a piece of paper or card as you work your way down the page.

Please look at the following pictures.

Showing text from underneath.

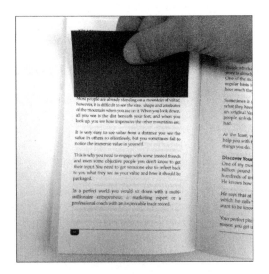

Covering text from the top.

Read the next chapter without the pointer. Instead, use a piece of paper or a card to help you to read faster. Just try; if you like it, you can do it more often.

Measure your improvement

You can test yourself again and let's see how fast you are going.

You can measure it yourself reading the next chapter with or without the pointer for one minute.

2.3.17 Breaking an old habit

A picture is worth a thousand words

You know that if you look at a picture you understand the image without having to describe all the details in words. You also know that a picture is worth a thousand words. This is very true because the left side of the brain deals with words by being sequential and linear while the right side appreciates and understands whole images.

Now look at a word like it was an image; a self-contained package of information that you don't need to read but you will recognise as a message. Logos make you aware of the cost of any purchase. In the same way every word is a logo or icon. You can understand it just by looking at it instead of reading them from beginning to end.

Silence the inner voice

The way to silence your inner voice is to look at words not as sound units, but image units that make sense and can communicate ideas.

For silent readers, they make micro-movements with their tongue as they associate the sound of their own voice. To break this habit you can apply pressure on your tongue with your teeth.

Clamp your tongue lightly with your front teeth and keep reading!

319

It is very interesting to notice that some people feel very strange and awkward by not having the freedom to move their tongue freely while reading. This is very enlightening because they will break an old and engrained habit. As soon as your brain starts to disconnect with the imaginary sound and the need to wiggle your tongue inside your mouth, you will naturally start to read faster. I bet you are experiencing this already.

Reduce the noise inside your head and switch off your imaginary voice

Firstly, your imaginary voice will never go away completely. Your voice is your friend and your identity; it will be with you whenever you start thinking to yourself, writing something or even when you read a headline or a small article. But there are ways to make the voice subside while reading. The voice will come and go and this exercise will help you get more detached from the need to speak words inside your head to be able to understand their meaning.

There is a way to silence the voice. The role of the voice is not necessary to understand the text – it is just a long, established habit.

Today you will break the pattern of associating comprehension with the sound of your imaginary voice.

Some people that can *touch type* can already write without the sound of their voice because they end up typing faster than they can talk. This is proof that you can process written information faster than the speed of your normal reading.

So, now you will try something a little different...

It will be fun and it will bring you amazing results. Your mind will start digesting knowledge without the sound.

To stop your imaginary voice saying the words inside your mind, you will create another voice that will be humming a sound like ma, ma, ma, ma, inside your head, or out loud if you are alone in the room. You will not be able to say two things at once so your imaginary voice that says the words from the text will start to subside in order for you to keep repeating a syllable.

Comprehension will develop as you practise because you will start to understand the message visually.

This exercise will help you develop this detachment while you say something like ma, ma, ma, ma, and keep reading. As you can imagine, it is difficult to understand the text but your brain is cleverer than you think.

Keep reading this chapter and saying ma, ma, ma.

Start doing it now! Start humming!

Your attention will start to split and you will begin to feel confident, saying something that is not in the text you are reading, while understanding the text. You will start improving your reading speed straight away; just persist on the training reading while saying ma, ma, ma, for a few pages of a book. This is a great warm up. Once you start feeling lighter from having to say all the words inside your head it is time to gather speed again on your book. Get your pointer, stop humming and start reading faster than before.

Your brain will start to feel free from the imaginary sound of the words you read. You are not really sounding the words out inside your head, you are just imagining doing so and you distort that voice because it is not real and can be silenced with a bit of training. I think that it is a great idea practising to read while repeating the same sound to trick your mind.

It's not as difficult as it appears. Just relax, take a deep breath and keep reading slowly for good comprehension while you keep humming. To get the best results I would recommend that you read two pages a day while humming for about two weeks. Your brain will get detached from the sound of the words and go much faster whenever you read and push your speed.

Let me tell you a short story to illustrate the power of humming while reading.

Years ago I used to practise Thai Boxing. If you've never seen it before I can explain how it works. It's like normal boxing but you can also use your legs to kick the opponent's body or head. It is a very fast-paced martial art and it is very fun too. One of the exercises we used to do was to kick a punch bag or have a buddy to throw some high kicks. Before starting, we would wrap lead pouches around our ankles. We would go and kick those bags until we got tired and then we would take the lead pouches away and I felt that I could fly like a bird. I still remember that my first experience of walking the walls was immediately after exercising with the pouches. I'd run towards the wall and try to walk on it. To my surprise, I gave three solid steps on the wall. It was an incredible experience! I was faster and more powerful than ever. What felt like weighing me down was in fact liberating me.

The same will happen to you if you weigh yourself down a little by humming. It feels like it is holding you back but in fact it will help you feel liberated. When you stop humming and start reading for speed you will feel so much lighter to go faster. Try it for a few minutes and the results will start to appear immediately.

Practise repeating a sound while reading and then stop and just go for speed. Put the metronome on and select a track, and then give it a try. If it works, then keep working with it; if not, you can always change the pace and go slower or faster. Whatever suits you best.

Stop humming ma, ma, ma.

Now I want you to try an extension of the ma, ma, ma exercise.

While reading, start counting numbers from one to 100 inside your head. This seems a little difficult but it is not.

It will definitely break the old pattern of associating comprehension with the imaginary sound of your voice.

Keep reading and counting until the end of this chapter and you will benefit from getting more detached from your voice and you will become faster as a result.

If you are counting and halfway through you forget where you were, just take an educated guess and then continue with the process. It doesn't matter providing you keep reading and counting. Once you get to 100, return to the beginning of your count and continue reading.

Start doing it now!

Keep reading and counting in your head from one to 100.

Listen to music or watch TV while reading

This is another way of getting detached from the little voice that torments our minds. If you listen to music while reading, you might pay attention to music and it will help you silence your little voice and then you get to read faster with less effort.

Try different kinds of music and, if it works for you, do more of it.

2.3.18 Selecting the keywords to sub-vocalise

Saying the keywords in your mind can help you, too

Another way of tricking the mind is by reading and saying (in your mind) the keywords – or the bigger words – without the need to worry about saying linking words like "and", "the", "or", "but" or any other small word. Just focus and look out for the keywords to grasp the meaning of the sentence. You probably remember that this was one of the first ideas I shared with you to help you read faster, but only now you have the understanding to use this technique effectively.

Initially, you will make a conscious effort to instinctively distinguish the keywords in the text. The Reticular Activating System will kick in and start to give it to you. In next to no time you will be automatically finding the message because the keywords will start to stand out from the page to give you the message you are after.

Read actively looking for connections and important messages. Sound out the important words inside your head – usually the big words – and continue to practise.

Start saying the keywords in your mind until the end of the chapter.

Now be aware that you will be reading quickly for a few minutes; while reading complex material, you may slow down to allow yourself to grasp the subject. That's OK, you can go faster and slower. Just use your pointer as much as you can and keep pushing your boundaries and become more flexible.

After doing this exercise, try to read without using the pointer. You will be surprised by how much the words begin to stand out, which will give you a clearer understanding of the overall text.

2.3.19 Sub-vocalise only half of the keywords

Now that you are aware that you can understand a text well without sub-vocalising the linking words, I will present you with another challenge.

I want you to say half or just part of the keywords on purpose and understand the meaning of the text. It feels like you are mumbling the words to yourself rather than reading them completely.

You will start saving time on every word. It is fractions of seconds saved all the time. This will result in having a substantial improvement on your reading speed and will stretch your comfort zone to become more flexible while reading different kinds of material.

Ensure you are aware that you are saying the words inside your mind; make every effort to say only part of the important words and you will start developing an excellent strategy that will become second nature in no time at all.

2.3.20 Developing your memory

Stop to think and you will remember more

To help you perform better and remember more of what you read, I would like to emphasise how important it is to stop and think about what you've just read. This is when memory is created.

After reading a few paragraphs that have good content, stop for a moment and try to remember the most important information there. Stop again at the end of a chapter and visualise what is important or essential; also remember some details.

This is the moment that you will be creating a book inside your head because instead of reading it passively, you will be recreating the entire story in your mind in a few seconds, and by doing so, you will keep that information alive and dynamic.

So, stop now and think for a few seconds; try to remember the most important information from this book. What was more relevant to you? Make the effort and try to remember, as this is when your memory will be created. Do it now!

Stop and think after a chapter, before and after a class or an important conversation. When you stop and think about the new information, you reorganise ideas in an order that is particular to you, filtered by your own experience.

To begin with, you will have to make a conscious effort, but soon the brain will start to retrieve information on autopilot.

If you are engaged in formal education or taking a course, pay attention to the teacher and when the lesson is over, try to remember what was important. At the beginning of a new lesson, try to remember what was discussed in the previous one. It will take you just a few seconds to retrieve the information but the results will surprise you. Your memory will get better and better! You can always take notes, too.

Finally, as you are reading words, these words will help you create images. It is also important to focus on these images and add more colour, more detail and motion to them. Instead of thinking in pictures, try to think like you are watching a film. You will remember these moving images you create more vividly than the words written on the page. Practise using Mind Maps and you will integrate the left side and right side of the brain with obvious improvement on your memory.

Talking is another way to improve your memory. Talk about what you've just learned and you will make all that information become yours. If you have the chance to teach, the retention will be even better.

Marking your books can help you to remember

I know that a lot of people are against writing or marking books and I respect that, however, my books are full of marks in pencil or even pen, post-its or highlighted in yellow. This way I pay more attention to what is really important.

Another use of a pencil is to mark exactly the last line you've read whenever you have a break, or you are interrupted by a phone call or someone enters the room and starts telling you something.

If you don't mark the last line you read, you will inevitably close your book, slipping in a book mark between two pages and by doing so, create a problem the next time you revisit the book. It is likely that you will begin reading from the opening passage on the left hand page and therefore re-read part of the text.

Psychologically you end up not wanting to go back to the book because you feel that you are a bit lost there. You've probably had the experience of watching a movie and stopping it halfway through only to find yourself searching for the last bit you remember watching before falling asleep. It is very frustrating to keep rewinding and fast forwarding until you find the place that you know you already watched for sure.

The same happens whenever you read a book. Marking the last line you read will let you get back on track straightaway. It's like a pause button. So, whenever you go back to the book you don't waste time re-reading one whole page that you already read. If you know where you've finished at the last reading session, you are more likely to start reading again sooner. If you don't want your book having lots of little marks in the margins, then you can always use a rubber whenever you start reading again from that point onwards. You can use a post-it or a bookmark that you insert from the side of the page like an arrow and it tells you exactly which line you read last.

You should skip back to re-read when you find something outstanding. Be on the lookout for a great idea.

I know that at the beginning of the book I was advising you to avoid skipping back if you don't understand something.

Here's the surprise!

I would recommend that you skip back to re-read a passage if you see something that seems important, because you want to mark or highlight those lines and make that information stronger in your brain. Use a pencil or even a pen to mark the book. If you don't like writing in your book, then just use a post-it note. Making notes can be useful so that you can find that nugget of information at a later date.

A tech savvy alternative to highlighting or marking your books is the App called TextGrabber. Take pictures of text, select the lines you want to keep and it will convert the pictures into editable text. It also instantly translates restaurant menus, magazines or any text into your native language.

Your books will become a powerful reference if you start marking them. In the same way you create files on your computer to gather similar information, you can start marking your books and writing down on the side the point of reference. This way you will start to recognise that whatever is higher on your values system will start to appear more in the margins of your books.

For example, my books have marks with words like "Memory" or "For Book 2" or "Focus" or other things that can be useful at a later date. Sometimes, I forget what I've marked and I need to flick through the book quickly to find the good stuff. But many times if something is important and I've put a post-it there with a title or have even written a paragraph about it on the post-it note, I'm very likely to remember the information by heart.

By doing that, I get more out of the books or documents I read, especially if I write something on the spot because then I'm creating information in my own right. You can do the same.

Some people don't know what their passion in life is but if they start reading and marking their books, the passion will start to become more apparent. Well, it certainly helps me to find what I want to get more involved with.

Just the act of marking the book sends a strong message to your brain, reinforcing the need to remember that particular topic.

By having a pencil and being willing to find something interesting in the book, you become an active reader instead of a passive reader. It will direct your attention to what you're reading and activate the RAS to find things that are relevant.

Just stop and think about what was said in the book in your own words or recollect your thoughts, images, feelings, whatever works for you. By thinking about it you develop extreme focus and it is not difficult to do so. Just think for five seconds to enhance the possibility of remembering something and things will stick there for longer. That's my experience.

Detectives use torches to focus their attention

Have you ever noticed that in detective films detectives constantly walk into a crime scene and switch their torches on even if the place is well lit? Why is that?

It is easier to see the detail if you have a smaller area to cover. The flashlight helps them to get focused; it guides the detective's eyes to what might be important. If you have too much to take in, your mind gets overloaded and you can miss important details.

The same will happen when you use a pencil or a pen. Your RAS will be turned on and you will find more relevant information because there is a purpose to your reading.

If you are reading on your iPad or Kindle, it's easy to mark the book and make notes too.

So, if you flick through the book you will find little drawings and keywords that will trigger your memory. This way you are active, searching for meaning and finding it. If you don't search for meaning you will not find it so easily.

328

I would like to recommend an App, which is great for gathering information on subjects that you may be interested in. It's called *Evernote*. I use it a lot.

You can remember names and faces easily

Another example of using your whole mind is remembering names and recognising faces.

The right side of the brain works with images so you may recognise someone's face immediately, even if you haven't seen them for five years. It's great if you recognise them; however, the question is, can you remember their name? Well, names are the responsibility of the left side brain.

So, even though they work together, the left and right side of the brain have different and complementary roles to perform.

Just follow me for a second. Can you spell the word "POWER" inside your head? Look away and spell the word while you are not looking at it.

Did you do it? That was easy, wasn't it?

Now I want you to look away again and spell the word "POWER," but this time attempt to spell it backwards!

Go ahead, look away and try it!

Did you get it right?

If you spell a word backwards, you use the right side of your brain to imagine the word as an image in front of you so you will be able to read it backwards. Because the left side is responsible for the language, we tend to use our imagination less and stick to the sound of the word to guide us when we have to spell a word.

I used to be dyslexic, and I found this to be a great strategy to help me spell correctly. I found it very useful to learn the Raviv Method to overcome my dyslexia.

If I start seeing a new word a few times I end up looking it up in the dictionary.

I like taking a mental picture of a new word to help me remember how to spell it. It is effortless to take a mental snapshot of a word; just look at it and blink both eyes for a second or two. The image imprinted in the retina will show itself to you as if you were still looking at the word but it won't last, the image will fade away. But just a second is enough to create this mental picture inside your mind. This picture will be accessible in your memory banks and will help you access the right spelling whenever you need it.

If you want to reinforce the image just look up and imagine the word floating in space and spell the word backwards. This way you will use your powers of imagination to create an image that is stored as one whole image, so when you need to spell it back, you will be able to read from your mental picture. But first, you need to put it there by slightly changing the way you see new words, so the brain learns that shortcut and then starts to apply the same method to all the words automatically.

Sometimes I imagine the new word in bold black letters against a red background, and the more you play with colours and shapes, the better.

To reinforce the learning process, I also used my body to learn (or the kinaesthetic channel in NLP terms). I would trace the words backwards in the air, letter by letter using my finger and drawing each letter in the air against a wall or even trace them with a finger in the palm of my other hand. If you imagine the words in your mind, they are real in one way or another. Just imagine them, and you will have them in your memory banks for long.

A couple of years ago I was teaching a group of professionals proofreaders how to proofread and speed read at the same time. This is the fundamental principle: to see words as pictures that fit with our mental templates or not. You may come across a word or expression that is wrong, and it stands out from the text.

Now that you have the new word inside your memory banks as an image, you need to give it life. To do that you can use the new words in two sentences that you will make. For example:

I learnt a new word last week: "sleuth." I've read the expression "I was sleuthing on the net to know if he was a credible guy." Sleuth means to search for information or act as a detective.

If I want to be able to remember or even use this new word I would recommend you to use the word twice.

For example:

"I'll be sleuthing some people on LinkedIn to find good joint ventures," or;

"I know people sleuth on me to see if I'm good at what I do."

I'm sure that you will know what sleuth means after this one.

If you create a silly sentence, it will produce the same effect. It is much easier to use a word that you've experimented with twice already, and therefore it becomes more natural to use it again.

The same principle serves to help you remember faces.

Whenever you are having a conversation with someone, you will passively look at their face because their face is right in front of you during the conversation. To make your mind active, try to focus your attention on just one part of that person's face, and you will become more aware of the details.

If the person has some unusual features such as a pointy chin, that can be a natural feature to focus on.

If they have intense eyebrows, then focus on it first. Zoom in and blow it out of proportion in your mind.

Let's do something easy to get started. Open your phone and look at a nice picture of you with a group of people with a few new faces. Choose someone who grabs your attention.

You will now focus your attention on a particular area of their face. Now look away and imagine what you saw.

It's interesting to pay attention to the colour of a person's eyes and the shape of their eyebrows. You will go from general to more refined observation.

As you start observing with more attention, you will start seeing the world more like an artist. So I will show you later in the book how to actually transform your ability to see like an artist into developing your powers to start drawing well.

The good news is that it is easy to have a massive shift and suddenly start drawing well.

It's all about having a new perspective and being able to slow down into the detail of a drawing.

Now look again at the same picture for 5 seconds. If you think you can see it clearly in your mind, close your eyes and focus on the image left in the retina when you close your eyes because, in a way, you took a mental picture of that image.

As you open your eyes again you will check if you can remember well or the image has vanished quickly.

Compare your imagination with the real picture in front of you. If you got it right, just keep adding more details to the face like the nose. Can you see the nose clearly? I'm sure you can. Now close your eyes and imagine the eyes, eyebrows and the nose. This way you will start remembering faces easily because your brain starts to use this neurological pathway to remember details of a face.

You've just created a strong memory with your mind's eye and you will be able to remember it because it's been created inside your mind.

Meeting and remembering new people

Now, whenever you meet a new person you can ask their name; ask to spell it out if you are not sure and imagine the name in front of you. If you try to spell the name backwards it will be locked in your memory as an image associated with that person. Now try to remember if you know someone else from your life or any famous personality with the same name. That way you can remember the name of your new friend by linking it with someone else's. If her name is Hannah you can create a link between her name and the other person you know.

Maybe you remember an actor or a celebrity. It doesn't matter if you are not sure why but there is some similarity. You can be wearing or doing anything you can imagine. If you can imagine and laugh about it, you can remember it.

The association ends up disappearing, and the name sticks to the face that you were imagining while looking away from the picture. Just a few seconds will do the trick. Practise more, and you will get better at it.

So, look at someone's face; pick one particular feature and then look away and try to picture it in your mind. This way you will be using your brain in a natural way and will easily remember other people's faces. It is all about interest, observation, and imagination.

It's helpful if you repeat their name out loud as much as you can.

Take pictures with your mind and create memories forever. In the beginning, it will be a conscious effort, however, by practising more, your brain will start building associations automatically.

In order to remember things you are studying you could make associations with other facts you already have in your memory. But it is creativity that will help you find better associations and remember more.

Children can move to another country and start speaking another language in a year or less because they are always playing and imagining things. We grow older, go to school, and stop imagining as much, and learning feels a little harder. Just be more playful in your mind, create cartoon stories and enjoy the freedom of linking new information to the already known creatively.

To keep improving your vocabulary, you can sign up to receive one new word a day that comes with its meaning, just as you would use a dictionary. You can use the principles I've described to help you continuously improve your vocabulary.

Just google "learn a new word every day," or go to the following website.

http://wordsmith.org/awad

I've been learning French for some time and I strongly recommend the free app "Duolingo" where you can learn a language in a simple and effective way. You can install the app on your phone or go to www.duolingo.com and begin your journey of learning a new language. Just remember what Einstein said:

"Imagination is more important than knowledge. For knowledge is limited to all we now know and understand, while imagination embraces the entire world, and all there ever will be to know and understand."

Memory training

To develop your memory further, I've developed a new training that will blow your mind.

I also recommend you to learn to develop your memory with the renowned memory coach Jim Kwik who has been helping Hollywood actors memorise their lines.

I have learnt a lot from him and so can you. Watch some of his videos on YouTube and enrol in one of his online courses if they suit you.

www.jimkwik.com

Correct misspelt words yourself

You can use the AutoCorrect feature to correct typos and misspelt words while typing a Word document, but if you don't know the correct spelling of that word, try to correct the word underlined in red yourself instead of using AutoCorrect. Your mind will become more active, and you will rely on your memory to find the correct spelling. This way you will add that new word to your visual vocabulary and you will win time by automatically writing the word correctly the next time.

A great way to take notes

There is a method for note-taking that is called *Cornell Notes*, which is very simple and makes your mind pick up the key concepts of a lecture or book, and helps you to develop your memory.

The steps to take notes are:

Divide the paper into three sections: From the top draw two lines one inch apart and a line two inches from the bottom. Draw another line two inches from the right of the paper like the drawing on the next page:

Note-taking for:	Date:
Purpose to read:	
Note-taking	Questions & Keywords
Summary	

In the left column you will take your notes, which include the main ideas of the text or lecture and you can use bullet points, short sentences and drawings. In the right column you can write the purpose of reading that book or the main questions you might have about it. Write also the keywords or key concepts from the message. Drawings are always welcome.

After taking your notes I recommend that you use the space at the bottom of the page to write a brief summary of the material you've been studying. This helps your mind integrate the new ideas in an active way.

Mind Maps can help you think clearer

Mind Maps are a great invention of Tony Buzan. I would recommend that you learn how to use them, as you will start to develop the right side of your brain and find new ways to memorise ideas.

Tony says that Mind Maps are great to make notes or summarise concepts. This is because we communicate mostly with key concepts and you can encapsulate them inside bubbles, draw colourful images inside, and write just the keywords on the lines that link each bubble.

He also says that we waste 90% of our time while making notes because we use far too many words which could be better represented by a little drawing.

The basic Mind Mapping Laws are:

- Use a plain sheet of paper in landscape position. In the centre of the paper draw a colourful image that represents the title of the Mind Map
- Create images throughout your Mind Map
- Use printed words on the lines that connect every thought bubble
- Your drawings can be very basic and what really counts is the energy you use to create something out of the ordinary; strange details or colours will aid your memory

Recently I was preparing myself to give a talk and I created a Mind Map. I could recall the Mind Map and knew what was next in my presentation. Below is a little example of it.

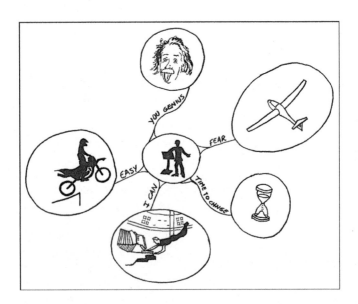

You can use Mind Maps for lectures to show how ideas and plans connect while explaining them. If you are running a meeting you can also apply the same concepts to present an idea or plan and invite people to contribute and visually fit new ideas in the Mind Map. This helps to reduce redundant ideas and calm people down when they see their idea clearly in the right place.

If you try to create a Mind Map at a meeting you will also have a clear summary about what took place. There are many types of software that can help you create a good Mind Map.

I think that by becoming more playful you will develop your creativity and have things done in less time. I like using Mind Maps and would recommend that you buy Tony's book. You will find more information on the website below.

www.imindmap.com

I'm getting more and more digital but I still like to keep a small notebook in my pocket to take notes. I believe that everything you focus on grows, so just by carrying a notebook I'm focused on having new ideas, and therefore they will come to me.

The curve of forgetfulness

We will remember things that are higher in our value system. I have some figures that illustrate, in a general sense, the *Cone of Learning* from Edgar Dale, with average retention rates according to teaching methods.

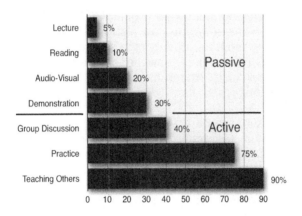

Mr Dale also arrived at some conclusions about the residual memory, and he says that after two weeks we remember:

- 10% of what we read
- 20% of what we hear
- 30% of what we see
- 50% of what we see and hear
- 70% of what we say
- and 90% of what we see, hear, say and do

Therefore, the secret to successful retention is to combine seeing, hearing, saying and doing and one of the best ways to do this is by using your imagination to see the information with your mind's eye, say the information to yourself or to others and take action using the new information. If you make it fun it will be even better...

The following graph shows you how we forget things the moment we stop receiving any information and you will have perhaps 5% residual memory after a month.

If you think about the subject again after one hour, you will create memory just by trying to remember what you've learnt, and this could improve your residual memory by 5% after a month.

By writing a blog after one day has passed you will be actively creating content that will reinforce your capacity of remembering that information, which might add another 5% residual memory after a month.

If you decide to give a short talk about the subject after a week you will probably enhance your residual memory by another 5%.

Every time you learn something you tend to forget details and the core information will leave a residual memory after a month, a year or even 40 years. Just by trying to remember you will remember more. That's exactly what you can see in the graph. Every time you try to remember something in any shape or form you go to another level of abstraction and create your own memory. I think this is amazing!

The more you think about it, you create more memory that will become more easily available.

The increase of residual memory graph

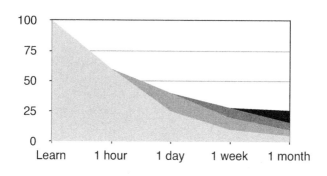

You learn something and start to forget the details
After 1 hour you think about it again
After 1 day you write a blog about it
After 1 week you give a talk about it

We are constantly being bombarded by new information and get distracted. By deciding to remember something you have learnt, you will become more focused and will also enhance your power of imagination, which will help you create new solutions for the problems that you will face in the future.

Memory is stored in the unconscious mind; so trust your unconscious to give you the answers, trust in your judgement and use the information you are receiving to remember more of what you read.

I believe that you should teach what you want to learn. To learn any subject takes years and if you are committed to sharing the wisdom you've received you will develop faster. As a result, you will be learning much more in less time.

Knowing that you might be sharing your knowledge in the near future will also help you because every time you read something interesting, you will be thinking about the main points of the book now that you have a bigger purpose to learn. This way you will be focusing more on the text you are reading and will remember more as a result.

What about writing a blog? It is easy to do and I think that it would be beneficial for you to do so. To get started, search for a blog on Google that helps people "create a blog". Create a profile for yourself and start writing.

I know it can feel threatening to expose yourself, but nowadays we can make a lot of money just by giving advice. So, if you want to be found and start to raise your reputation, you need to be found on Google. By writing a blog, your confidence will increase and you will remember what you've written. Every time you express an idea you will be helping yourself to remember more of what is important to you. You can start by writing a comment on someone else's blog, and whenever you feel a little more confident, you can then write your own. You will start to leave a legacy by writing some words that will be available on the internet forever.

Before you keep reading, stop and think about what you have learnt so far from this chapter. This way you will create memory as it is your own take on information.

HORSES READ QUEST

Vision Four

DEVELOP YOUR
PASSION FOR BOOKS

"Whatever your wildest dreams may be, they only scratch the surface of what is possible."

Michael Berg

Read on and improve your reading speed by a further 10–30% or more. You will become more inspired to read, and therefore you will apply your knowledge to settle down in a new comfort zone.

Some people are afraid of riding horses because they do not have the skills required to be in charge of the horse. Instead, they jump on the horse, hold on tight and let someone else pull the horse along. They think they are riding it, but they are not.

After learning how to read at different speeds, you will feel the difference between riding on a path in the woods, on the seashore or crossing a stream.

Horses like a rider who know where they are going, and gives clear directions when to turn or to increase speed.

In the same way, a marketing book will require a different set of reading speeds than a science fiction book. Instead of reading everything at one steady pace, you will be able to shift gears to speed up when you can and slow down when you need to.

Many people look at a book and think based on experience, that it would take one or two months to finish it. At the final step, you will learn how to work out the time required to read a book at your new reading speed, and will be surprised that a 200-page book might take you as little as two, three or four hours to read. You will also learn how to set up your reading targets to stay motivated to read more books, just for fun.

2.4.1 The final exercise

I've got an exercise that you might want to try while reading this or another book of your choice. Now you will be playing one of the ON/OFF video sequences that go up and down. For example, you can choose to play it from 40 beats per minute (BPM) until 60, and then you go back until you read again at 40 BPM. Alternatively, you can play other variations available.

This final exercise requires you to start using the pointer every time you start a new rhythm. After about 15 seconds, you should stop using the pointer and see if you can keep up with the pace and comprehension. This should be done while listening to the metronome, and when I stop the metronome you will keep reading in silence at the same pace. Feel the difference it makes. It might be easy to read without the pointer at 30 and 40 BPM, but the pointer might give you invaluable support while reading at 50 and 60 BPM. Observe how you feel and keep using the pointer to achieve your best performance. This is the big transition but be aware that even I use the pointer from time to time. Because each book requires a slightly different speed to read, I can get to the best pace to get the most out of it if I use the pointer. Sometimes I'm a little tired at the end of the day and I use the pointer when I start reading new material to help me to focus and perform to the best of my ability.

Go to the webpage below and start practising. Do it now!

www.humansinflow.global/audio

2.4.2 The 4% strategy for flow

I know that a new skill like speed reading is something that you will be developing over your lifetime, so I have a great piece of advice to help you improve further.

While explaining how to achieve the flow state I showed you that there is an optimum ratio between challenge and skill. The fundamental idea that you would be stretching your skill level to the maximum to tackle the challenge at hand is better understood if you follow the advice from Steven Kotler that, after doing a lot of research in Google headquarters, came to the conclusion that 4% is the amount of pressure you put on yourself to increase your performance in any activity and get into flow state.

If you feel that you are not reading fast enough, there is a simple way to keep improving.

As you find yourself reading at a comfortable speed, use the 4% strategy for flow. Always read the first paragraph of a chapter or an article at a comfortable speed and then push to read what feels like 4% faster on the next paragraphs or use the timer to measure your reading speed and then use the metronome to help you get into a new rhythm that is just 4% faster.

After getting comfortable again, push to reading 4% faster and you will be developing incrementally without noticing. It works the same way as compounding investment strategy. You push just a little every time you read and the final development will be much bigger than you could have ever imagined with the extra benefit of helping you to get into flow. Once in flow you will actually forget that you are reading and just enjoy the experience.

Read in bursts

To help you focus your attention I suggest you try reading in bursts. Read faster until you reach a coma, period or any other punctuation sign. Because you make a micro pause after every burst you might notice the difference in relevance between different passages. It's like swallowing little bites of information that might contain interesting content or not. This is a simple and effective way to increase your reading speed and focus.

2.4.3 Calculating the time to read a whole book. Surprise, surprise!

Now for the best part of this book

Do you remember that I promised that you would look at a book like you look at a DVD?

Let's say you want to choose a DVD to watch. Firstly, you are attracted by the picture on the cover; you then read the title, small description at the front and big description at the back; which is essentially what someone would do if they were selecting a book to read. The big difference is that the DVD has a number on the back cover that states the time it takes to watch the whole movie – and the book doesn't. In a general sense people will avoid starting a task if they have no idea about the time it will take to finish it. Therefore, I will show you how to work out the time to read any book of your choice. You will be surprised with the results.

Now, let's say you decide to read a book of 200 pages. How long will it take you to read the book?

Firstly, flick through the pages and notice how many empty pages you will find in the book. Some books leave a lot of dead space between chapters, or they are full of pictures and graphs. If that's the case, just have an approximate guess of how many pages you have as real text to calculate the time to read the book.

Assuming that the book you are reading has many pages lacking content at the beginning, some blank space between chapters and also pictures and graphs, you will estimate that 20 pages are basically empty of content – so you will delete them from the total.

To find out the time to read this book, I will round the numbers down to make it even easier.

Just multiply the number of words you have on one line by the number of lines you have on one page.

For example, if a book has 10 words per line and 25 lines per page, multiply 10 x 25 = 250 words per page. Now multiply 250 by the number of pages in the book. If the book has 200 pages of real text, the book will have 50,000 words (250 x 200 = 50,000).

This means that we have about 50,000 words in the whole book. You can round it down because there are lots of lines in the book that don't have 10 words per line and quite a few empty spaces.

Now just divide 50,000 by your reading speed.

If you are reading at the pace of 300 WPM, you will take 167 minutes or 2 hours and 48 minutes to finish the book.

By reading at 400 WPM, you will take 2 hours and 5 minutes to finish. By reading at 500 WPM it will only be 1 hour and 40 minutes. Now at 600 WPM it's only 1 hour and 23 minutes, while if you are reading at 1000 WPM, it will take 50 minutes to finish the book. Incredible, isn't it?

I would recommend you to take longer than that to read the entire book. Give yourself an additional 30-90 minutes as you will be stopping to mark the book, make notes, while reflecting on some of the main points. However, the actual time to read the book will be reduced because you now know how to speed read effectively. Congratulations!

2.4.4 Saving time table and ROI

To have a quick overview of how much time you will be saving every day as a result of your improvement, please take a look at the following table:

Time saved by improving your reading speed by 62%			
Reading hours per day (5 days a week)	Time saved per week	Time saved per month	Time saved per year
1 hour	2 hours 20 min	10 hours 1 min	13 working days
2 hours	4 hours 38 min	20 hours 4 min	27 working days
3 hours	6 hours 57 min	30 hours 7 min	41 working days
4 hours	9 hours 16 min	40 hours 8 min	55 working days
5 hours	11 hours 35 min	50 hours 9 min	68 working days
6 hours	13 hours 54 min	60 hours 11 min	82 working days

I've used 62% improvement as an example of your future average reading speed but I believe that after reading the book you might even have an overall improvement higher than 62%. Most of my clients can read 112% faster at times but they don't necessarily read 112% faster all the time.

If you read for work for on average three hours a day and have an average improvement of 62%, you will have 41 extra days of work every year. If you have employees, they will work 41 extra days for free every single year. I think this is a great *return on investment* (ROI) and you will hardly notice that you are reading faster because it will become second nature to you!

2.4.5 You are limitless

I will quote some wise words from Krishnamurti:

"The mind is so powerful that it can create an experience to support any belief. Then we believe the experience proves the belief, not knowing that the belief created the experience."

I believe that you can expand your knowledge by believing in yourself and daring to do things you have never done before.

Now, how long has it been since you did something for the first time?

You brain works as a whole organism. I believe that if you learn something new, your brain gets motivated to learn even more, which will reflect on your reading performance too. So, how about taking up a new hobby?

There is a field of knowledge called thematic interconnectedness that explains how we can learn from unusual sources. If you start learning how to dance you will feel challenged, but it is really refreshing to think with a beginners mind and see things anew. It can have profound effects on your life, and you can learn valuable lessons that can be applied to activities that didn't seem to have anything in common on the surface.

So, what about learning how to meditate and open the doors of perception?

There are many ways to get a taste for it. You can try either silent or active meditation. You can see the effects of meditation on your brain by watching biofeedback software mapping your brainwaves in real-time, or you can listen to frequencies that will make your brain vibrate in a new way, and you will be meditating like expert yogis in no time at all. There is also the 10-minute guided meditation that has been used by over 5 million people to date.

Read on if you want to explore the secrets of your mind. You can also visit the webpage below, and choose the right meditation technique to suit you.

www.humansinflow.global/meditation

347

If you think meditation is too serious, and you just want to have some fun, why don't you try some cookery or music lessons?

You could even join a book club. Information is about timing, too. Certain books will attract serendipity; read more books and make your own luck.

Nothing is stopping you from becoming the perfect version of yourself. You are limitless.

Get out of the rut and create magic in your life.

Hack your way to become a leading expert fast.

The **Sharks Think Quest** has five visions to help you position yourself in your field.

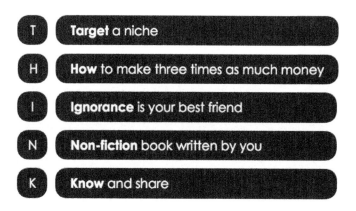

T — **Target** a niche

H — **How** to make three times as much money

I — **Ignorance** is your best friend

N — **Non-fiction** book written by you

K — **Know** and share

Time to read the Third Quest

Reading Speed in Words Per Minute	TIME	Reading Speed in Words Per Minute	TIME
At 100 WPM	1.7 hours	At 600 WPM	17 minutes
At 200 WPM	51 minutes	At 800 WPM	13 minutes
At 300 WPM	34 minutes	At 1000 WPM	10 minutes
At 400 WPM	26 minutes	At 1200 WPM	9 minutes
At 500 WPM	20 minutes	At 1400 WPM	7 minutes

To illustrate the process, I will compare the journey of creating your strategy to position yourself as an expert in your field to the body of a shark. Once you understand the links between the steps, you will be ready to start your journey, get into the flow and stay motivated until you achieve your expert status.

The challenge

Sharks are one of the very first vertebrates on Earth, and they have been around for the last 450 million years while humans developed only 0.3 million years ago. Researchers at The University of Copenhagen have estimated that Greenland sharks can live more than 400 years, so they are the vertebrates that live longer than any other species.

Can you imagine how much luck, good genes, great mutations it needed and how much quick thinking it had to do to survive while millions of other species became extinct?

I use sharks as an analogy to strategically finding a niche, becoming more effective than the competition, be willing to learn new things and share your discoveries in a book format and also overcome a possible fear of public speaking to really master your trade and teach others to achieve something that will change their lives.

This quest is very important because you will put your new abilities of reading faster to work with a solid objective in mind.

The good news is that knowing which direction you are taking will help you build the platform from where you will be able to take off to the following quest.

The most desirable state to work and have fun in life is definitely connected to getting into the flow or being in the zone. The Eagles Flow Quest will take you to a place where making great progress can feel effortless. You will learn how to obtain extreme focus to accomplish your goals faster, but first, you will clarify the objectives that will be used as fuel to achieve your full potential.

SHARKS THINK QUEST

Vision One

TARGET A NICHE

"Contrary to popular belief, there is no such a thing as an educated person. You are either learning or you are not."

Bob Proctor

Sharks are fascinating creatures that have been around since the dawn of time. They have an incredible sense of smell that gives them remarkable abilities of orientation, no matter if it is day or night. They can smell blood from three miles away.

As they lock the direction they have to travel to reach their goal in their mind, they use their tail as the main source of trust to reach their target. I use the tail analogy to represent targeting a niche.

This first step will help you become an expert by improving your metaphorical sense of smell and your propulsion power.

Once you are clear on why you chose your line of work, you will become not only inspired to serve, but you will inspire others to follow you. This is certain to propel your career forward and help make you stand out from the crowd as an expert.

3.1.1 The never ending learning cycle

Bill Gates and Warren Buffett were giving an interview at the University of Nebraska, and were asked:

351

"What superpower would you like to have?"

Bill Gates answered first: *"Being able to read super-fast! Yeah! That would be nice!"*

Warren Buffett replied: *"Yeah, that would be huge! Well...Bill can read super-fast. I mean, he reads about three times as fast as me. I probably wasted ten years reading slowly."*

Your education defines you and when you know how to do something that not many people are able to learn you have an edge. And, even if you can read much faster than before, you can always still develop further! The world is constantly changing, but are you keeping up with the times?

Learning is important at all ages and stages of life, but most people are proud of finishing a degree and do not take learning seriously afterwards. Many people read three or four books a year and think they are doing quite well.

How many books did you read in the last 12 months?

10X thinking

Google founder, Larry Page, believes that it is often easier to make something 10 times better than it is to make it 10 per cent better.

To do that, you need to make the shift from traditional linear thinking to entrepreneurial, exponential thinking.

10x thinking implies that you are willing to think big, embrace change, and disrupt both yourself and the industry you work in.

10X yourself

So, how can you improve yourself 10 times?

By not focusing on your existing skills and assumptions, and not putting extra effort on top of an existing solution. Instead, explore new fields of knowledge, be open to creative concepts and solutions and have breakthrough ideas that will make a big change in your life and, crucially, position yourself as an expert in your field.

Can you imagine the impact of reading 30 to 50 books in your field? You could certainly become an international expert in your area of knowledge just by keeping up with new developments. What about being the source of future thinking?

According to David Cottrell, if you read one book a month you are in the top one per cent of all non-fiction readers in the world [4]. How hard can this be?

I think that you can accomplish anything if you have a vision, stay motivated and employ the right strategy.

3.1.2 Read more and succeed faster

I understand that people make decisions in life in search of pleasure or to avoid pain.

If you want to read more, it could be because you want financial freedom to be able to travel the world. This is a motivational strategy that comes naturally to many people; especially entrepreneurs. They take that risk with the self-belief that the future will bring them a fortune.

Contrary to being motivated towards success, some people are motivated to avoid pain. For example, you might want to read more to catch up with your colleagues at your new job because you are afraid of being fired if you don't start contributing at meetings.

There is nothing wrong with either of the options above; however, be aware that some people might run faster by seeing the carrot on a stick while someone else might run even faster just by the thought of a whip.

What is it for you?

Do you work hard to buy a bigger house or do you work harder because you are afraid of not being able to pay the mortgage, which may result in the loss of your home?

I'm a bit dramatic here but this is the truth that lies behind our desire to get things done. You are either searching for pleasure or you want to avoid pain.

The difference between motivation and inspiration

Most people join a gym because they intend to get fit. However, once the novelty of the gym wears off, they may decide to hire a personal trainer to achieve their goals.

Someone else may choose to go running for an hour each morning to get fit.

For some, the idea of waking up an hour earlier each morning may be an arduous effort, while for others, they feel the inspiration to do so.

If you were to plan to run the marathon in six months from now, would you require someone to urge you on to go running? I don't think so because you create a big vision of crossing the finishing line and you stick to your training regime. If you decide to run for charity, the commitment is even bigger and this way you might start creating gravity around your dreams and inspire others to join you and start running too. This way you become more inspired.

This is the difference between motivation and inspiration. Motivation comes from the outside; inspiration comes from the inside. You can hire a coach to help you perform better at anything but you don't rely on them because you have a burning desire to succeed.

So, I want to help you get inspired, and one good reason for you to start reading more could be that you want to make more money. Would you like to make more money? Read on to find out how.

SHARKS THINK QUEST

Vision Two

HOW TO MAKE THREE TIMES AS MUCH MONEY

"You are never given a wish without also being given the power to make it come true."

Richard Bach

The shark's dorsal fin is famous. Just by seeing their fin above the waterline, you can see power and direction.

The uniqueness of their fins is enough to make you ten times more scared than seeing a fish as big as the shark that doesn't have a fin. Even though their fin seems to be a dangerous weapon, they don't use them to hurt anyone. Their fin is there to broadcast their superiority, and make everyone respect them. What a creative marketing approach.

Now, your way of demanding respect is by demonstrating your knowledge and insight. Reading the news is commonplace, and it will not give you a competitive advantage. If a shark focuses on eating tiny fish as main course, it will end up spending more energy to chase these little fish than the energy it will get from eating them.

Sharks like a challenge and hunt for bigger prey to satisfy their appetite and you should focus on reading big books to quench your thirst for knowledge. Learning from books will be your best weapon to spot trends and create strategies that will directly reflect on your capacity to innovate and make more money.

If you want to become more aligned with your purpose in life, you will benefit if you become inspired to pursue the incredibly helpful habit of reading more business books.

3.2.1 Read seven business books a year

"According to the U.S. Labor Department, business people who read at least seven business books per year earn over 230 per cent more than people who read just one book per year." [4]

Many of us spend huge amounts of money, time and perseverance to take a degree and end up making more money as a result of acquiring targeted knowledge.

We are living in exponential times, and anything is possible. Rest assured that just reading books you can double, treble or even increase your income by a factor of ten.

How many books would you like to read every year?

If you read 15 pages of a business book a day, you will be reading two books of 225 pages every month. This is 24 books in one year!

What about that for a challenge?

Anything related to business would count here so, if you like watching programmes that show a selection of good advertising campaigns on TV, then maybe you would find it interesting to read a book or two about advertising. You will broaden your knowledge with new ideas and perhaps one day you will be having a chat with your boss and suddenly you say something inspirational and who knows where that might take you in the future.

Business coaches

It's worth considering that any successful sports person has a coach to help them maximise their performance; in the same way, I believe that a business coach will help you improve your game, and be able to recommend many inspirational books.

I had a few business coaches that challenged me to develop my potential as a visionary. I can see myself impacting the whole world with this book, my online courses and by training others to ignite people's passion for reading books and get in flow.

Once I had crystallised my exciting vision, I had invaluable help to execute it from a business coach from ActionCOACH called Parag Prasad, who told me to read a thought-provoking book called *Eat That Frog* by Brian Tracy. Brian's book is so short that I read it for the first time whilst still in the bookshop. It was so good that I bought a few copies to give as gifts to clients and friends.

My other coaches have been helping me with planning and committing to bold outcomes. I've been working hard and I'm having a lot of fun with them while reinvent myself. I hope you also have the privilege of being coached by someone inspiring that will challenge you to be your new self.

Start searching for your business coach by following the link below or by searching around.

www.humansinflow.global/businesscoach

So, you may be reading books on marketing and a friend informs you of their desire to open a shop. Having listened, you come forward with some clever promotional ideas, which make an instant impression. So much so that your friend offers you a partnership deal of 20% stake in the business. Partnerships like that happen all the time because knowledge is a valuable commodity.

Now let's say that you have a good job, and you live comfortably. If you read books about how to buy a house to rent or invest your money, you might stay in the same job, but you will start making money by investing wisely, which is a great way to become financially independent.

If you have an important business meeting with a professional that has written a book, or that mentions his favourite business book in his LinkedIn profile, can you imagine the impact you would make by reading the book before the meeting? Even if you don't read it from cover to cover, you will understand a lot about that person and by showing interest in them, you will be miles ahead of the competition.

Kids and books

If you have kids, you can help them become interested in reading books by suggesting good books to read. But it's never easy to make them sit down to read, right?

Parents are usually happy to give some money to their kids if they do some chores at home. I would suggest that you give them money for reading a book which is much more useful than washing a car.

I would say they need to read at least five pages of a book to decide whether they like or not and still be entitled to receive 1/10 of the amount intended for the whole book. You could also read the book to them to get them hooked.

They can listen to the audiobook for five minutes to see if they like the book or watch a video book summary on YouTube to get the gist of it or find a reliable summary by following the link below.

www.humansinflow.global/summaries

The most important reason to incentivise a kid to read books is because the main objective is to help them find the kind of book that will really touch and interest them. When they start spending the money you give them on books to give as a present to friends you know you are on the right track.

The reward should be accompanied by a friendly chat about the book or a written highlight of great ideas found in the book.

I would also suggest that your kids have an unlimited budget, if you can afford, to buy books on Amazon. Open an account on their new site Gift.Amazon.com because a small percentage of the money spent on books will go to a charity that they can choose, adding another feel-good to the purchase.

They can always download the sample of a book on their phone and start reading anywhere they go.

Reward the kids when they read and learn, link the process of understanding that reading books can help them make money and perhaps you can give them a much larger reward if they write a book or start a blog, which is something that will change their outlook on life.

SHARKS THINK QUEST

Vision Three

IGNORANCE IS YOUR BEST FRIEND

"The best effect of any book is that it excites the reader to self-activity."

Thomas Carlyle

The shark is constantly swimming, even while sleeping. Can you imagine being that restless?

Many people have a mind that never stops. They feel that they need constant stimulation, and keep jumping from one subject to the next. Their judgement and decision-making power can get fatigued, and they become less responsive to changes.

Sharks can see in the dark, and they have the best sensitivity to detect electromagnetic fields that all animals produce; so they can find prey even without seeing it. Similarly, you will be able to see opportunities that others are blind to because books don't only give you new information, they stimulate your creativity and imagination, which can produce incredible insights. On top of that, you will start noticing that serendipity will make you read the right book at the right time.

The shark's body represents your body of knowledge, and the focus here is your information diet.

If you are allowing the media and social media feed your mind with content that is depressing and pointless, you can make a stand and decide to

361

experiment living a low information diet. You will be less informed about unimportant news/events, and more informed about things that matter. The benefit of being ignorant about the news and your social media 'friends' latest sock purchase / latest holiday plans / etc. is that you will finally find the time to start reading books and watching videos that can help you progress in your career. I read a daily digest with ten headlines and only click on one or two to read the full small articles. This way I am up to date, but I also avoid distractions like following sports.

Another source of insight and intellectual nourishment is the daily practice of meditation. So, I urge you to boost your mental health by trying one of the many forms of meditation, or start exercising, pick up a hobby or just have more nourishing downtime.

3.3.1 Become a thought leader

Recently I met Lynne McTaggart, who is the author of a fantastic book called *The Field*. She talks about a new way of understanding how we access and store information. The interesting twist here is that, based on scientific observation, she believes that we store memory outside our brains or in the "field" around us, which means "in the air". The brain is used to tune to our memory or to new ideas that can be downloaded from this immense field of knowledge that surrounds us. She points out that no one has ever proved that we store memory inside our brains, we can only observe some parts of our brain lighting up while we think or remember but this would be just the activation of our receptor station.

I believe that if you know what makes you tick, the magic key will turn on whenever you start reading more about the subject you are passionate about and you will access information that has been developed by other people because everything is stored in the "field".

While writing this book, I had many moments of profound inspiration where new ideas or concepts just crystallised in my mind, and I felt like downloading the information from a higher level of awareness. I've heard and read that many authors have the same feeling of downloading information while creating fiction or making new discoveries. The interesting phenomenon is that certain discoveries in science happen simultaneously in laboratories that are not connected and are placed in different countries. This synchronicity is proof that some people find a way to access this immense field of knowledge and come up with similar findings in different parts of the world.

Expert knowledge

If you read from 30 to 50 books on a particular subject, you can become an international expert in that area of knowledge. It is like taking another degree by yourself. If you read one book a week, you would read 52 books in a year and change your life.

Now take a look at these reading statistics from The Jenkins Group in the USA and get excited about reading a few extra books. You might get very inspired to read more and in doing so, awaken your hidden potential that will give you creative solutions to your challenges.

- 33% of high school graduates never read another book for the rest of their lives
- 42% of college graduates never read another book after college
- 80% of US families did not buy or read a book last year
- 70% of US adults have not been in a bookstore in the last five years
- 57% of new books are not read to completion

Aren't these numbers incredible? Just make an effort to read a little bit more. When you apply this knowledge to your profession, you will be ahead of the masses that don't read and you will have the potential to generate more business and, ultimately, make more money!

Cultivate selective ignorance

It is interesting to note that we end up reading a lot of news and information that wastes time. I read a book called *The 4-Hour Work Week* by Tim Ferriss and he talks about cultivating selective ignorance. I think it is a brilliant concept that helps people to become more focused on subjects they want to learn and stop overloading themselves with trivia, social media and the news. If I read the paper, I am totally aware that I want to find news that can propel my business forward. I want articles with good random ideas or that have a direct connection with what I do, so that I can have new ideas or perhaps I will reach out and contact the journalist.

I glance through the paper and only stop when I find something that I really want to read. Similarly, I am ruthless about not opening emails just because they have a catchy subject line. Most of the time, I keep up-to-date by reading a *News Digest* App. They select 9 to 11 of what they consider to be the most important headlines of the day, and I click on them if they really grab my attention and interest. Another great source of news is Apple's *News* App. You select the sources you prefer and the more you read, the more personalised your News becomes. As I have already mentioned, I avoid watching the news on TV and, in this way, I create between 30-60 minutes in my day that I can then use to read a book and learn something that can really have an impact on my life.

Avoid decision fatigue

Yes, it is exciting to read the news and trivia on Twitter and Facebook. You release dopamine in your bloodstream and you get turned on, but by forcing your brain to decide to read or ignore every single entry, you will get fatigued very quickly, and you will have less energy to focus on things that really matter. This is called *Decision Fatigue*.

My advice is to make fewer decisions and become more pro-active. Did you know that Facebook founder Mark Zuckerberg wears the same clothes to work every single day? Yes, grey T-shirt and a darker grey hoodie. His wardrobe has lots of the same pieces. He thinks that we can only make a limited amount of assertive decisions a day and he doesn't want to waste this power by having to decide which clothes to wear every single day, not to mention the decisions required while buying clothes. He is saving his decision power for things that are really important to him. Does it make sense or not?

Find your mission in life. Focus on just a few things that you care about every day of the week, and say NO to everything else that doesn't help you fulfil your dreams.

If you must check your Facebook and Twitter, limit the time spent to 10-20 minutes a day because this is usually a reactive activity. Do not let them hijack your life, instead find a meditation course or search on YouTube for a free lesson and learn how to focus your mind. I practice meditation to develop clarity and to fine-tune my purpose.

The idea is to start reading and researching about things that you like doing or about which you wish you had more information. Do not be restricted to reading books; browse the internet, follow people you admire, have a RSS Feed Reader, read book summaries, watch videos, listen to podcasts and audio programmes or talk to people about areas you want to develop.

What would you like to know more about?

If you like drinking wine, you could start by reading a book about a famous winemaker and understand a little bit about wines. You will inevitably end up having new, stimulating things to talk about whenever you sit down with your friends around a good bottle of wine.

Why not learn about meditation, football or psychology? The choice is yours and I believe that by reading more you will expand your world and more opportunities will present themselves.

It is not by chance that many wealthy people have lots of books in their houses. Do you think that because they are rich, they find the time to read more books or because they find the time to read more books they end up becoming richer?

Whatever the case, reading simply brings you more knowledge and knowing more is fundamental in this changing world. Read a bit more and decide what you want to learn next. Ask your friends for recommendations and make a list of books you want to read. The possibilities are endless.

3.3.2 Find your limiting beliefs about reading

To improve your reading speed, it is important that you read more. I know that you have lots to read at work but you will need to choose a few books to start practising the principles I've introduced you to throughout the book. So, I would like to know what is your reason for not reading more than you are reading at the moment? This is a very important question, because just by identifying what is stopping you reading books, you will become aware of your limiting beliefs and therefore, you will get over some of them and start to develop your love for reading.

Please tick below all the reasons or excuses for not reading more books than you are actually reading. You might find many of them relevant to you; write down your private thoughts or reasons that are hindering your overall development. It is crucial to know why you don't read because I want to inspire you to read more and this is the first step. It will only take a minute to think about it.

Now tick all the reasons for not reading more books.

☐ I watch TV/movies instead
☐ I work late
☐ I'm already studying
☐ I go out to socialise
☐ I play video games
☐ I have a drink
☐ I'm too tired
☐ I think reading is a boring and slow activity
☐ I lack focus
☐ I have children to look after

- ☐ I'm not motivated
- ☐ It is not part of my routine
- ☐ I feel guilty about spending time reading instead of doing high priority things
- ☐ I like to spend time with my family

Add your own reasons or excuses below:

_____

_____

_____

OK, now I want to ask you a critical question that might shake your limiting beliefs. Please read again all your reasons for not reading books and ask yourself after each reason. Is it true? Is it really true?

We always want to be right and to be so, we justify our actions with a few untrue ideas. I do it too!

I believe that it is with the best of intentions that you might think that you don't read more books because you work late, or because you like to go out for a drink and socialise. But now thinking carefully, is it the real reason for not reading more? I would suggest otherwise. You could always find the time to read 15 pages of a book every day if you were really inspired to do so; excuses are just justifications, not true reasons.

I overcame some of my limiting beliefs by walking over hot coals with Tony Robbins. If you can do that you can pretty much do anything else.

Follow the link below to know more about this event.

www.humansinflow.global/tony

3.3.3 Being addicted to TV can slow down your brain power

On average, people watch three hours of television a day. Some, however, can waste their life sitting in front of the TV.

I see it as an addiction like smoking or drinking. If you have a habit that is making you waste time it is possible that you are addicted to it and don't know how to break the habit. Perhaps you want to feel free to choose other alternatives to have fun, enjoy your free time or find new ways to become more productive and progress in your profession much faster. So, let's see if I can motivate you to read more and stop watching so much TV.

If you want real information, you need to read. Reading is a much faster way to gain knowledge than the TV and it brings much more content.

I believe that you could learn ten times more reading the newspaper for 30 minutes than watching the news on TV. To me, it seems that the newsreader is just reading headlines from a newspaper and making superficial comments about them. The worst thing is that you can't even choose what you want to know, they just throw information at you that is seldom relevant in your life. I would recommend that you spend time choosing what you want to watch. Be careful not to watch just anything, just because you can't be bothered to switch the TV off. Make an extra effort to switch it off and you will have more time to live.

By the way, I've been living in London for 19 years and I didn't have a TV for at least 12 of those years because I feel happier this way. Could you get rid of yours? You could do an experiment and leave your TV at your friend's house for a month to decide if you really need it or not.

You can find the news on the internet and use filters and alerts to be notified about specific subjects in text or video format. Follow the thought leaders in your field and be ahead of the masses.

SHARKS THINK QUEST

Vision Four

NON-FICTION BOOK
WRITTEN BY YOU

"Imagination grows by exercise and contrary to common belief, is more powerful in the mature than in the young."

Paul McCartney

Printed books are the basis of our civilisation and writing one is a powerful statement.

Sharks date back to over 450 million years ago, which is double the time when the first dinosaurs roamed the Earth. Can you imagine how many stories they would be able to tell if they could write?

They are one of the very first vertebrates on the planet, they survived four global mass extinctions, and they are so old that the first trees on Earth only grew strong when sharks were marking their 100 million years of existence on the planet.

The shark's brain is responsible for coordinating all its bodily functions and interactions with the environment, so I would recommend you integrate all your knowledge, and position yourself as an authority by writing your book. The word 'authority' contains the word author.

You have the privilege of having so many life experiences that you can write a book of 150-200 pages if you decide to. All you need to do is to choose the field in which you want to be known, write what you already know, but also do some extra research to make it really up-to-date and use it as your new business card or valuable marketing material.

This is not as challenging as you might think it to be. Many resources can help you in the process of writing, and I have recommended some courses to help you accomplish writing a book in a matter of a few months. You can even write your book by recording yourself giving an interview and paying someone to transcribe and organise your ideas into chapters. You will be amazed by the sense of achievement that comes from having your name on the front cover of a book. Incredible opportunities appeared in my life just because I invested the time to write this book.

So, what will your book be about?

3.4.1 Capture your dream

By developing your reading speed, you will be able to read two books a month by reading 15 pages per day.

That is it.

Which subject or subjects would you like to become an expert in?

Sometimes it is painful to decide to change direction drastically, but I guess I've learnt to make important decisions out of the need for leading an inspiring life.

Now I invite you to take a deep breath and try to guess some answers to these questions by filling the blank. Just exercise your mind by finding new possibilities for your life. Enjoy!

I want to learn how to _____

I want to study _____

I want to be better at _____

I want to understand _____

What would you like to learn more about? This could be the first step to developing a new hobby or a new way to have fun or make money. Please spend a minute or two thinking about the areas you would like to develop your knowledge in, write it down, research on the internet the best books for you and buy them. Do it now!

If you took some action, I invite you to look into the unknown and fly five years into the future. Are you doing anything different other than your day-to-day job? By starting to read more, you will enhance your knowledge and broaden your horizons. Just for fun, what would you like to be an international expert in?

I would like to be an international expert in

_____

I hope I got you thinking about that big dream that you want to make real. Keep thinking about it and be very specific because it will help you get started and find the books and people you want to learn from. This way you will attract your dreams. Open your eyes to the possibilities.

3.4.2 Getting inspired

Another good question is: What would be a real reason for you to read more?

If you say that it is to have more knowledge, then the answer is good, yet there is no strength in it. You need to be more specific.

Please select the appropriate answers and then elaborate a little on them so you will have a clearer vision about the good reasons for reading more. Anything is possible once you are committed to a big vision.

If you would you like to have your own business, which business would it be? What could you do to get things started?

_____
_____
_____

Would you like to get a promotion at work? What would you like to do at the company you work for?

_____
_____
_____

Would you like to show off your knowledge while with friends? What would you like to be able to talk about?

_____
_____
_____

If you could choose where to work where would it be? Which country would you like to be living in?

_____
_____
_____

Would you like to have fun reading? Would you like to read some comedies, famous plays or classic literature?

_____
_____
_____

Would you like to make more money? How much are you planning to make and by when? If you are specific, chances are that you can achieve your target in less time. Start dreaming and planning now!

_____
_____
_____

I believe that if the reason is good enough, you will start buying and reading those books that support that dream; having a dream motivates us to accomplish incredible feats in life. Have you ever heard of Simon Sinek? He wrote a book called *Start With Why* and I think the book is fantastic. Google him and watch his talk on www.ted.com to get really inspired.

Please stop for a minute and think about the main reasons to read more. Jot them down and identify yourself with that feeling of accomplishment. This is just the beginning of an amazing adventure.

3.4.3 Become an author

Read more, capture the essence of the text and make notes. This way you will be actively remembering the information and will be able to play with it whenever you need.

I will be repeating myself here by suggesting that you could start your own blog. It will help you build your confidence and raise your profile on the internet. If you already have many blogs posted, then perhaps you can compile the information and write a book.

It started with a dream

The first time I thought I would be able to write a book was at a very inspiring presentation by Gerry Robert. He planted a seed inside my brain. This seed grew for seven years, and now I have my book ready. The most surprising thing was to go to a seminar for entrepreneurs in London and meet him again after all those years. The timing was perfect and, with the book proof in hand, I enrolled on his course and got to learn the final steps to make the most out of publishing my book. He has a wonderful method of helping you write your book in a matter of months, not years. If you want to get your book done fast, follow the link below, attend one of his talks or enrol on one of my workshops to help you write and publish your book. I regret not taking the plunge years ago; it would have saved me a lot of time and heartache. You will never be the same after deciding to write your book.

www.humansinflow.global/writeabook

Now, I will share some practical ways to put your ideas into words.

If you prefer handwriting instead of typing, I discovered a pen that you can use to write as normal on a piece of paper, and then the words are sent to your computer as text to be edited. This is really fantastic if you keep writing notes on paper and want them organised on your computer. It also captures any drawing with accuracy. To find out more about it visit their website:

373

www.e-pens.com/uk

If you read a great passage from a book or document and decide to copy it for later editing, you can take a picture of it using a fantastic App called TextGrabber, and the text becomes editable.

Speed writing

I strongly advise you to learn how to touch type because this way you will stop the imaginary voice that sounds the words inside your head, which will create more flow to your thoughts.

It is interesting to notice that, by learning how to touch type, your body will start learning how to spell correctly; this is called muscle memory, and it will guide your fingers to spell correctly without you having to think about the right spelling. Most people rely only on their visual memory to recall the right spelling and this might come as a surprise to most of you.

A web-based company called Read and Spell helps anyone to touch-type, including people with dyslexia and other learning difficulties. To learn more visit their website.

www.readandspell.com

Take advantage of using a software that fixes your grammar as you write with, Grammarly, and you will feel more confident that you can reasonably explain your ideas. Check it out.

www.grammarly.com

You can also start to practise dictating your own book. There is an amazing App called *Dragon* that types whatever you are saying; just search for *Dragon* dictation. Another way is to dictate an email using a Gmail.com account on your phone. This tool is not available on the desktop. If you don't like dictating or the software makes too many mistakes, you can Google "transcription", and you will find a lot of people on Fiverr, PeoplePerHour or Upwork, amongst other sites that will charge you very little to have it all typed up. You can record a lesson, conversation, or talk you might give. You will start using the content you have in a written format without much effort.

Whatever your field I would say that even a small printed book will give you an enormous sense of satisfaction and it will help you position yourself as an expert in your area.

You can also re-purpose previous work and transform it into a book or eBook. You can always find extra help if you ask your friends, colleagues or search for professionals at Upwork.

www.upwork.com

I hope you find these tips inspiring and I hope that you decide to get serious about leaving a legacy in the form of a book. If you need help, please get in touch and I can recommend some professionals to help you structure your thoughts.

And if you write a book someday do let me know, I would like to celebrate this incredible achievement with you!

SHARKS THINK QUEST

Vision Five

KNOW AND SHARE

"Action makes more fortune than caution."

Luc De Clapiers

The last scene focuses on the shark's mouth. After all, that's what makes them famous.

They have several layers of teeth that keep growing and replacing themselves, so they always have sharp teeth and stay a top predator.

As an expert, your mouth can also make you famous. You need to express yourself and your ideas in order to make an impact on other people's lives. Sharpening your communication skills is crucial.

I recommend you find professionals that can help you create the perfect pitch, speak from the stage with confidence, or record your ideas and sell them as e-Learning or online courses.

As you keep learning and teaching, you will improve your power of persuasion.

By having your book written, you will have a solid platform to speak from and will be surprised with the media attention, and admiration from family, friends and peers.

3.5.1 Relax with a book

A lot of people think of reading as a serious task, and I believe it is useful to try new approaches to make the act of reading a more enjoyable activity.

Why don't you try to combine your leisure with reading?

I have a few suggestions:

Why don't you choose a good book and try to read it in the bath, pub, park or at the coffee shop?

If you like exercising, perhaps you can go to the gym and try the bicycle or cross trainer, and read your Kindle or iPad at the same time. If you prefer to run or cycle, you could try an audio-book.

Instead of going out for a drink with a friend, why don't you have a glass of wine while reading a great book? By the way, I think that one glass is usually enough to keep your mind alert. After that, you are at your own peril!

I think this is a good way to be more relaxed while reading, and to feel more confident to speed read and grasp the meaning of the text with less effort. Have a go and see if you like it! Make sure you are older than the age limit in your country to be able to drink!

Why don't you read out loud to your friend or partner? Children like to be read to and adults love it in the same way! People stop reading beautifully written or interesting books to us just because we know how to read. I don't think it makes any sense. So, why don't you grab a book of your choice and read for a person you love? You will have food for thought and good reasons to think about different things. I like to read about subjects that the other person would choose themselves. Select chapters that they might like from a psychology or history book. Be clever with your choices and you will have great fun reading to each other.

3.5.2 Creating a challenge and a strategy to accomplish it

To make the most of what you have learnt, I invite you to take the *Read Three Books In Three Weeks Challenge*. This way you will start a habit that can last a lifetime.

Read Three Books In Three Weeks Challenge

By now you know that a 200-page book might take you approximately two to four hours to read. So if you stop watching the news, and start reading 30 pages a day, you will be on target to read one whole book every week.

You will see how easy it is, if you plan it in advance.

This is the strategy to read one book a week:

Start with books with less than 200 pages. Divide the number of pages of your book by seven, to know how many pages to read per day. Use seven post-its to mark the targets for each day. To estimate how much time you will read each day, measure your reading speed. Calculate the time to read each day. I am sure it will be less than you think. 30 minutes a day could well be enough.

Now decide which TV programme you will not watch (what about not watching the news?), or what other activity you will avoid to create time for reading your book. Decide what time you will start reading each day, and stick to it.

To stay focused, skip any paragraph or chapter that you are not really interested about.

Jot down the big ideas from the book, and decide how to apply them to your work or life.

The key is to have an exciting list of books to read and have a routine for reading your books. It could be when you commute to work, or alternatively, once a week you decide not to watch another movie and use the time to read a good book instead.

I would suggest that you choose books with less than 200 pages for the *Read Three Books In Three Weeks Challenge,* to maximize your chances of successfully accomplishing your goal.

3.5.3 Creating your booklist

To start the challenge, you need to create your book list. If you already have some titles written down, compile all the books in one Excel spreadsheet. This will help you to get organised and start the process of keeping track of your development. You can also rate the titles and summarise the important points from the books.

To help you select the books for your reading list, you can search the web for lists of the best, or most recommended, books in your field. You can ask your friends for their recommendations, but the best people to go to are your boss, people you admire in your organisation, or some of your best clients. Tell them you have learnt how to speed read, and ask them if you can borrow some of their books. If they agree, borrow one book at a time, and give yourself a time limit to give it back. This way you will be more motivated to start and finish the book, and your friend/boss/client will not be worried that you will keep the book forever. If you have promised to give the book back within two weeks, and you do not finish reading it on time, call them and ask for an extension of a week to finish it. Keep your word and return the book before the due date. This way you will start understanding how they think, you will have informed conversations, and it is very possible that you will be promoted sooner than expected.

Ethical cheating

If your list becomes too long and you want to get through it faster, you can start reading book summaries too.

Some people might think that reading a summary would be akin to cheating, but I think otherwise.

By reading the summary, you can identify the key messages of the book and learn precious concepts in a fraction of the time and, in addition, you can use it to increase your reading speed.

If you read the summary and conclude the new information learnt was sufficient, you can start reading another summary. However, if you think of the summary as a trailer for the book or a preview, you will spend five to ten minutes evaluating if you really want to read the book or not. If you decide to read the book after reading the summary, you will be able to read your book faster and avoid skipping back to re-read, because you have already found the key messages. Therefore, you will not be afraid of missing anything out and will be more confident reading the book at a faster pace.

I have selected some sources for book summaries for you to choose from. Some of them you pay for, and some are totally free of charge. Some of them are inconvenient text, audio and video formats. There is also a website called *Read It For Me* that provides well-produced, 10-15 minute videos that summarise the books in a memorable way. There are websites that specialise in summarising business books, personal growth books and biographies. There is also a website called *eNotes* that has study guides, literature criticism and also summaries of fiction and non-fiction books.

I have also selected an incredible online tool to summarise emails, documents and even entire websites on the spot. Copy and paste the text or the URL into the tool, select the number of lines you want the summary and you will get it instantly. The best thing is that it is totally FREE.

If you like learning with video, make sure you take a look at the TED Talks with their remarkable speakers that convey an idea in 18 minutes or less. Many of the speakers are also authors. In addition, there is the relatively less famous YouTube Education and the iTunes University.

To wrap it up, you can buy software that changes the playback speed of any video, and you can save valuable time by fast-forwarding a video 2, 3 or 4 times, while still understanding the message.

Go to the following website to find the links to all the summaries, videos and resources.

www.humansinflow.global/summaries

3.5.4 Creating targets for the month with the *Minaxi Target*

I have explained to you how to use the *Minaxi Target* to set up your reading target for each day (check it out at 2.3.14 Set yourself a realistic routine and great goals). Do you remember how it works? Now, let us set some targets for the month.

I have a target of reading two books a month. If I read 15 pages a day (my daily target), I will read 225 pages in 15 days. I can read half a book or, at least, browse the book and read some parts that are of interest to me. I do not think I need to read the whole book on every occasion. I prefer to move on unless the book is one of those that compels me to read on. In this case, it is possible that I will create more time to read and finish the book sooner. If it is not that exciting, I read half of it and skip around to get the general idea and move on to another one, ever hopeful that it will be a great one!

I think it is much better to get as much as you can from a book in about a week, even if you skip parts of it, because the content is fresh and condensed in your mind and you get a great overview of the book. You will have a more complete memory of it than reading it slowly and carefully for three months because by the time you get to the end you will have probably forgotten the beginning! Would you prefer to watch a movie in one sitting, even if you have a few distractions along the way, than watch a movie in ten sittings throughout three months? Books work in the same way.

So, my *Target* per month is to read two books. But my *Mini Target* is one book a month, and the *Max Target* is four books a month.

By the way, you can adapt the *Minaxi Target* to other activities you want to introduce into your routine, like exercise, organising your house, learning a language or anything else you might think of!

3.5.5 You can remember more of what you read if you have a big why

We learn something and start to forget about it very quickly. Most people believe that it is difficult to remember information from a book, but, in fact, we also forget things we say very quickly. If you have a chat for two hours with a friend and try to remember what you've talked about, you would say that you remember just a few subjects of the conversation. But as you start to talk about it, you start to remember more.

We are very hard on ourselves when we think about comprehension from books or text; in spite of that, I believe that you will comprehend and remember more of what is higher up in your list of values.

I did a bit of acting while at University, and I remember that while rehearsing for a role, I had to feel like the character I was playing while having to memorise a lot of text. I had a buddy to help me to go through the lines – but it was tough. Nowadays, a lot of people want to become actors and get famous, but the question is, do they have what it takes? Do they have a good memory to remember all those lines with great detail?

Now another question for you:

Do you think that actors who succeed get ahead because they already had a good memory?

I don't think this is true. I believe that if they really want to succeed, they will develop a good memory. Be aware that they might be great at memorising lines; however, they will forget their partner's birthday or forget to put the rubbish out when it is collection day.

I think that good memory is all down to values. You always have time, money, focus and a good memory for whatever you value the most. The hard thing is to find out what you really like from your own heart and not by trying to copy other successful people. You can emulate other people but you need to develop your own authenticity to support your personal growth.

In the same way, do doctors have a good memory?

Not necessarily; they will develop good memory, because if they get confused about the name of a drug to prescribe to a patient instead of curing them, they can kill them. This is enough reason to see medication as high value, and therefore, they will remember all those confusing names of drugs. If you can remember this example, you will be able to help yourself to find out what really inspires you.

Whenever you understand what makes you tick, you will find more reasons to support your learning, and you will develop your memory automatically.

I wish I could understand what singers are saying when they sing. Most of them are very hard to understand. I like music and I can cope with not understanding the message because I'm not a singer. If I were, I would search on the internet for the lyrics. I would read and memorise them to have a great understanding of the song. But I like dancing, so for me, it is enough to listen to the music and shake my bones.

Decide what you want to focus on and more of it will start showing itself to you. Based on my own experience I can say that what you think about you bring about!

So if you want to develop your memory, many techniques can help you develop a great deal. You can search for a book or a course on the subject or get in touch with me and I might be able to help.

3.5.6 Share your knowledge to lead your field

By teaching, we really master our abilities and I would recommend that you help someone to read faster and give them the incentive to read more. Just help them using a pointer and they will thank you for that.

Why don't you start writing a blog with some of the good ideas you've been having or quotations from books you read? Make comments on other people's blogs, posts or randomly find people on the internet to talk about things you like in all those forums or chat rooms.

Once you become strong in your area of knowledge, you can start exchanging information and also start forming joint ventures to leverage your value through other people's connections.

A great place to share your ideas is called *"Toast Masters International"*, which is a great place to learn and practise public speaking. These are very supportive groups and they cost nothing if you want to visit a group and feel the atmosphere of excitement when people go on stage to share great information. If you decide to join a group, they will give you a lot of support, and because they are a not for profit organisation, they cost around £100 pounds each year. There are other options on the market that might suit your needs better. If you are serious about building a career delivering content from the stage, or by creating online courses, you can visit the webpage below to understand why I recommend Andy Harrington as one of the best professionals to help you structure your presentations and succeed in this profitable market.

I had a premonition, on the Synchronicity walk I went in London, that I would be working with Brian Rose from London Real, so perhaps you too can take a look at his work if you get a hunch. Adventure!

www.humansinflow.global/stage

3.5.7 Learn how to pitch your ideas

Telling stories and creating analogies are an incredible way to draw attention to whatever you are saying. Stories paint pictures in other people's mind and they are very effective to convey emotion, which ultimately dictates our decisions.

But you also need structure to ask for what you want and I've learnt the pitch architecture directly from a man that create three multi-billion pound companies.

His name is Mike Harris and he didn't have much to start with, just a great idea and a presentation. He heard lots and lots of "no thanks" while refining his methodology, and he finally nailed a way to engage and sell ideas. If I hadn't learnt from him I would certainly not have met all the celebrities I met, or even been invited to speak from the big states in the world.

You can start by reading a few books on the subject or learn about the "Key Person of Influence Programme" as they have a few accelerator programmes to help you do just that. They are in the UK, US, Australia and Singapore.

www.dent.global

Join a business club

There are lots of clubs or groups you can join and you can start searching at Meet Up www.meetup.com

for a diversity of subjects, but I'd like to recommend you to search for "private members club" or "business club" in your city to find people you can make acquaintances with and do business.

Some famous organisations that have a worldwide reach are the BNI (Business Network International) which operates in 70 countries, Toastmasters that helps you with public speaking in 143 countries, Lions Club in 190 countries, Rotary Club in 200 countries, and many more organisations and charities that will expand your relationships and give you the opportunity to pitch your ideas and develop your business, or perhaps introduce you to new work opportunities and to have fun.

3.5.8 Join or create a book club

If you join a book club, you will have the opportunity to have a peer group to help you discover a new world through books. The more you talk about books, the more you learn from them. You learn how to structure your thoughts by having to give your opinion about a book or a subject. It helps you to gain greater confidence in discussing new subjects.

You can find real or online book clubs where they discuss books of different genres, such as business, science fiction, gay, short stories, Asian subjects or anything you can think of.

If you Google "Book Club" you can find a group to join and also make new friends. If you don't find the book club you wanted, just start one and lots of people will join your book club in no time. We are living in incredible times and you can meet up over Skype and even Invite a friend to try it with you.

Hack into the meaning of life and dare living forever.

The *Dragons Live Quest* has four visions to help you stretch the fabric of time and enjoy your life more.

L   **Legacy** will be left by you

I   **Invent** the impossible

V   **Verify** the real value of your invention

E   **Extinction** and creation process

Time to read the Fourth Quest

Reading Speed in Words Per Minute	TIME	Reading Speed in Words Per Minute	TIME
At 100 WPM	1.1 hours	At 600 WPM	11 minutes
At 200 WPM	34 minutes	At 800 WPM	8 minutes
At 300 WPM	22 minutes	At 1000 WPM	7 minutes
At 400 WPM	17 minutes	At 1200 WPM	6 minutes
At 500 WPM	13 minutes	At 1400 WPM	5 minutes

To illustrate the process, I will compare the search for the meaning of life and the understanding of time with the existence of dragons. Once you understand the links between the steps, you will connect with your higher self to facilitate flow.

The challenge

The dragon's analogy is undoubtedly the most powerful as it goes into the possibility of you being able to leave a legacy in this world and change the future generations. Yes, you are already doing it, but you can be much more assertive.

The dragon is somebody's imagination, so I invite you to invent new possibilities, then verify if their existence can be proven or if they can contribute to a better world.

To end the book, I question mortality and your perceived life expectancy. Read the last part to understand how to stretch, create and distort the fabric of time to live a more challenging and fulfilling life and perhaps you will decide that living almost forever is also a possibility for you.

Perceived reality and life span

According to quantum mechanics, reality might not exist without an observer, and by observing reality, the person will automatically change it.

For example, I believe in Jesus Christ and he lives forever in the heart of Christians but did he really exist as described in the translated version of the Bible? Many authors wrote the Bible's New Testament, but Jesus didn't write a single line. The church selected the books to create the Bible and the Vatican removed 14 books in 1684. Since then the church split in three main denominations: the Catholic, Protestant, and Orthodox. Now there are around 43,000 different established churches that don't agree with each other on many levels.

I respect all religions, so what we believe to be the truth can be reduced to a matter of opinion or faith.

Dragons, for me, are real and I use the analogy of the dragon as a starting and ending point. Apparently, life as we know, started from the Big Bang explosion and the lasting legacy of that explosion keeps burning in our sun. So the creature to represent transcendence had to be the dragon as it breathes fire.

Dragons exist inside our minds and have been not only enduring through centuries but reproducing at an incredible speed. I will explore the possibility of you leaving a legacy if you dare to learn more and create something new.

In chaos theory, the "Butterfly Effect" is depicted by the creation of a tornado that was triggered by the flapping of the wings of a single butterfly many miles away from the actual event. Therefore, significant changes in your life might have been shaped by seemingly insignificant events.

The impact you have on a single person creates a domino effect, so by having higher aspirations, you are more likely to change this world. Everyday counts, or perhaps every single second counts and you have a more significant responsibility to shape the next generations than you give yourself credit.

Be aware that if there is a dragon, there is a fight. So your willingness to positively impact the world will inevitably find opposing forces, so prepare yourself to deal with the real or imaginary presence of haters and win.

From creation, there is the inevitable decay and destruction, so I question the possibility of living almost forever by challenging the way you see chronological time. I believe you can create more days worth remembering, and I will give you a recipe to slow downtime, and you will be able to stretch your life until the inevitable day that you will transcend.

DRAGONS LIVE QUEST

Vision One

LEGACY WILL BE LEFT BY YOU

" If you can dream it, you can do it."
Walt Disney

The fire from the dragon's mouth represents legacy.

Dragons can create fire from nothing; similarly, you can create meaning in your life from nothing. You need to be willing to contribute to the development of the world in a way that will impact others in your community. You need to think bigger than yourself and use your focused attention to create the impossible.

4.1.1 The future of science and your role as a revolutionary

My intention with this book is not to teach you how to flow, it goes beyond that by questioning your default way of thinking.

I am leading the Humans In Flow Revolution, and I invite you to break the boundaries of traditional knowledge, to disrupt new industries, and create your own revolution to help us move towards the future. Regardless of your field of work, something must change and evolve. By changing, you will not please everyone, there will always be people who will hang on to the past and oppose your new ideas, but this is part of the challenge of creating a new world.

Many well-established theories will be replaced, and I hope that my insights in this book will contribute to the evolution of the way we read and learn. Please don't trust me on everything I say; I would rather have you questioning me because that is the way to creating the future, thinking!

Now, I want to share something that has hugely challenged my way of thinking. I hope it can also expand your way of seeing how to live longer and become healthier. My plan is to live healthy until I'm at least 205 years old.

My grandfather, called Alcebiades Cartaxo, was the Chancellor of one of the most prestigious Agriculture Universities in Brazil for seven years. He was an eccentric scientist who had a fantastic impact on my life.

Since an early age, I've learnt about chemistry and alchemy with my grandfather. Alchemy includes the creation of the philosopher's stone, and the development of the elixir of life amongst other goals. He proved to me, and many of his students and colleagues, that stable elements like silicon (atomic number 14) can transmute into carbon (atomic number 6) and oxygen (atomic number 8) without releasing extra energy from splitting an atom into two. Conversely, the atomic bomb works on the principle of releasing an enormous amount of energy from splitting atoms.

As global warming is such an important topic, I want you to follow my thought for a moment so perhaps you can see what's been hiding in plain sight and, this way we can step forward to find new solutions to our climate challenges.

The Amazon rainforest soil is notoriously thin and poor in nutrients, so once deforested their resources quickly dwindle and the formation of deserts becomes almost inevitable.

All the majestic trees in the rainforest had to grow from a soil that is mostly hard clay and sand, and the deep roots of trees had to penetrate into it to grow tall. Compacted sand is very tough to break through, nevertheless around one quarter to one half of the size of a visible tree will be invisible to us as it will be their roots.

Half of the composition of a typical tree is made up of water and the other half is composed of 50% carbon, 42% oxygen, 6% hydrogen and 1% nitrogen. As you can see, the plant would have to extract enormous quantities of oxygen from the atmosphere to grow and that would be a way to endanger human life on the planet, but the opposite is true, trees actually release oxygen into the atmosphere.

The photosynthesis process explains that plants absorb CO_2 from the air and transform it into the body of a tree. I can see this as a partial truth because the carbon in the atmosphere is a trace gas and its concentration is just 0.04% by volume as it has risen from 0.03% from pre-industrial times. To put things in perspective, the air contains 78% nitrogen, 21% oxygen, 1% water vapour and 0.04% CO_2.

As CO_2 is a trace gas, we would need a constant circulation of air, at very high speeds through the leaves to allow the plants to extract enough CO_2 to grow the timber and leaves, but the wind blows gently at low speed.

The transmutation theory highlights that the roots will penetrate the soil not by forcing themselves into a hard crust but by transmuting silicon (or sand with atomic number 14) into carbon (atomic number 6) and oxygen (atomic number 8), therefore using this carbon and oxygen to create the wood and the leaves.

In practical terms, if you go to a park in your town, you will see very tall trees that were planted many years ago. If the composition of the soil is mostly sand (silicon), the tree would have to dislodge the sand to penetrate its roots and, as a result, you would have the earth raising tall around the tree. However you know that this doesn't happen and instead the ground stays flat around the tree for as many years as the tree is alive. Conversely, if you decide to dig around the tree's roots you will not find compacted earth but soft ground because the tree dissolved and transmuted the sand into carbon and oxygen.

Another startling observation is that trees that lose their leaves during the winter will sprout new leaves very quickly during springtime, without photosynthesis, as they have no leaves. Trees don't store liquid carbon in their branches or accumulate enormous amounts of carbon and oxygen in their roots and use it to grow all their leaves all at once. So where does the stuff to form the sprouts come from? I believe this reinforces the transmutation theory again.

Although very simplified here, the transmutation theory already has many sympathisers and a new breakthrough is bound to happen, so we can understand this intriguing phenomenon and, perhaps creating new elements out of simple building blocks is possible after all.

The dream of many alchemists is to transform lead into gold, and I believe that we will be able to create gold from other elements and disrupt the whole market. We already create artificial diamonds so, why not gold or platinum? I've developed my scientific mind and have become very curious about finding alternative ways to challenge the status quo. It was exciting to be able to challenge my teachers with advanced theories that questioned their obsolete way of seeing the world. I had learnt about my grandfather's controversial theories, and I ended up studying Agricultural Engineering at University.

The most incredible thing was when my grandfather was giving an interview for his city's newspaper after turning 100 years old, he told the reporter that he was always reading and studying, and that over the years his eyesight improved, so he didn't have to wear glasses anymore.

He was really active at this point and would regularly take the bus to go to his farm, to work on his transmutation experiments. The most surprising thing was the answer to how many more years he would like to live. He said:

"I would like to live 20 years more to see my Carbon Transmutation theory being proven right, and this way change chemistry at a fundamental level, by explaining that nuclear fission and fusion are possible at low energy emission." And this is alchemy in action.

He died two years after the interview, but I still have his theory written down and I am carrying his legacy forward by reminding you that alchemy is present today in many ways. Epigenetics proves that the mind turns good and bad genes on or off and that miracles are happening every day. On a pragmatic level, you can see all the powerful pharmaceutical companies making expensive drug trials just to beat a placebo drug that really cures an infinity of ailments with no side effects.

Creativity to innovate grows if you have constraints, so use your boundaries and dissatisfactions to create a new world and leave a legacy.

DRAGONS LIVE QUEST

Vision Two

INVENT THE IMPOSSIBLE

" It always seems impossible until it's done."

Nelson Mandela

Dragons don't exist in the real world, no fossils were ever discovered to prove that dragons existed, and nothing similar to dragons was ever recorded in history.

So the dragon's body is represented as an invention. Someone thought of it and gave it shape and colour. Many others followed and created their dragons. Now stories all over the world have adventures that are more real than ever, because someone had to fight with a dragon, and the reasons for the battle will draw you in as nothing else would.

4.2.1 The limits of your imagination

When Sergey Brin and Larry Page decided to find the new CEO to lead the expansion of Google in 2001, they had a very big challenge at hand. By choosing a powerful leader they would risk everything. So what was the final stage to find the right person for the job?

After a gruelling period of selection they invited the best candidate to join them at the Burning Man festival in the USA. This isn't an ordinary event but rather a thriving place where visionaries and thinking leaders hang out for a week. They gather once a year in the middle of the desert, erect a city with an infrastructure for 60,000 people where the event is held, and mind-enhancing states are achieved by music, art and freedom to create the world of the future. During the festival there is a "no money" policy, since money requires to giving and getting something in return, and the festival is a commerce-free event. With very little sleep a revolution is created by people that want to expand their own limitations to create a brand new future. Elon Musk, founder of Tesla and Sun City, may be found there with many other top executives as normal people to explore the synchronicity and serendipity that will result in expanding the possibilities of the new world.

Eric Schmidt endured the marathon of interacting and thriving at the Burning Man and was hired as the CEO of Google, building a company with a pioneering culture and one of the most successful organisations in the world. [5]

If you think you would dare to challenge the status quo, and to join other people that are keen to disrupt new industries, you better read more books, meet strange people and act on your thoughts.

To introduce this concept, I will discuss two theories to improve your health and stretch your imagination.

My grandfather was in perfect shape almost until he died, aged 102, so I know I've got good genes, but I'm concerned about the way degenerative diseases are becoming more frequent even though scientists are developing more treatments and drugs. We are catching fewer diseases, and we are becoming ill from the inside out, i.e., diabetes, Aids, cancer, Alzheimer's, coronary diseases, allergies and many more illnesses that were not commonplace when my grandfather was young.

Medicine has developed enormously, yet we are getting sicker; why is that? Is it the result of a sedentary lifestyle with too many ready meals, a lot of sugar and the dreaded stress?

Well, one of the theories about the development of chronic diseases that also explains why we age, is called the Free Radical Theory of Ageing. According to this theory, our cells damage because they accumulate free radicals, causing ageing. Free radicals are atoms with unpaired electrons, or in simple words, these atoms need more electrons to become stable. If you eat fruit, vegetables and nuts with high levels of antioxidants, you supply extra electrons to your body, and the chances are that you will become healthier, and will not develop cancer or other chronic diseases.

Now comes a new theory that I find intriguing.

4.2.2 Earthing theory

In the book called *Earthing*, the authors, Clinton Ober, Stephen Sinatra and Martin Zucker say that we can tap into an abundant source of electrons that are bioavailable, from just under our feet, and it costs nothing.

Their theory takes into account the fact that the introduction of rubber and synthetic soles for our shoes changed our electrical stability. Rubber is insulating in the same way as wooden floors or carpet, so we lost contact with the earth, that we used to have 50 years ago, while using leather-soled shoes. Our electrical appliances are connected to the earth to avoid damage, and we should do it with our bodies too. We are electrical beings, and we generate electricity which can be measured, for example, by the electrocardiogram (ECG).

By grounding ourselves we become electrically stable, because the earth has abundant electrons that can be absorbed by the body, if you earth yourself by walking barefoot, or touching a conductive material that is grounded.

This is a theory based on science, that is still controversial, and it states that by grounding yourself you will reduce inflammation in the body and boost your immune system.

If you are a health practitioner or you are concerned about your longevity, you can visit their website for links to their book, videos, and resources, that can help you become a healthier person, and perform better at work and in life.

www.groundology.com

4.2.3 Ice Man method

Another person I've been learning from is a Dutchman called Wim Hof. He is revolutionising the way we can boost our immune system, treat chronic diseases and also fight mental illnesses. He teaches simple breathing techniques that have scientifically proven to affect our bodies, in ways never seen before. If you are curious about it, you can google his name and watch some videos of his endurance to cold exposure challenges and interviews. I'm convinced that his method has great power and I have been doing his breathing exercises and taking only cold showers for the last 25 months.

Visit his website for an introduction to his method.
www.wimhofmethod.com

If you think that all this science is nonsense, that's fine, do your research and make your own decisions. Remember that you can start thinking about how to revolutionise your field of work. How would you do what you do today in ten years from now? What could you invent?

DRAGONS LIVE QUEST

Vision Three

VERIFY THE REAL VALUE OF YOUR INVENTION

" Doubt the conventional wisdom unless you can verify it with reason and experiment."

Steve Albini

Although dragons are mythological creatures, they are alive all through the world, and they are now a part of the collective consciousness.

4.3.1 The difficulty of verifying an invention

The Bible describes the creation of our world as something very intriguing. It says in John 1:1:
"In the beginning was the Word."
It is fascinating that a declaration in language created all that exists. So if you think of a possibility in your mind and declare it publicly, you start the process of creation. By honouring your word, you not only create something from nothing, but also enrol people on your vision and execute your invention.

To verify that something intangible is real, you might assume there will be opposing forces to deny it.

So every truth will be contested. Even God is not a unanimity. Many people deny its existence, and they have the right to do so.

Therefore, in order to verify the existence of something, we can go to basics and search for the word.

Google "God" and you will find 2.2 billion entries, which are 10% of all 25.2 billion entries available. Now if you search for "Bible" you will find only 682 million entries, "Devil" has 621 million entries and "Christ" would give you only 493 million entries.

The surprising fact is that "dragon" has a staggering 1.2 billion entries, which demonstrates enormous popularity as it has more entries than "Bible" and "Christ" searches combined.

So I am comparing the existence of God to the existence of Dragons to motivate you to come up with something new.

Arthur Schopenhauer said 200 years ago that:

"All truth passes through three stages. First, it is ridiculed. Second, it is violently opposed. Third, it is accepted as being self-evident."

So if you want to impact this world you can expect to be violently opposed, as your ideas are innovative, the opposition will only appear if you stand for something big. Be willing to use the resistance they create as fuel to further promote your cause. You will face criticism and rejection if you focus on building something that will have an impact in the world, so be prepared, because even without intending to do so, you will offend or upset other people.

4.3.2 How to respect your opposition

Another quote from Schopenhauer highlights the importance of understanding the resistance visionaries encounter.

"Talent hits a target no one else can hit; Genius hits a target no one else can see."

Our society preaches that we should be inclusive and politically correct so we can develop in harmony, but the conflict is part of the evolution and development.

Unlike the sentence written on the Brazilian flag "Order and Progress," you cannot be a control freak to have order and progress simultaneously. Progress implies breaking free from an established order that doesn't work anymore to create a brand new reality.

If you dare to create something new, or join some group that wants some reform in the social, political, scientific, religious, sexual or any other area of human interaction, you will find some resistance in being accepted by the vast majority just because you became a minority.

If you stand for a cause and dare to impact your whole city or your country, you must face reality and consciously expect to find opposition along the way. They will challenge you and give you the strength to get your message clear and poignant.

I teach people how to focus so they can double their reading speed, get into the flow and that way ignite a passion for reading books and for learning.

I see it as such a noble cause that I shouldn't expect opposition, but as I grow my reach I inevitably find people strongly opposed to what I do. Just because in nature there are always two sides to any circumstance.

Likewise, a great movie or a video on YouTube will have a percentage of viewers giving it the thumbs down. I will undoubtedly find people that will not agree with my views in the media, in debates, in my classrooms or big talks. It's just an indication that I am having a significant impact on my city, my country, and the world.

We need opposition, and we should respect them because they magnify our cause. The challenge is to use their criticism as fuel for your mental engine, and not to feel discouraged. Let everyone voice their thoughts and find a way to express their creativity, so that this world can create innovation, despite the criticism.

DRAGONS LIVE QUEST

Vision Four

EXTINCTION AND CREATION PROCESS

" Every act of creation is first an act of destruction."

Pablo Picasso

Can you accomplish all you desire during the time you have left on this planet, or are you cutting yourself short by having distorted expectations about the power that you have to change and transform this world while alive?

My ambition is to leave a lasting legacy, and also see this legacy transform the centuries ahead, so I will explore new ways to live longer, or perhaps to live more intensely inside the life I have been granted.

The Big Bang theory explains that space and time emerged together 13.8 billion years ago, and we think that the chronological time of clocks and calendars measure our life. Albert Einstein's Theory of Relativity explains that you can perceive time running faster or slower, and I will show you how to slow time down so you have a longer life.

4.4.1 How to distort the fabric of time

My childhood summers used to last forever, as I jumped on rivers, rode horses, climbed trees, visited other people's houses, had crushes and also had my heart broken.

Everything was new, but now summers pass in a flash, and I forget entire months where nothing exciting happens.

I use the analogy of the Dragons life because they can live forever, and you too can live almost forever, if you understand the power of using your Brain Time and enjoy your life longer.

My obsession of creating new ways to speed up my reading led me to research a few ways to slow time down.

You can measure time with precision, but in your head time is not linear. It speeds up, it slows down, and it can also stop. This is Kairos.

Now using some simple math, I will come up with a bad prognostic for the coming years. I'm 53 years old, and my life expectancy is supposed to be 82 years old today, so I have already lived 65 per cent of my life. This appears to be right, but it is not, as my life seems to pass much faster than when I was nine years old.

If I plot my Brain Time in a graph, I need to create some parameters, and establish that a summer when I was nine years old would be equivalent of a year when I was 20 years old, which could be the same as the last five years of my life.

So it's possible to think that I lived half of my life by the time I was 23 years of age, which leaves me with approximately 4 per cent of my life left, not 35 per cent, and this can really mess up all my future accomplishments. So I've done some research to fix this discrepancy, and I have good news for you. With great insights from John Coyle talk at TEDx Naperville, I understood some principles that can buy you extra time, and they are inversion, contraction, and expansion.

Then it's time to look into what science is promising to achieve to keep us alive forever.

And finally why Okinawa's old population don't retire at old age and stay younger as a result.

4.4.2 Inversion - Live faster to remember slower

You already know that time flies when you are having fun, so you might be concerned that if you get into a flow state, more and more of your life will be over in a flash.

Now think of a dreary day at the office when you are already tired of doing the same task every single day, time drags and 15 minutes feel like two whole hours.

To understand this paradox, imagine your memory as two different kinds of video recorders. The one at the office is a black and white security camera with low-quality imagery and is fixed in a corner in the office room. Now the memory on which you record your holidays is like a portable HD video camera that you can zoom in and out, with high fidelity surround sound, and one that allows you to rewind to any scene and play it again in slow motion.

Now you understand that planning new adventures for your life will help you have more vivid and exciting memories, and you will feel like you have lived much longer when you look back and remember those memorable moments.

4.4.3 Contraction - The conduit of time is shrinking

Now, think of time passing through your brain as water passing through a water pipe. If your brain has a wider aperture it will let less time pass, and it will go slower, but if you make the diameter of the pipe smaller, time will have to run faster to alleviate the water pressure. The two important variables to change the diameter of the pipe would be, how new is the experience (Novelty), and how intense the experience is (Emotion).

For a nine-year-old, most of the experiences during the summer will be novelties and also involve high levels of emotion. This way the pipe is wide and time trickles through it, making summers seem to last a very long time. At 25 years old, you have less variety in your life, start to avoid discomfort and get a steady job. But when you hit 50 years old, your life is pretty much routine, even your holidays are predictable, so your novelty and emotion are small, the time pipe contracts a lot and time passes very quickly through it.

To compensate for the feeling of life starting to speed up, and to avoid missing out, we look for new things to buy and also new experiences. So even though we have novelty, the emotional factor is missing because there is no risk involved in buying a new set of pans. But the moment you decide to take some cooking lessons, you experience the pressure of performing well and cooking for others.

Play at high stakes and expose yourself to failure that might bring pain into the experience. You can play the game of a nine-year-old if you look for novelty with risk and time will start stretching out again.

So begin to avoid living a very comfortable life, look for something challenging to do, commit to an outcome, enrol people in the experience and have a deadline for many of the stages of development of the new skill or activity you decide to have a go at. A new life will start bursting out of your pores, and I'm sure that you will begin by laughing more often too.

4.4.4 Expansion - Stretching brain time

Einstein's Relativity Theory states that gravity can distort time, so a precision clock would start running slower if it approaches the increased gravitational pull of a bigger planet, and it could almost stop if it approaches a massive star.

Now, considering a famous actor or actress, a movie star has a profound effect on the way we perceive time. Movie stars create gravity around themselves, so we are pulled towards them by the fascinating effect they have on us. For a ticket, you can enter a cinema room and believe that fiction is real life and you can live many years inside a two-hour movie.

I had the good luck of spending two days with a Brazilian superstar named Ana Paula Arosio in London, and I remember so many details of our time together. I totally understand the effect her gravity had on my brain time, as I have such long and vivid memories from being with her.

In the same way, you can create or expand time by giving people or events more value and importance. To do that, you should be planning to catch up with people you like, even if you need to go on a long trip to see them and it is also important to put yourself forward to experience the unpredictable results of making unreasonable requests. As I described at the beginning of the book, I asked to speak to a business mogul named Tony Robbins, and just because I asked a few people to help me with my impossible dream, I materialised the encounter, had a chat with Tony and offered him a partnership in my business. My life completely changed because of my boldness, and then a few months later I asked to speak to Randi Zuckerberg. When we met I had the chance to tell her that we could double the speed that people read their Facebook feeds, gave her my book, and who knows what that will lead to in the future.

These are just a few memorable moments I've created in my life in the last few years, and I'm accelerating the speed that I stretch time.

In practice, a Rolex that is moving away from an observer on earth will run slower than a Rolex on someone's wrist. This evidence can be extrapolated, and we could create the possibility of a passenger in a fast-moving spacecraft to advance into the future, in a fraction of their own time. So one year of travel could correspond to twenty years on earth, and if we could maintain an acceleration of ten meters per second, which is the acceleration of gravity on earth, we would be able to travel through the entire universe in one human lifetime, and the traveller would come back to a different earth in the distant future.

I want to create more memorable events that can change the direction I'm going. I've seen the impact a day had on my life.

So what if I could put the focus and effort to create ten or 20 memorable events during a single year? The result would be that I would be living the equivalent of 400 extra years inside the expected 29 years, until I reach 82 years old, or 2,700 more years if I manage to live beyond my 205th birthday.

So creating memorable events in your life is possible by practicing using your creativity and doing one small new thing every day in the following week, like changing your furniture around, putting a note on your bathroom wall, running to the train station in the morning, or not having breakfast. However, if you really want to make big changes happen you can start by writing a to-do list and doing the hardest thing first, in the morning, expand your comfort zone, embrace uncertainty, live more intensely. A book called *Eat That Frog* by Brian Tracy explains that if you do the most challenging thing first you will be taking actions that will be remembered, and will change your life, instead of doing the mundane and trivial tasks that will surely drag all day long and will be forgotten.

You will be surprised of the effect that it will have on you as you start seeing new possibilities in your life, you will begin to be alive while awakening and the more daring the experience, the better. If you want to read an inspiring book about creating new options in your life, you might like to read *The Dice Man* by Luke Rhinehart. You don't need to be so radical in choosing life-threatening situations but just daring to think about something dangerous can help you understand that it's possible to look back on a life where you accumulated many lifetimes worth of memories and experiences, just by avoiding the predictable routine of a retired person that doesn't want to learn anymore and spends their time pottering in their garden.

So to live longer, you could perhaps follow Steve Jobs' advice:

"Stay hungry. Stay foolish."

Life has no meaning except for the meaning you give to it, so spice your life up and enjoy your everlasting minutes with a smile because you know something new is going to happen soon. I recommend you write your bucket list, create a vision board or a Goal Mapping, practice public speaking at a Toastmaster's session, enrol in an online course, walk on fire at a Tony Robbins' "Unleash the Power Within" event, learn about a new religion and attend one of their meetings, decide to write your own book to stay hungry for unique experiences and share them, learn how to draw, go camping at a summer festival, take a cookery lesson, learn a foreign language for a year, (free on the App Duolingo), and visit the country for three months to master the language. Other ideas include; to watch less TV and videos, record more live videos, do some charitable work, learn about investments in property, stock market and cryptocurrency, start writing a diary, set daily goals, invite people you like for a coffee, make more friends and ask them what could you do differently the next day. Make it up and Kairos will be more present in your life!

4.4.5 What if you are about to start living forever

Serious efforts are being made to extend our life expectancy, and according to Google's chief futurist Ray Kurzweil, humans will start having access to eternal life as early as 2029. In case you never heard of him, he is considered a genius by predicting many of the modern technologies available today and received honours from three U.S. presidents.

Millions of scientists have been working to extend life expectancy, and Ray predicts that by 2029 we will have resources to add more than a year to one's life for each year that passes, and therefore manage to stay alive indefinitely. Google his name to find out other surprises that the future holds.

If preserving our life as it is has its limitations, what about creating a way to metamorphose the old human into a new one? The caterpillar and the butterfly have the same DNA but, under environmental and hormonal influences, there is a change in which genes are turned on, to what extent, and where. They have the same brain, but the body dissolves to fill the new mould or energetic field that predetermine the future shape.

Some worms can regenerate their whole head and brain due to stem cell activity, so maybe we will be able to do the same and, like a worm, remember things after losing our head!

There is a jellyfish called Turritopsis dohrnii that is officially known as the only immortal creature on earth. With this precedent I'm fully committed to living at least 205 years of age, and everything that becomes a reality starts in the mind. So perhaps living forever is not too farfetched, after all.

If people start to believe that living forever is a possibility we will certainly have a bigger chance of seeing people treating our planet with more respect.

411

Ikigai

Studies with twins that lived their lives apart from birth say that only 10-30% of how long a person lives is dictated by our genes.

The Okinawa island in Japan is famous for having an incredible number of people living healthy far beyond 100 years of age, usually dying in their sleep, often after sex.

The most valuable insight from their lifestyle is that they keep working until they die, in fact they don't even have a word for retirement, instead they have the word "ikigai," which indicates the source of value of someone's life, so everyone that lives beyond 100 has a reason to wake up in the morning and contribute to someone else's life.

Perhaps now you understand why Queen Elizabeth II keeps working at the age of 93. She understands what ikigai means.

To value your life more, you can write your obituary, visit a home for the elderly and chat to the residents, and if you want to have an enlightened conversation with friends about life and death, you can find great guidance at the Death Over Dinner website.

www.deathoverdinner.org

You will never guess what the future holds, and the future is already happening today. Please take more risks and don't live a comfortable life, look for challenges instead and perhaps you will indeed live forever.

PAY IT FORWARD

Hey, I hope you enjoyed the quests and are transforming your life in a powerful way, one day at a time.

In the event that you got more value from my book than the amount you have paid, I suggest three ways to pay it forward.

I hope I can inspire you to impact the world.

Achieve high flow by supporting a friend or a community

What about directly teaching a friend something you learnt in this book or something you already know?

They will be grateful for the lesson and you will have a buddy to talk about new ways to improve your access to flow.

You will only reach the highest level of flow if you find a way to combine high flow and purpose.

Therefore flow will become a driving force in your life if you start a small project. Think of new ways to impact the communities you belong to.

You can get started by promoting a gathering with close friends to discuss the possibility of creating a project that resonates with you. Think of subjects that are high in your values system, something you are interested or curious about.

It could be raising money for the homeless, organising talks in schools about mental health, starting a recycling awareness group in your neighbourhood, mobilising your contacts to build a school in a third world country or anything else that will make you stand for something you cherish.

Many people set a challenge for themselves to raise money for a charity and I admire them, but if you decide to do the same I suggest you think bigger and enrol others to join you to accomplish a challenge themselves and the impact will be many times bigger.

If you start a movement you will automatically promote group flow, develop your leadership skills and make a lot of people smile in the process.

Start a list of possible projects you could start, call a friend to discuss your ideas and get started today.

Take more risks and live more in flow.

It will be fun, I promise!

Impact the world by gifting a book

If you are still not sure on how to start a project and want to motivate your friends to start thinking beyond themselves, you could inspire them by gifting them a powerful book. They will develop a new mindset to create change in the world with you.

Most people don't realise that a little act of kindness can have a ripple effect with unimaginable results.

For example, if you decide to gift this book to two friends today, they might be surprised to receive the book (or audiobook) out of the blue.

You can then explain that you are paying it forward because you are grateful for all the blessings you had in your life and you think this book will help them find more satisfaction in life.

You can always choose another book that impacted your life or a book that would give your friend a new perspective about the cause you are planning to support, it's entirely up to you.

The important message you want to send across to your friends is, that if they pay it forward by doing the same and gift their favourite book to two friends within a week of receipt, they could impact the whole world in just 32 weeks.

I know that you might be puzzled by my statement so let me explain the logic behind it.

One person at the time

If you gift one book to two other friends, you would have helped two friends in the first week, six people in the second week, 14 people in the third week and the whole population of the world in 32 weeks.

That's right. One friend alone could impact 8,589,934,588 people by giving just one book to a couple of friends and ask them to pay it forward.

If we make this happen, we will be able to find solutions to problems we don't yet know exist, and perhaps contribute to saving this world. So, take a look at the "Impact the World Chart" below and start thinking about who you could gift a book today.

Impact the World Chart

Look at the exponential number of people reached in 32 weeks, if you gift a book to two friends and they do the same within a week.

You will reach 8,589,934,588 people within 32 weeks, which is a bigger number than the total population of the whole world.

Incredible, isn't it?

# WEEKS	Week 1	Week 2
# PEOPLE REACHED	2 people	6 people
Week 3	Week 4	Week 5
14 people	30 people	62 people
Week 6	Week 7	Week 8
126 people	254 people	510 people
Week 9	Week 10	Week 11
1,022 people	2,046 people	4,094 people
Week 12	Week 13	Week 14
8,190 people	16,382 people	32,766 people
Week 15	Week 16	Week 17
65,534 people	131,070 people	262,142 people
Week 18	Week 19	Week 20
524,286 people	1,048,574 people	2,097,150 people
Week 21	Week 22	Week 23
4,194,302 people	8,388,606 people	16,777,214 people
Week 24	Week 25	Week 26
33,554,430 people	67,108,862 people	134,217,726 people
Week 27	Week 28	Week 28
268,435,454 people	536,870,910 people	1,073,741,822 people
Week 30	Week 31	Week 32
2,147,483,646 people	4,294,967,294 people	**8,589,934,588 people**

Now you know that you have the power to impact the whole world as any little act of kindness can spread and multiply.

If you found value in this book you can help thousands of people find it by giving me five stars on Amazon or other media channels.

I thank you very much for your support.

To make it easier to give me a thumbs up, using your preferred channels, just follow the webpage below.

www.humansinflow.global/fivestars

Thank you a million!

I'm just paying it forward myself, so what are you going to do?

God bless you,

Zander

CERTIFICATE - LEVEL ONE

YOU ARE NOW A FLOW STATE COACH

As you finished reading this book and practiced the exercises proposed, you are allowed to teach what you have learnt and charge for your knowledge and expertise.

As you have completed the Quests, you deserve your certificate of completion.

Send me an email with your full name and address and I will send you a certificate to improve your CV.

Visit the website below now to request your certificate.

www.humansinflow.global/certificate

THE NEXT LEVEL

According to Albert Einstein, *"Wisdom is not a product of schooling but the lifelong attempt to acquire it."*

I shared, at the beginning of this book, that out of desperation, I learnt how to cheat at school. Now I don't cheat, I inspire people to keep learning and experimenting with everything they find on their way that inspires them.

The future of learning

I'm leading innovation, and I've been invited by Success Resources' CEO, Richard Tan, to coach thousands of people from their platform all over the globe. They already organise 500 events in 30 countries a year to promote great speakers, and they are creating a global community, to help you learn how to succeed in this competitive world with practical knowledge that is not taught at school or university.

My first big speaking engagement was at an associate Success Resources' event for 1,100 people in Kazakhstan in November 2017. In the future, I hope to have the privilege to share the stage with renowned people, and I'm looking forward to speaking alongside presenters like Tony Robbins, Sir Richard Branson, Robert Kiyosaki, Larry King, Steve Forbes, Randi Zuckerberg, Bill Clinton, Tony Blair, Les Brown, Jay Abraham and Baroness Mone of Mayfair.

In a bold move, Success Resources is revolutionising education using cutting-edge technology. New stages will start popping up around the globe because they are partners with ARHT Media, the world's first complete end-to-end solution for the creation, delivery and monetisation of human holograms. They are already beaming presenters live for a two-way interaction with an audience.

And it doesn't stop there, because Tony Robbins, leading presenter at Success Resources' stages, is a partner with NextVR, the only platform that can deliver live events in virtual reality with the energy and the passion of a truly immersive experience.

FOX Sports, Live Nation, NBC Sports, HBO/Golden Boy and CNN have all partnered with NextVR, and they are delivering one live event per week to 100 million people at the beginning of 2018, and education is on the agenda for a dramatic and profound transformation. Tony is preparing new VR presentations to change your life.

I'm creating a VR session that will blow your mind, and I've already started the production of an animated 3D feature film with stories that involve these four powerful creatures so you will be able to learn in an immersive experience.

Advanced techniques

Now, if you would like to improve even further, I can coach you how to use advanced strategies to find flow and also hold you accountable to achieve ultimate performance.

Learn how to get in flow state and become more creative.

Keynote speaker

I can deliver a keynote speech at your organization, or a course to your team or your family anywhere in the world. Please get in touch for information.

The Practitioner course

Please get in touch if you want to take the Practitioner Flow State course and become a certified Flow State Coach at a higher level. You will be able to help your family, friends and clients while creating an extra source of income.

You can also be listed on my website as a coach, and build a thriving career. Send me an email describing how reading this book changed you and a reason why people should learn how to get in flow with you.

I'm training and certifying new coaches to cope with the demand and perhaps you will be the next coach to touch and inspire millions of people to achieve great accomplishments while in flow.

Teach the flow state with my support and charge well for your lessons. I can give you scripts, PowerPoint and further training so you will be a Master Practitioner in flow.

Give me your feedback

What is working for you? Please share with me your discoveries about how to be more efficient while reading and learning.

Email: zander@humansinflow.global

Or connect with me on Twitter, LinkedIn, my Facebook page or any other media. Visit my website to stay connected...

www.humansinflow.global

I teach what I want to learn, and I like to say that:

"To learn and not to share your ideas is not yet to learn. Action is necessary to hold information alive in your mind."

So share the love...

ABOUT THE AUTHOR

Zander Garcez is Managing Director of Humans In Flow Consultancy, where he empowers top executives and ambitious professionals to lead their fields from the bleeding edge. Zander navigates through complexity and uncertainty by living in London, and he splits his time between giving talks around the world and coaching professionals to achieve 'impossible' goals.

Zander gave up his Engineering degree in the third year because he was dyslexic and a very slow reader. However, his weakness became his strength when he took up a speed reading course and decided to become an entrepreneur. He then took up a Business Degree, Masters in Marketing and Advertising, and developed the *Humans In Flow Method*.

He has 13 years' experience and he personally coached more than 3,600 people, including professionals from Goldman Sachs, J P Morgan, Google, GE, Bloomberg, eBay, *The Wall Street Journal*, The Walt Disney Company, KPMG, Ernst & Young, Home Office, Thomson Reuters, Adecco, Foreign and Commonwealth Office, Lloyds Bank, Citigroup, Sage, Bank of America, PwC, HSBC and O2.

Zander is leading the *Humans In Flow Revolution* because he discovered that you have what it takes to transform your life and disrupt your market.

Zander's mission is to empower busy and ambitious professionals to achieve flow to promote innovation in their company and in their life.

ACKNOWLEDGEMENTS

I'm fortunate to have met some fantastic people that definitely changed the direction of my life.

Special thanks to my wonderful mum Marly and dad Jayme, Tuc Garcez, Gizela Quefaz Garcez, Miki Garcez, Otto Garcez, Cynthia Garcez Rabello, Ricardo Rabello, Rodrigo Garcez Rabello, Marina Garcez Rabello, Alcebiades Guarita Cartaxo, Carmen Pereira Cartaxo, Manuel Garcez, Miuda Garcez, Edgard Cotta, Betty Cotta, Fabio Cartaxo, Dulce Cartaxo de Souza, Silvio Modesto de Souza, Romilda Dessimoni Cartaxo, Eduardo Pereira Cartaxo Jr, Eithel Horta, Wanda Horta, Cid Horta, Alex Horta, Carolina Paiva Ferretti, Tevo Durães, Beleza Ferreira, Marcelo Pires, Alfredo Bufren, Aryon Lobo, Liss Barducco, Lizie, Carla Choma, Amaury Cortes, Sarita Paciornik, Lais Katz, Mini Boscardin, Conde, Ernani de Oliveira, João Candido Pereira de Castro Neto, Jamil Snege, Graciela Ines Presas Areu, Claudio Roth, Liss Barduco, Ana Paula Arosio, Nitzan Leon, Paul Bailey, Charlie Taillard, Sam Heath, Dan and Aurelie, Jim Cousins, Geoff Brownlow, Ruth Brownlow, Eve Brownlow, Oliver Brownlow, Marcus Fumagalli, Sonia Maria Rinaldi, Caio Rinaldi, Mark Smith, Kathryn Lovewell, Liz Walker, Gal Stiglitz, Daniel Browne and my lovely friend Esther Helfen for inviting me to come to Europe and introducing me to the amazing Regis and Catherine Justome, which I'm forever grateful for.

The business insights from Roger James Hamilton, creator of the Wealth Dynamics profiling system.

The love and trust of my eternal love, Lollie Erb. You are a truly inspiring woman that opened my heart to love. You deserve the best in this world.

The support to develop a leading brand from the Key Person of Influence programme. Highlighting Daniel Priestley, Marcus Ubl, Darshana Ubl, Andrew Priestley and Tom Banjanin.

The inspiration to dream big came about from seven inspiring magicians that I had the opportunity to meet and learn from: Tony Robbins, Dr Richard Bandler, Paul McKenna, Chris Howard, Paul Dunn, Jonathan MacDonald and Dr John Demartini.

The support to be bold comes from my mentor Steve Bolton, founder of the successful franchise Platinum Property Partners.

Invaluable knowledge about social media came from Penny and Thomas Power. They are the founders of Ecademy, one of the first online networking communities to grow big, ages before Facebook and LinkedIn were on the map.

The support from Nili Raviv, creator of The Raviv Method, gave me the understanding and tools to get out of dyslexia.

The inspiration to start creating video products and reach out beyond my little world was from Darren Shirlaw, founder of Shirlaws Coaching.

Thanks to Mike Harris, creator of three iconic billion-pound brands, for helping me communicate to the world what I do best in very simple words.

Invaluable criticism and excellent copy-editing of this book are from David Pilkington. Second copy-editing is from Kim Kimber.

Final touches under the supervision of my great friend Namita Kapila, founder of Interlanguage London, which is an English school for business and high-level students.

The cover design took shape after great criticism from Shaa Wasmund MBE and Matt Thomas, Mark Attwood and Andy Coley.

The cover and back cover content would not be clear without insightful contribution from my friend Rebecca Redwood. She also suggested that I should explain the reason for choosing Arial type font for the book.

Last minute inspiration to write a compelling tagline from Master Theta Healing Practitioner and Instructor Anna Kitney. Final touches supervised by my friend Richard Cotton.

Understanding how to be a top keynote speaker from bestselling author Andy Harrington. Thanks to

Andy Harrrington, Rima Aleksandraviclute, Marion Bevington and Jessen James for helping me write my story. Great feedback from my presentation from Mastanee Ati and Steve Talbot.

Insights into the publishing world from bestselling author Shaa Wasmund MBE, Mindy Gibbins-Klein at Panoma Press and Gerry Robert at Black Card Books. Their support and friendship were very important in finishing this book.

Inspiration to create the books of the future from Simon Woodroffe OBE.

Business development sprung from my business coaches from Action Coach, Parag Prasad and Shweta Jhajharia; Ian Christelow, master licensee of Action Coach in the UK and also Brad Sugars, founder of Action Coach.

Clarity to communicate my vision and mission from my friend Alistair Lobo. He is one of the most insightful business coaches I've ever met.

Help to contact the media and spread the news from business strategists Shaa Wasmund MBE, Matt Thomas and Rafael dos Santos.

Invaluable lessons about changing my internal reference points and contributing to a better world from my coach JT Foxx.

Profound inspiration to become a better communicator and expand my reach by building a strong team from my friend and Millionaire Mind Intensive presenter Mac Attram of Mindspace Associates.

New insights and expansion of my ideas were facilitated by my friend Fabio Amendola.

I want to express my gratitude to Lydia Tan for shining her light on me and introducing me to Jennifer Cao, Cofounder of New Tycoon, which led me to meet Tony Robbins and eventually opened the doors of a portal to a new dimension where I met Success Resources' CEO Richard Tan and Veronica Chew. That led to me being invited to become a speaker at their international platform, and also one of the first NewTycoon Ambassadors in the world. Oliver Tham for the spiritual guidance, Vivien Leow and Ken Sapp for the business leadership, relentless support from

425

Emileigh Tan, Casper Chen, Evon Lian, Debbie Dela Cruz and Alex Yeoh. Incredible videos created by talented media guru Ken Okazaki. Thank you to fellow Ambassadors, Krishna Gurung, Richard Wombwell, Harry Sardinas, Lily Patrascu, Hock Chong and my friend Annie Le for all the support and inspiration to grow an idea into a thriving business.

Inspiration to reinvent myself from Totka Spasova, Alex Roseman, Riyaz Lakha, Dan Warburton and René Deceuninck.

The strengthening of trust inspired by fellow coaches Jerry Baden, Susann Ribeck and Amit Bhanot.

The inspiration to create a movie out of this book from Georgie Barrat.

Special thanks to all my students, you keep inspiring me to become a better teacher and an eternal learner.

I feel indebted to the United Kingdom, and I thank Her Majesty Queen Elizabeth the Second for inviting me to become a British citizen. I will do whatever it takes to improve the quality of our education to standards never imagined before, by helping everyone, from children to adults, develop their passion for learning, and the UK will lead the way to a prosperous and peaceful world.

Finally, I thank God for blessing me with my life that hasn't been short of challenges. The adventure continues.

A NOTE ON THE FONT

Traditionally we find serif fonts in print, but according to bonfx.com which automatically tracks usage of the most popular web fonts across Alexa's top 10,000 sites, the most popular font in 2015 was Arial (20%) and Verdana (10%), which are both sans-serif fonts.

As we are increasingly reading on screens, I decided to use the sans-serif font Arial, because you will be more likely to improve your reading speed if you are reading a familiar font than an obscure font.

I considered using the new font OpenDyslexic that was recently launched by Amazon on Kindle, that aims to help dyslexic people read easier, but I was swayed by the benefits of a familiar font.

After a lot of research, I found more evidence that my choice was justified:

- Arial and Times are read faster than Courier, Schoolbook, Georgia and all the other fonts. [11]
- Arial and Courier are considered the most legible fonts. [12]
- Arial was considered the most Youthful & Fun type and Times the least, from 12 popular fonts. Not surprisingly Times appeared to be the most Business-like font. [12]
- Arial has been the most preferred font in studies that examined children, older adults, and college students. [12]

REFERENCE LIST

[1] Mindvalley podcast (2018). [Transcript] Steven Kotler on Accessing Flow States. Retrieved April 25, 2018, from <https://podcast.mindvalley.com/transcript-1/>

[2] Harvard Business Review (2019) The Case for the 6-Hour Workday. Retrieved December 11, 2018, from <https://hbr.org/2018/12/the-case-for-the-6-hour-workday>

[3] Flow Genome Project (2020). Advanced Brain Monitoring & DARPA. Retrieved March 12, 2020, from <https://www.flowgenomeproject.com/>

[4] David Cottrell (2013). Book title: Tuesday Morning Coaching - ISBN: 978-0-07-180615-2, MHID: 0-07-180615-6, or ISBN:978-0-07-180614-5, MHID: 0-07-180614-8

[5] Peter H Diamandis & Steven Kotler (2012). Book title: Abundance: The Future Is Better Than You Think – ISBN: 978-1-45-161421-3

[6] Deloitte's report (2018). Medtech and the Internet of Medical Things – July 2018.

[7] Mihaly Csikszentmihalyi (2013). Flow: The Psychology of Happiness – ISBN: 9781448177707

[8] Steven Kotler & Jamie Wheal (2017). Stealing Fire: How Silicon Valley, the Navy SEALs, and Maverick Scientists Are Revolutionising the Way We Live and Work – ISBN: 978-0-06-242965-0

[9] Steven Kotler (2014). The Rise of Superman: Decoding the Science of Ultimate Human Performance – ISBN: 978-1-47-780083-6

[10] Alexei Vyssotski (2009). Peering Inside a Bird's Brain. https://www.technologyreview.com. MIT Technology Review. Retrieved June 25, 2009, from <https://www.technologyreview.com/s/414121/peering -inside-a-birds-brain/>

[11] Michael Bernard, Bonnie Lida, Shannon Riley, Telia Hackler, & Karen Janzen (2002). A Comparison of Popular Online Fonts: Which Size and Type is Best?. usabilitynews.org. Retrieved April 25, 2016, from <http://usabilitynews.org/a-comparison-of-popular-online-fonts-which-size-and-type-is-best/>

[12] Michael Bernard, Melissa Mills, Michelle Peterson, & Kelsey Storrer (2001). A Comparison of Popular Online Fonts: Which is Best and When?. usabilitynews.org. Retrieved April 25, 2016, from <http://usabilitynews.org/a-comparison-of-popular-online-fonts-which-is-best-and-when/>

Printed in Great Britain
by Amazon

54905002R00244